WITHDRAWN FROM
THE LIBRARY
UNIVERSITY OF
WINCHESTER

D0410418

The political economy of industrial policy

In memory of my father
ROBERT F. GRANT

The political economy
of industrial policy

Wyn Grant, BA, MSc, PhD

Senior Lecturer in Politics
University of Warwick

Butterworths
London Boston Sydney Wellington Durban Toronto

All rights reserved. No part of this publication may be reproduced
or transmitted in any form or by any means, including
photocopying and recording, without the written permission of
the copyright holder, application for which should be addressed to
the Publishers. Such written permission must also be obtained
before any part of this publication is stored in a retrieval system of
any nature.

This book is sold subject to the Standard Conditions of Sale of
Net Books and may not be re-sold in the UK below the net price
given by the Publishers in their current price list.

First published 1982

© Butterworth & Co (Publishers) Ltd 1982

British Library Cataloguing in Publication Data

Grant, Wyn
The political economy of industrial policy.
1. Industry and state—Great Britain—History
—20th century
I. Title
338.941   HD3616.G73

ISBN 0–408–10765–0

KING ALFRED'S COLLEGE
WINCHESTER .

338·942
GRA   2465

Typeset by Scribe Design, Gillingham, Kent
Printed by Cambridge University Press, Cambridge

Contents

Preface

This book is principally concerned with the conduct of British industrial policy from the 'U turn' marked by the 1972 Industry Act to the completion of the 1979 Conservative Government's first two years in office in May 1981. Although the main emphasis is on the United Kingdom, an effort is made to learn from the lessons of foreign experience, and the analytical framework could be applied to other western countries.

The book focuses on the attempts of successive British governments to influence industrial investment by the private sector, although the adoption of the state holding company model in the form of the National Enterprise Board is also examined in depth. Less attention is paid to the conventional nationalized industries, not because they are unimportant but because they are already the subject of a substantial academic literature. This book concentrates on topics which have been relatively neglected.

There are a number of topics treated in this book which could have been the subject of a book of their own, e.g. British Leyland, the steel industry, industrial democracy. However, some important subjects have had to be dealt with in a short space in order to allow full treatment of the central theme of government attempts to influence the level and pattern of industrial investment, particularly in the private sector.

No one can write a book on industrial policy without being aware that not only is it a subject on which many individuals have strong political views, but is also a subject on the treatment of which many academics have strong intellectual views. In this book, a particular effort is made to develop a political science contribution to the study of industrial policy in such a way as to complement the insights derived from the study of economics. A genuine political economy will develop only if the economics and political science disciplines develop to the full their own distinctive contributions to the study of problems of common interest.

The Social Science Research Council provided me with a one-year personal research grant which enabled me to write this book and I am grateful to the SSRC for their financial support. The University of Warwick granted me a year's leave of absence and I would also like to thank the University for allowing me to teach, over a number of years, with Shiv Nath of the Department of Economics, a course on the Making of

Economic Policy, and to conduct a course on Industrial Policy in Britain. Thanks are also due to the lively students who have taken those courses and who, through their questions and observations, helped me to shape my ideas about industrial policy. Liz Anker of the Government Publications section in the University Library responded to my frequent requests for obscure government publications with her usual courteous efficiency.

I would like to express my thanks to the civil servants in the Department of Industry, the Treasury, and six other government departments, who spared the time to talk to me about various aspects of industrial policy and I am particularly grateful to those civil servants who read parts of the book in draft form. I am also grateful to a number of senior industrialists who found the time to talk to me and to officials of the Commission of the European Communities.

Various parts of the book have been 'consumer tested' at different stages of product development in the form of seminar papers presented at the London School of Economics, the University of Reading, the University of East Anglia and at the annual conferences of the Public Administration Committee and the Political Studies Association. I am most grateful for the helpful comments I received on those occasions.

Dr Peter Burnell of the Department of Politics, University of Warwick, read the manuscript from the viewpoint of someone whose academic interests are in a different area and I would like to express my appreciation for his meticulous comments on chapter drafts. Professor Malcolm Anderson advised me from the viewpoint of someone with an interest in the area and I greatly appreciated his comments on the intellectual strategy I adopted. My chairman, Professor Jack Lively, has been highly supportive throughout the project.

Special thanks are due to Hans Platzer of the Institut für Politikwissenschaft, Universität Tübingen and Wolfgang Streeck, Internationales Institut für Management und Verwaltung, West Berlin, not just for their advice on West German industrial policy, but for enabling me to visit Germany just before starting, and just on completion, of the manuscript. Quite fortuitously, they enabled me to brace myself for, and recover from, the sense of pessimism which must afflict anyone writing on recent British industrial policy.

Others who deserve thanks for their prompt and helpful responses to requests for advice and assistance include: Heidrun Abromeit, Gesamthochschule Wuppertal; Professor Hugh Berrington, University of Newcastle upon Tyne; The Rt. Hon. Sir Ian Gilmour, Bt., M.P.; Paul Hare, Department of Economics, University of Stirling; William Plowden, Director-General, Royal Institute of Public Administration; William Paterson, University of Warwick; Helen Wallace, Civil Service College; Shirley Williams, Policy Studies Institute. None of the individuals mentioned are responsible for the interpretations contained in the book or any errors or mistakes which have remained undetected.

The Confederation of British Industry gave me permission to quote from the letter in the CBI archives at the Modern Records Centre, University of Warwick, which is referred to in Chapter Two. Robert M. Worcester of Market and Opinion Research International kindly gave me permission to reproduce the results from a MORI opinion survey referred to in Chapter Three.

Last but not least, thanks are due to my wife, Maggie, for helping me to work at home free of interruptions.

Wyn Grant
Leamington, May 1981

List of Abbreviations

ACARD	Advisory Council for Applied Research and Development
APS	Accelerated Projects Scheme
BMFT	Federal Ministry for Research and Technology (Federal Republic of Germany)
BNOC	British National Oil Corporation
BRD	Bundesrepublik Deutschland: Federal Republic of Germany
BSC	British Steel Corporation
CAP	Common Agricultural Policy
CBI	Confederation of British Industry
CoSIRA	Council for Small Industries in Rural Areas
DEA	Department of Economic Affairs
DES	Department of Education and Science
EDC	Economic Development Committee
EFTA	European Free Trade Association
GATT	General Agreement on Tariffs and Trade
GDP	Gross Domestic Product
GMWU	General and Municipal Workers Union
IDA	Industrial Development Authority
IMF	International Monetary Fund
IRC	International Reorganization Corporation
MAP	Microprocessor Application Project
MISP	Micro-electronics Industry Support Scheme
MORI	Market and Opinion Research International
NEB	National Enterprise Board
NEDC	National Economic Development Council
NEDO	National Economic Development Office
NIC	New Industrializing Country
OECD	Organization for Economic Co-operation and Development
PPDS	Product and Process Development Scheme
RAM	Random Access Memory
RDG	Regional Development Grant
REP	Regional Employment Premium
SDA	Scottish Development Agency
SIS	Selective Investment Scheme

SPRU   Science Policy Research Unit (University of Sussex)
SSRC   Social Science Research Council
 SWP   Sector Working Party
 TUC   Trades Union Congress
WDA   Welsh Development Agency

Chapter One

Introduction

1.1 What is industrial policy?

Industrial policy has come to play an increasingly prominent part in British politics over the last fifteen years. One of the central issues in the British general election of 1979 was whether more or less intervention by government in industry would be most likely to halt the nation's economic decline. Interventionist measures which attempt to tackle the problems of the industrial economy have not been confined to Britain, but have been taken by many other western countries

There is nothing new about governments taking an interest in the pattern of industrial activity (or inactivity) within their borders. However, it is not without significance that the old concept of government–industry relations has generally given way in the terminology to the newer notion of industrial policy. Whereas the former concept implies a continuing dialogue between government and industry based on mutual acceptance of an essentially passive role for government, the latter implies a wider, deeper and hopefully more systematic involvement by government in industrial affairs. In Britain and elsewhere, as macro-economic measures have increasingly come to be seen as an inadequate means of dealing with the structural problems of the economies of western countries, there has been an increasing resort to micro-economic measures as an alternative approach to economic revitalization.

It is, of course, far from generally accepted that the way to deal with these problems is for government to involve itself more in industrial affairs. In the British case, it has been contended that industrial policy measures have weakened the economy by favouring declining firms and industries at the expense of growing ones, thus slowing down the process of industrial change. Certainly, whatever ideological position is taken about the desirability or otherwise of government intervention in industry, it is difficult to be sanguine about the policies that have been developed to date. As Mottershead has argued in a review of British industrial policies, 'industrial policies seem limited to a peripheral role of tidying up the edges of the economy, rather than providing any central thrust to alter and improve industry's performance and that of the economy as a whole'[1].

1

Ohlin has noted that 'a decade of fairly lively discussion of industrial policy has not produced any sharply defined notion of what it embraces'[2]. Much of the international interest in the subject has been stimulated by the work of the Organization for Economic Co-operation and Development's (OECD) Industry Committee, but their own definition of industrial policy—'a focus of attention on a set of objectives related to industrial activity and development'[3]—is the kind of weak compromise definition one would expect a committee to produce. In this book, industrial policy is taken to refer to a set of measures used by governments to influence the investment decisions of individual enterprises—public and private—so as to promote such objectives as lower unemployment, a healthier balance of payments and a generally more efficient industrial economy. Investment decisions are taken to cover not only the creation and expansion of production capacity and re-equipment, but also decisions about research and development and product development.

One of the most difficult problems that arises in any attempt to assess the merits of different industrial policies and of different policy instruments is that the level and pattern of industrial activity is often more profoundly affected by decisions taken within the ambit of a government's general economic policy than by decisions taken as part of a government's industrial policies (Corden, 1980). Decisions about, for example, the exchange rate, taxation, money supply, interest rates and public expenditure often have more far-reaching consequences than the succession of *ad hoc* initiatives and small scale palliatives that often seem to be regarded as constituting an adequate industrial policy.

However, even if industrial policy often looks like little more than a series of hastily erected sandcastles built in the face of the incoming tide, a distinctive policy arena concerned with industrial activity does exist, even if its boundaries are imprecise. From an analytical viewpoint, the most difficult boundary problems are not those between 'primary' economic policy and 'secondary' industrial policy, but between industrial policy and other 'secondary' areas of economic policy. Thus, energy policy, transport policy and agricultural policy all refer to particular industries which are the subject of extensive government intervention and whose level and pattern of activity have important consequences for other industries whose affairs are regarded as falling within the ambit of 'industrial policy'. The conduct of commercial policy can have significant consequences for domestic industries, particularly where they are vulnerable to import penetration. Employment policy covers both questions of industrial relations and measures affecting the size and skill composition of the labour force which have major implications for manufacturing industry. One categorization problem that arises is that 'job saving' measures are often taken within the ambit of industrial policy, whereas 'make work' measures may be the responsibility of employment policy agencies.

It has been necessary to draw fairly tight boundaries round the subject matter of this book in order to exclude questions of employment policy and trade policy except in so far as they have a direct bearing on what has been defined as industrial policy. There is a danger that by focusing on the activities of government in this area, government's influence on the overall pattern of industrial activity may be exaggerated. In many ways, industrial policy offers a classic example of government's reach exceeding its grasp. However, the fact that the industrial policy measures taken by successive British governments have often exacerbated the problems they were meant to cure, enhances, rather than detracts from, the importance of studying such measures.

1.2 Academic disciplines and the study of industrial policy

Political economy

'Political economy' has become an increasingly fashionable academic term in recent years, and, like many fashionable terms, much of its attraction resides in its ambiguity. Some academics use the term simply to indicate that they have an interest in the politics of economic policy-making. For others, it is a code phrase used to quickly identify fellow Marxists striving to creatively adapt Marxism to the analysis of the specific problems of contemporary industrial society. Another use of the term is to refer to a particular period in the history of economic and political thought when the two disciplines seemed closer together than they are today. However, one of the most influential usages has been among those who, disillusioned with the results of the efforts to develop a distinctive theoretical apparatus for political science, have turned to the more advanced social science of economics and attempted to apply some of its theories and terminology to the study of political phenomena.

The purpose of this book is not to offer excuses for the limitations of political science, but to show how its insights can be applied in a positive way to complement the insights of economics. In talking of 'political economy', one is not advocating a hybridization of the two subjects which would inevitably mean that the economics strain would be the more dominant. Rather it is argued that both disciplines need to bring their own particular insights to bear on problems of common interest: to use a horticultural analogy, political economy should be an 'F_1 hybrid'[4]. By proceeding in this way, not only is understanding of the specific problem enhanced, but the two disciplines can each be enriched by a better understanding of the theories, methodology and terminology of the other discipline. Such a pooling is particularly necessary in the study of industrial policy where it is often difficult to disentangle the economic and political forces surrounding a particular decision or policy.

Organization theory

Hogwood has argued that 'the most fruitful new insights' into industrial policy might come from an approach which emphasized 'the importance of organizational and interorganizational factors in shaping industrial policies'[5]. The application of organizational models to the study of industrial policy-making can yield many insights, and the second chapter of this book takes up Hogwood's concept of an industrial policy community and considers the organizational setting of industrial policy-making in Britain.

However, although an organizational approach has much to contribute to the study of industrial policy-making, it also has particular defects and limitations. Whilst politics in a modern industrial society is conducted largely through and within organizations, a perspective derived from organization theory may fail to take sufficient account of the ways in which the organizations involved in the political process are different from other kinds of organizations. In particular, the state cannot be reduced to the status of one organization among others and, although other political organizations (such as interest groups) lack its special status and character, they are shaped by their relations with the state. Apart from the branch of organization theory concerned with the study of bureaucracy, it is doubtful whether modern organization theory affords sufficient attention to the special character of political organizations. Above all, organization theory does not give us much assistance in the study of the ideological perspectives which are of such great importance if we are to fully understand the actions of political decision-makers.

Science and technology policy

Another academic approach to industrial policy is to study it as a form of science policy or technology policy which has to anticipate and cope with the economic and social consequences of technological change. Apart from the significance of work on science and technology policy as an area of intellectual effort taken notice of by decision-makers, it provides a neat illustration of the scepticism displayed towards political interpretations of industrial policy in many reputable quarters.

One of the most influential exponents of the perspective which sees industrial policy as being primarily concerned with the 'efficient management of technical change'[6], Professor Freeman of the Science Policy Research Unit (SPRU) at the University of Sussex has argued that 'In our view rigid general doctrinal positions are of little help in the development of British industrial policy'[7]. It is difficult to defend the adoption of rigid doctrinal positions, but if one substitutes the phrase 'ideas emerging from the democratic process' for 'rigid general doctrinal positions', opposition to Freeman's point of view seems a little less unreasonable. One could then go on to argue that such ideas are of little value unless they are placed in the context of an overall political strategy which may indeed be informed by coherent doctrinal positions.

This is not to deny the value of the work being done at SPRU and elsewhere which, at the very least, serves to remind us that technology policy is not 'concerned mainly with rather esoteric and very expensive nuclear and aircraft projects'[8] but should be concerned with the broader adaptation of the industrial economy to technical change. However, without some sense of political direction, an undue emphasis on the importance of new technology can easily encourage a 'Tomorrow's World' version of industrial policy in which every technical innovation is seen as something which should immediately be brought into full production regardless of market demand or considerations of social need.

Political science

Hogwood sees the contribution of political analysis in terms of the application of vote-maximizing models to the study of industrial policy (Hogwood, 1979a). Such models certainly have something to contribute and they will be deployed in Chapter Three to attempt to explain the preference of successive British governments for location-specific forms of industrial policy.

However, political science has more to offer than models which borrow the terminology of economics. In particular, there are two important tasks for the political scientist to tackle in the analysis of industrial policy, each of which will be attempted in this chapter. The first is the exposure of assumptions or orthodoxies which, although generally unchallenged and often unexplored, have a profound effect on the ways in which industrial policy problems are perceived[9]. These orthodoxies are more than simply the prevalent conventional wisdom regarding various aspects of the policy problem. Rather, they are unquestioned or, at any rate, generally accepted premises which limit the range of permissible policy options, harmless as symbols of good intentions, but dangerous once they are thought to possess real meaning.

The second task, the construction of a typology of policy content, contributes to the elucidation of the purposes and limits of different kinds of industrial policies. Such a typology is necessary, if analysis is to proceed satisfactorily, for three reasons. First, it assists the task of description. Industrial policy really consists of a series of policies, in turn made up of a number of discrete decisions, often of a highly discretionary character. A typology assists the teasing out of the underlying premises of policy from the mass of rhetoric combined with specific decisions that make up industrial policy. Second, it assists the task of explanation. It helps the understanding of the obstacles which different policy strategies face; the explanation of the changing functions which continuing institutions perform under different strategies; the exploration of the ideas regarding the promotion of a more efficient or socially equitable industrial economy which underpin particular policy measures. Third, it assists the task of prescription. A typology can assist in the identification of the 'blind spots' in decision makers' appreciation of the policy problem and hence help the formulation of less bad industrial policies.

In particular, it is important to appreciate the difference between the inherent and self-imposed limits of different policy strategies. Inherent limits are those which are imposed by the logic of the policy strategy and which can only be avoided by adopting an alternative policy strategy (with, of course, its own particular problems and disadvantages). Thus, for example, all selective intervention policies face the dilemma of reconciling a belief in preserving the autonomy of the firm with a concerted effort to exert a significant influence on its behaviour. Self-imposed limits result from an imperfect appreciation by decision-makers of the character of the policies they are following and the conditions for, and obstacles to, success. For example, it could be argued that it is difficult to successfully pursue a selective intervention policy unless it is accompanied by some form of selective import controls.

1.3 Three orthodoxies of industrial policy

Three orthodoxies have dominated the prevalent conventional wisdom about British industrial policy: the belief that the preservation of the mixed economy must be a primary objective of British economic and industrial policy; the view that British industry has suffered from the inconsistency of the policies pursued by British governments; and the belief that the British economy is 'deindustrializing' at a rate that is dangerous and unacceptable. In examining each of them in turn, it will not necessarily be argued that they are heresies rather than orthodoxies. Each orthodoxy has, at the very least, some relevance to the political debate about the conduct of industrial policy. The problem is that the assumptions underlying each orthodoxy are too often taken for granted with the result that the orthodoxy suffocates rather than stimulates the critical examination of policy objectives which is so important.

The mixed economy

The 'mixed economy' is a favourite touchstone of British politicians and it is therefore unfortunate that very few people seem to have any clear idea what the mixed economy is, other than that it represents some happy British compromise standing between the economic systems of the United States and the Soviet Union. Trevor Smith had great difficulty in locating an adequate definition, but he goes on to argue that 'No succinct or pithy definition of the mixed economy is possible and, even if it were, it would not be very useful.'[10] Whilst agreeing with Smith that 'The mixed economy can be properly understood only if it is considered in a wider context than the matter of formal ownership and control'[11], there would seem to be little point in searching further for a definition if one can pinpoint what government's understanding of the concept is.

Unfortunately, official definitions of the concept are hard to find and the clearest one is to be found in a rather obscure source, the 1976 consultation document on transport policy. On page one, we learn that the national transport system should be based on a mixed economy which amounts to 'significant Government intervention in the market in order to meet social as well as purely commercial objectives'[12]. The important point about this definition is that it reminds us that the mixed economy is a modified form of market economy. Although government intervenes to replace the market where it is believed to have failed, and resorts to financial inducements to modify the behaviour of market actors to conform with government economic and social objectives, the allocation of resources in the economy is still carried out largely through the market mechanism.

It is difficult to derive from such definitions criteria for resolving the crucial question of which activities in a mixed economy should be the subject of state control or influence and which should be left entirely in private hands. Admittedly, the definition used by Smith envisages that nationalization in a mixed economy is 'confined to the basic public utilities and industries which occupy a crucial power position within the economy'[13]. However, the first part of the definition refers to an equally vague concept, that of the public utility. Although we may feel that we all know intuitively what a public utility is, in fact it is not so easy to identify as the proverbial elephant. For example, if it is argued that a public utility provides a service which is of crucial importance to the maintenance of accepted standards of life, is used by the greater part of the population, and requires an extensive distributional network for the provision of the service, one would not only encompass traditional public utilities such as electricity and water, but also include clearing banks and chemists shops. The second part of the definition, 'industries which occupy a crucial power position within the economy', could in fact justify the nationalization of the 200 largest monopolies which loom so large in the minds of some members of the Labour Party.

The Manifesto Group of the Parliamentary Labour Party have been among the most enthusiastic supporters of the mixed economy, but even they are unable to explain the magic formula by which this supposedly successful form of economy operates. They state, 'In the "mixed" economy, in which a dynamic private sector coexists with a substantial public sector, those activities which are most effectively pursued through the market are wisely left in private hands'[14]. But how does one decide *which* activities are most effectively pursued through the market and by the dynamic private sector, and which are to be consigned to the (implicitly sluggish) public sector?

A belief in the mixed economy orthodoxy is shared by a wide range of conventional British political opinon. Its greatest admirers are to be found among moderate Conservatives, Social Democrats and the mainstream of the Labour Party. However, even professed socialists like Stuart Holland admit to their support for the idea, calling for a remixing of the economy to provide a 'new and more balanced mix'[15].

However, it is argued that, other than being a reassuring political symbol which is usefully vague, the concept is meaningless. It gives no assistance in the development of criteria for intervention—which are essential if one is going to have a coherent industrial policy that is to some extent insulated from the political pressures that can turn it into that form of 'low politics' in which politicians trade off hastily and furtively one set of priorities and local needs against another. Moreover, adherence to the notion of a mixed economy does not necessarily lead to a 'best of both worlds' economy offering a unique blend of market and socialist principles, but can produce a confused and inefficient combination of the worst features of both types of economy—what one commentator has termed the 'mixed-up economy'[16]. In addition, discussions of the mixed economy usually ignore the existence of a significant 'third sector' of private, non-profit-making organizations such as building societies, the co-operative movement and working mens' clubs. (Levitt, 1973; Weisbrod, 1977).

However, the principal objection advanced here is that the uncritical use of the notion of the mixed economy is simply misleading. Because some forty-three per cent of the United Kingdom's Gross Domestic Product (GDP) in 1979 was accounted for by general government expenditure, it should not be assumed that there is some rough balance between private profit-seeking and public welfare- regarding principles in the economy[17]. It is arguable that the principles of the market permeate large parts of the economy, as is evidenced by the importance attached to commercial criteria of operation in most nationalized industries, even if there are sectors in which market principles have to be modified or even abandoned.

The mixed economy bears all the hallmarks of a classic orthodoxy: it is frequently referred to by both decision-makers and academics in terms approaching reverence, yet it is not clear what is being preserved or why it is so especially desirable. As Metcalfe and McQuillan comment, 'The mixed economy is a flawed concept from a prescriptive as well as a descriptive viewpoint.'[18]

Consistency

The need for greater consistency in the industrial policies pursued by British governments is a recurrent theme of much of the writing on the subject, particularly in reports by or for practitioners. The committee sponsored by the Hansard Society under the chairmanship of Sir Richard Marsh to compare political and industrial 'lead times' pointed out that 'Widespread criticisms have been made of changing and inconsistent Government policies'[19]. Similar views have been expressed by the Confederation of British Industry (CBI) (CBI, 1976b, 1978a).

No one would dispute that there have been a considerable number of reversals and changes in British industrial policy. Even where a general commitment to a particular type of assistance has been maintained over a long period of time, e.g. regional policy, the form of assistance has been subject to frequent variations. The CBI have a case when they state: 'It is obvious why companies put such a high priority on consistency of government policies, from investment incentives to technical standards. Frequent changes can clearly disrupt investment projects and add to costs.'[20] A study of investment lead times sponsored by the CBI found that larger projects, defined as having a 1976 value of over £2 million, took around four years to reach completion (CBI, 1978b). After one has also made allowance for the time taken by a company to learn about and digest the implications of a new government industrial policy initiative, it is clear that most new incentives will not start to produce significant results until about five years after they were first launched—more than the average lifetime of a Parliament.

There are, then, strong practical arguments for longterm industrial policies lasting longer than the normal lifespan of a government, even allowing for the absence of 'U turns' midway through the period of office. It would seem difficult to argue against consistent policies, as one is then placed in the position of arguing for inconsistent policies. Nevertheless, one does not have to be a political mad hatter to be sceptical about the consistency orthodoxy. Too much stress on the value of consistency can lead to an excessive rigidity in policy. After all, there is no point in being consistently wrong! One of the key tasks of government is to monitor policy to ensure that it is adjusted in the light of experience. The emphasis of the need for consistency in recent discussions of industrial policy seems to have reinforced other influences which led the 1979 Conservative Government to take the attitude in its first two years in office that any modification of policy in the light of experience was tantamount to a confession of political failure. Consistency in regional development grant policy has been attained at the expense of a failure to adjust to evidence that considerable sums of money have gone to capital-intensive projects which create few jobs and which would probably have gone ahead without government assistance. Many of the points that are made about policy changes creating a climate of uncertainty that does not encourage invest-ment could be met by phasing-in policy changes over a suitably long time period.

The sudden changes that have taken place in industrial policy in the past, the practical arguments for relating government decisions to the time scale of decision-making in industry, and the common sense attractiveness of the notion of consistency, all lend weight to what has become a popular orthodoxy among commentators on British industrial policy. It is impor-tant, when making changes in industrial policy, to take account of the inevitable time lags before such policy changes are effective at the level of the firm, even though political pressures may encourage more rapid but less effective action.

However, arguments that 'The prime ground rule must be continuity and consistency of government policy towards trade and industry, whatever party may be in power—a bi-partisan policy'[21], extend beyond relatively technical recommendations on how changes can be made more quickly effective to prescriptions about the nature of the whole political process. It is no accident that the Hansard Society committee commended a system of proportional representation which would lead to 'governments of the centre'[22]. Industrial policy is so important that it cannot be 'taken out of politics' into the protected but stifling atmosphere of a bipartisan consen-sus; equally, it is not so important that the need for a better industrial policy should be allowed to determine the nature of the country's democratic arrangements by changing the 'rules of the game' to benefit centrist politicians.

The Social Democrats in Britain have succumbed to the seductive charms of the consistency orthodoxy, calling in their initial list of policy points for a consistent economic strategy not disrupted every few years by political upheaval. The consistency orthodoxy is an attractive piece of homespun British philosophy, which does lead us to some of the real constraints on the effectiveness of industrial policy, but treating it too seriously could produce an inflexible and rigid policy which took too little account of indications of inadequacy and changing circumstances.

Deindustrialization

The notion of 'deindustrialization' has enjoyed a considerable popularity in recent discussions of British industrial policy. Like many terms in popular usage, it has benefitted from a certain ambiguity (Cairncross, 1979). However, whatever the term may lack as a precise definition of an identifiable economic process, its political attraction is as a convenient shorthand for a readily recognizable trend whereby formerly prosperous British industries have gone into a seemingly irreversible decline, marked by rising import penetration, factory closures and increasing job losses in the manufacturing sector.

A very influential explanation of these phenomena was offered by two

Oxford economists, Robert Bacon and Walter Eltis, initially in the *Sunday Times* in November 1975, and subsequently in their book, *Britain's Economic Problem: Too Few Producers*. Although it has been suggested that 'they employ an identity to search out a cause'[23], there is no doubt that their articles and book had a considerable influence on the thinking of the Labour Government in office and the then Conservative opposition. Their 'quite intricate and qualified argument' has suffered from 'popular over-simplification'[24], but nevertheless it has remained politically attractive because its essentials can be readily understood even by those who are not literate in economics. Bacon and Eltis argue that the deterioration in Britain's economic performance can be explained in terms of the fact 'that successive governments have allowed large numbers of workers to move out of industry and into various service occupations, where they still consume and invest industrial products and produce none themselves'[25]. The authors draw an important distinction between the market and non-market sectors of the economy which is not the same as the distinction between the private and public sectors. As the proportion of the nation's labour force producing marketed output has fallen, so the numbers of those (such as civil servants and social workers) who rely on others to produce marketed output for them has increased and 'they have had to satisfy their requirements by consuming goods and services that diminishing numbers of market-sector workers are producing'[26]. Perhaps the most serious consequence is a squeeze on industrial investment which influences the whole future development of the economy.

Bacon and Eltis have made an important contribution to the debate on British economic and industrial policy by reminding us of the dependence of the non-marketed public sector on the productive economy, although, conversely, industry is ultimately dependent on the infrastructure that these services are intended to provide in the form of a healthy and well educated population. It has been argued that the concept of deindustrialization really offers little more than a 'new label for an old problem— the relatively poor competitive performance of British manufacturing industry'[27]. New labels can be useful, but in this case they have not apparently led to any agreement among economists on 'the appropriate diagnosis and treatment of the problem'[28].

Nevertheless, although the prescriptive economic value of the notion of deindustrialization is apparently limited, its impact on contemporary political thinking has been profound, and, it will be suggested, not altogether helpful. The attraction of the idea in political terms is that, apart from being simple in its essential form, it strikes a receptive chord in both major political parties. Although much of the expansion in the non-marketed public sector took place under Macmillan and Heath, the ideas put forward by Bacon and Eltis hold a certain attraction for a less moderate Conservative leadership which often seems almost to want to repudiate actions taken by the party in government in the past. References to the extra goods that have to be produced by manufacturing industry 'for the consumption of the vastly larger numbers of teachers, social workers and civil servants, and the extra buildings to house them'[29] and to the fact that 'Oxfordshire County Council now employs more workers in Oxfordshire than British Leyland'[30] are music to the ears of Conservative supporters anxious to find a cloak of intellectual respectability for their new-found fundamentalism. Indeed, one commentator has suggested that the Bacon and Eltis book 'provided an intellectual rationale for Conservative claims that unproductive government activities have expanded at the expense of profits and employment in the private sector of industry'[31].

However, Bacon and Eltis discuss both 'left' and 'pro market sector' strategies to deal with the problems they diagnose and it is certainly true that their analysis fits well with certain strands of thought within the British Labour Party. A longstanding vein of puritanism in the party, which can be traced back to its nonconformist origins, have often led its spokesmen to treat the 'candy floss economy' of the non-industrial sector with suspicion and disdain. In a major speech on Labour economic policy in 1964, Harold Wilson emphasized that the measures he proposed were designed to assist 'essential manufacturing': 'I am not particularly keen to provide Exchequer assistance for the computerization of betting shops or roulette establishments.'[32] The most important manifestation of this tendency was the introduction of Selective Employment Tax in 1966, which was intended to transfer workers from services to manufacturing. Ten years later, the same line of thinking continued to influence the Labour leadership, with the Chancellor, Mr Healey, declaring: 'The TUC and Labour Party are united in believing that the steady contraction in our manufacturing industry is the main reason for our disappointing economic performance since the war.'[33] Thus, for the Labour Party leadership, manufacturing jobs were seen as preferable to jobs in marketed services for a curious mixture of economic and moral reasons.

The deindustrialization thesis clearly encapsulates in a simple form an important aspect of contemporary British industrial reality. If it did not do so, it would not have received such widespread acclaim, however much one believes in the existence of a good market for 'Emperor's Clothes'. The danger of too ready an acceptance of the orthodoxy is that it is possible to jumble up description, explanation and prescription without realizing that a shift from one task to the next requires careful thought and justification. Unless appropriate caution is displayed, it is easy to confuse symptom, cause and solution, with disastrous consequences for policy-making.

A particular danger of the orthodoxy, as it has been popularly interpreted, is that it distracts attention from two possible lines of approach to the problems—particularly that of loss of jobs—resulting from the relative decline of the manufacturing sector in Britain. The first possible line of approach would be to encourage the expansion of that part of the services sector producing marketed goods such as insurance and tourism which contribute to the balance of payments. Bacon and Eltis explicitly recognize the contribution made to the balance of payments by marketed services. They are not making a crude statement to the effect that labour in a factory is inherently superior to all other forms of labour, but there is a danger of their argument being misinterpreted in that way in public discussion.

The drawback of placing too great a reliance on the potential contribution of marketed services to the economy is that UK 'exports of services already command a relatively large share of what is still a relatively small market'[34]. Nevertheless, there may be a case for doing more to stimulate the more labour-intensive foreign currency earners among the service industries such as tourism. The deindustrialization orthodoxy reinforces already strong tendencies towards an industrial policy that adopts a narrow and somewhat old-fashioned definition of what constitutes an 'industry'. Although there might seem to be a case for confining industrial policy to industries that 'make things', such a policy perspective is too narrow and excludes consideration of some policy initiatives which might be helpful.

A second possible line of approach to the problems resulting from a declining manufacturing sector is that of reducing the total size of the labour force and/or the number of hours worked by the labour force. The point here is that the deindustrialization orthodoxy directs attention to the distribution of the labour force between the marketed and non-marketed sectors and away from the question of whether the reduction in the number of jobs in the manufacturing sector could be compensated for by reductions in the length of the working day and the working life. Moreover, the distinction between marketed and non-marketed sectors is often trans-muted into a distinction between the industrial and non-industrial sectors in political discussions of what is often referred to as 'the erosion of the country's manufacturing base'.

All of the three orthodoxies that have been discussed here have something to contribute to the discussion of British industrial policy. However, they inhibit the discussion of policy alternatives in a number of ways. The assumptions they embody are too rarely subjected to critical scrutiny. By deploying them as slogans, politicians can avoid public discussion of the immense difficulties that arise in any attempt to formulate a more satisfactory British industrial policy. Above all, they structure the debate about industrial policy in a way that emphasizes some problems at the expense of others and obscures some possible solutions by highlighting others. Industry ministers could benefit from a self-denying ordinance not to mention the mixed economy, consistency or deindustrialization during their terms of office. Lacking the shelter of familiar assumptions, they might surprise themselves with the policy possibilities they discovered.

1.4 A typology of policy alternatives

In the rest of this chapter, four strategic approaches to industrial policy are set out in a typology of policy alternatives. The four categories used in this typology are:

1. Pure market
2. Social market
3. Selective intervention
4. Socialist approaches

The inherent limitations and defects of each approach are examined in turn. It is not argued that a government's industrial policy will display all the characteristics of one approach and none of the characteristics of any other approach. Each approach merges into the next one and a certain amount of blurring at the boundaries is unavoidable. Nevertheless, it is maintained that the categorization employed does have descriptive and analytical value, both in providing an overview of the main alternative types of industrial policy and in identifying the major difficulties likely to be encountered in pursuing any one policy strategy.

In the ensuing discussion, more space is devoted to the social market and selective intervention strategies than to the pure market and socialist strategies. The approach to industrial policy adopted by British governments (and by other western governments) in the post-war period has been either of the social market or selective interventionist form. Hence, the analysis can benefit from the experience of policy implementation, whereas any discussion of the other two approaches is necessarily more speculative.

In any case, a government pursuing a pure market strategy will not have an industrial policy as such. Communist countries face rather different problems in their industrial policies from western countries, in so far as the central problem of industrial policy in western countries—devising effective means of influencing the decisions of the autonomous enterprise—should not arise in a Communist state. However, as Communist countries have developed economic policies which allows the enterprise more autonomy, they have started to encounter problems which are familiar to students of western industrial policies. These problems will be discussed in the light of Hungarian experience later in the chapter.

The pure market approach

Strictly speaking, there is no such thing as an economy in which all allocations of resources are made through the market. Even the most extreme exponents of the efficacy of markets as distributive mechanisms have to make some exceptions. As Hirsch points out, 'Even under the most favourable conditions for market society, certain things have to be kept off the market.'[35]

Nevertheless, the pure market approach is important as a theoretical model which exerts an intellectual pull on social marketeers, shifting them in the direction of a version of the social market approach which is more market than social. The absence of anything that would be recognized as an industrial policy within the framework of the pure market approach means that the case against it cannot be made in terms of the industrial policy it produces. Two general arguments may be advanced against the pure market approach. First, it has a corroding effect on social relations, e.g. by strengthening the selfish aspects of the individual character at the expense of values which stress obligation to others, so that even if it results in a more efficient economy, a high price is paid in terms of a less tolerable society (Hirsch, 1977). Second, the attempts by proponents of the pure market approach to justify those small areas of state intervention and regulation which are to be permitted produce principles which could be applied in such a way as to justify intervention on a far wider scale than the advocates of the approach would ever envisage.

In his discussions of the role of government in a free society, Milton Friedman accepts that there cannot be exclusive reliance on the market mechanism. He accepts that once paternalistic justifications for government activity are allowed, for example in relation to the mentally ill or to children, 'doing so introduces a fundamental ambiguity into our ultimate objective of freedom'[36]. The particular cases of children and the mentally ill discussed by Friedman illustrate the difficulty of erecting watertight barriers against further government intervention, once one has allowed even a little intervention. After all, if one can help the mentally deficient on paternalistic grounds, why not the unemployed? To use Friedman's own words, 'There is no formula that can tell us where to stop.'[37] The boundaries to government intervention then become no longer a question of the general superiority of market over political mechanisms, but rather the subject of a practical political judgement about the relative effectiveness of different kinds of policies.

Social market approach

Advocates of a social market approach to industrial policy recognize the inevitability of some intervention by government in industrial affairs, but they regard such intervention as inherently undesirable and consider that it should as far as possible be infrequent, temporary and limited in scope. Perhaps the major difference between the social market and selective intervention approaches is that advocates of the former believe in a policy *for* industry rather than the comprehensive industrial policy advocated by selective interventionists. As the Conservative Party put it in a 1977 policy document, after they had shed their 1972–74 selective intervention strategy for a social market approach: 'Should government have an industrial policy at all . . . Of course, a government must have an economic policy . . . but an economic policy that is not primarily directed to creating the conditions in which wealth-creating . . . industry can develop and flourish is bound to fail. An "industrial policy" which consists largely of interference, tinkering and providing palliatives for structural defects is no kind of substitute for it.'[38]

The stress placed on the general economic framework rather than on a specific industrial policy in the social market approach leads to an emphasis on economic and fiscal controls and legal regulation, and to policies that are neutral between firms and industries[39]. In particular, there is an emphasis on competition policy as a means of curbing monopoly and other hindrances to the effective operation of the market mechanism. Instead of the enthusiasm for tripartite discussions between government, industry and unions which is a hallmark of the selective intervention approach, a social market approach to industrial policy involves a more 'arms length' relationship with economic and social interests.

Nationalization in the social market model is largely confined to what are viewed as public utilities with the boundaries of their operations being strictly defined. Although the desirability of natural monopolies being in public ownership is acknowledged, the length of time that a public monopoly in a particular field has been in existence is not automatically taken as a guarantee that it is natural rather than artificial. Wherever the justification for industries remaining in public ownership is insufficiently strong, they should be returned to the private sector or converted into 'mixed enterprises' involving the participation of both private and public capital. Industrial innovation policy under the social market approach relies on integrating public research and development capacity with industry and disseminating and transferring technology or on 'climate' measures such as the adjustment of patent and licensing laws (OECD, 1978). In terms of the wider consequences of industrial activity, the social market approach favours the use of taxation to equate private with social costs in relation to such problems as pollution and congestion. Historically, the approach has been associated with a philosophy of 'welfare capitalism' involving state provision (although not a monopoly) of health services, disability and retirement pensions etc. and some redistribution of income through taxation and family allowances. However, there is no logical connection between measures to improve the functioning of the market and measures to assist the family, although both types of measure are likely to be frowned on by defenders of the pure market.

The two areas of industrial policy in which the distinction between a social market and selective intervention approach is least clear are regional policy and agricultural policy. Regional policy has its place in both approaches, although there is a tendency for proponents of the social market approach to favour more limited and discretionary assistance in the form of tax relief whereas the advocates of selective intervention tend to favour more generous cash grants. Despite these differences of emphasis, what is striking is that those who favour the social market approach are much less inclined to oppose industrial assistance to a particular locality than they are inclined to oppose government assistance to a particular industry. The reasons that have led politicians to take a generally favourable attitude towards regional policy are discussed more fully in Chapter Three.

In the case of agriculture, the reasons why the supply and demand mechanism does not generally work properly in relation to agricultural commodities have been extensively documented by agricultural economists and are well understood by the relevant decision-makers. However, government (and Community) intervention in agricultural markets has gone beyond what is necessary to keep inherent market instabilities within reasonable bounds. Agriculture has benefitted from some of the largest subsidies received by any industry—according to one set of figures, only the railways have done better in Britain (Oulton, 1976)—and this assistance has been provided within a framework combining selective intervention and protection which has no parallel in any other industry.

It is somewhat ironic that the CBI, in a 1976 policy document which roundly condemned selective intervention, goes on to say of agriculture, 'It is no accident that agriculture, which has been favoured with a bi-partisan policy since the war, has been one of the most successful sectors of the UK economy. If industry . . . could enjoy the same bi-partisan treatment, one of the major obstacles to the UK's economic recovery would be removed.'[40] Unfortunately, the general applicability of lessons drawn from the experience of agriculture is limited by the fact that one is dealing with an industry made up of a large number of independent producers enjoying generally harmonious industrial relations, even in those cases where the production unit is not worked by the family. These conditions could not be said to be generally applicable in British industry. Nor, indeed, would it be possible to reproduce the scale of assistance to agriculture in other sectors without bankrupting the government.

A major problem for the proponent of the social market approach is that of deciding where intervention should stop, given that it is regarded as a distasteful necessity. The same problem arises for the advocate of the pure market, but it is more acute for the proponent of the social market as he is prepared to tolerate more departures from the market principle. The list of circumstances in which intervention is permissible under a social market approach set out by the CBI in 1976, although overtaken by the CBI's advocacy of a more positive industrial policy in 1981, reflect the difficulty of establishing criteria which set effective limits to intervention under a social market approach. For example, aid to defence industries is justified on the grounds that 'defence is an overriding national consideration'[41]. However, such a statement still leaves open the question of how far it is necessary for Britain to have defence 'national champions' distinct from those of other western nations. The CBI also declares its support for assistance to industries facing 'unfair foreign competition'[42]. However, unless it is made clear precisely when foreign competition ceases to be fair and becomes unfair, this principle could be used to justify extensive sectoral aid schemes of a kind favoured by selective interventionists. Once one allows some intervention by government in industry, it is difficult to establish criteria which set limits to that intervention or provide intellectually sound grounds for resisting the political and economic pressures for more intervention.

Social market theorists believe that capitalism has been unable to work properly in Britain because of excessive political interference leading to prohibitively high levels of taxation and public sector borrowing which have 'crowded out' private sector investment and stifled entrepreneurial initiative. If an industrial policy based on the social market model is going to work satisfactorily, the first condition that has to be met is that businessmen will respond to the opportunities to increase profits offered by lower taxes and public expenditure by increasing investment and employment. Leaving aside the problem that many forms of capital investment lead to a reduction in available jobs, it is clear that not all British industrialists can be expected to behave in the way outlined. Not only may they fail to exhibit the characteristics of the classic entrepreneur, they may also not be willing to give way to others who are prepared to pursue a strategy of profit maximization through higher investment. For example, a study by the Department of Industry of the wool textile industry found that 'Most of the managers interviewed drew attention to the pattern of proprietorship in the industry in which owners identify closely with their companies and are unlikely to get positions of similar status and responsibility elsewhere. Many therefore prefer to continue to make low profits rather than sell out and be left without position.'[43]

Nevertheless, it could be argued that social market policies will at least ensure that some industrialists will be induced to behave differently from the way in which they would have behaved in the absence of policies designed to facilitate entrepreneurship. Such claims are, by their nature, difficult to either establish or challenge. Much of the social market case, however, rests on the argument that whatever the imperfections of the social market economy, these imperfections are fewer than the distortions and loss of prosperity which result from the pursuit of more interventionist strategies.

Burton has attempted to demonstrate the superiority of the social market approach by exposing the limitations of alternative policies. In particular, he deals with one argument favoured by supporters of more interventionist approaches to industrial policies—what he terms the 'excessive caution' argument: 'Private enterprises are too cautious in undertaking investment in infant industries that promise to be prodigies and senile industries that are in need of rejuvenation in one form or another. The government must step in with subsidy inducements to overcome this "excessive caution" in business behaviour.'[44] Burton agrees that 'people tend to be more cautious when allocating their own resources than when allocating somebody else's'[45]. Whereas businessmen are constrained by 'strong incentives to choose carefully and avoid mistakes', politicians and bureaucrats 'have considerably reduced economic incentives to act in such a careful manner'[46]. In fact, when one considers the long lead time for large scale investments and the rate of turnover of top management, it is by no means certain that those who made the original decision will still be there to carry the responsibility. Moreover, Burton's secondary argument that few cases of unprofitable allocation of taxpayers' money come to light is an argument for more open government rather than for a different kind of industrial policy.

However, the main deficiency of Burton's argument is that he fails to face up to the possibility that both propositions may be true, i.e. that governments may be too reckless, and, in particular, too vulnerable to short-run political pressures; but that industrialists may be too cautious in the sense that they do not invest to the extent that is necessary if the international competitiveness of the industrial economy is to be maintained. Should this be the case, it would point to the need for some government assistance to stimulate industrial investment, albeit within a framework set by firm criteria and subject to careful monitoring both by industrialists and by Parliament.

Even if one accepts the economic case for the social market approach, there are two powerful political arguments against such a strategy. First, it is difficult for a nation state to refrain from subsidizing its industries when its competitors are subsidizing their industries. In Chapter Four, there is a discussion on the ways in which the Federal Republic of Germany, the supposed bastion of social market capitalism, provides extensive aid to a range of industries. Failure to provide at least matching assistance to British industries would leave them competing internationally on unequal terms. Second, intervention may have to be on a significant scale if it is to blunt the harsher social consequences of the unrestrained operation of a capitalist economic system. In the concluding chapter, it will be argued that a successful social market strategy needs to be as much social as market if the political costs of such a strategy are to be contained. Moreover, whatever the general merits of a social market policy, one is left with doubts about whether Britain's weakened industrial economy is the place to attempt to apply it.

Selective intervention

The case for selective intervention by government in industry often seems to rest on a kind of world-weary pragmatic scepticism which sees it as the only possible policy strategy in the British context. Edmund Dell has argued, 'Industrial policy is based on the persuasive presumption, evidenced by long political experience, that when government is presented with specific problems, it will have to attempt to deal with them—however strong its *laissez-faire* instinct may be.'[47] Certainly, the experience of the 1970–74 Heath Government—and of the first two years of the Thatcher Government—could be regarded as instructive in this respect.

Selective interventionists believe that macro-economic measures are by themselves insufficient as a means of attaining such objectives as fuller employment and the avoidance of a chronic balance of payments deficit and that resorting to micro-economic measures by government is inevitable. Pursuing the right general economic policies, although important, will not be enough to prevent continuing economic decline. In particular, selective interventionists believe in the need for, and efficacy of, financial inducements that discriminate between firms and industries. In order to seek advice on the operation of such a policy, and to try and ensure the co-operation of the affected interests, one sees the proliferation of tripartite bodies of various kinds concerned with industrial policy. In addition, the selective interventionists, although not favouring the wholesale nationalization of major areas of industry in private ownership which is advocated by socialists, see a significant role for nationalization and various kinds of mixed enterprise as a means of both rescuing declining industries and stimulating emerging industries.

In general, however, the selective intervention approach is based on voluntary co-operation between government and industry, rather than compulsion. Although the use of compulsion is not ruled out, the emphasis is on persuasion. Industrialists must be induced by means of subsidy, exhortation and tripartite working party to take those decision which government considers to be in the national interest.

It is suggested that the selective intervention approach encounters three major difficulties:

1. The problem of seeking to influence firms whilst at the same time preserving their autonomy.
2. The risk that decisions will be based on short-run political considerations rather than be related to the pursuit of longterm strategic objectives.
3. The difficulty of ensuring that government has at its disposal sufficient relevant information at the right time in order to make decisions about intervention.

Young and Lowe argue, 'It is the search for means of bringing government influence to bear on the firm that do not involve the firm losing its commercial independence that has been at the heart of British industrial policy.'[48] Governments have based their policies on the managerial and commercial independence of the firm and whether a firm will respond or not depends on how the policy measure looks from the level of the firm. In Young and Lowe's view, the main consequence of the ability of the firm to maintain its independence is that it can frustrate the achievement of the aims of government industrial policy. Governments have sought to work through the private sector because the aims of the firm and of the government were thought to coincide. In fact, argue Young and Lowe, their aims are often poles apart, and relying on persuasion and inducements will not always achieve the government's end because the independence and autonomy of the firm enables it to resist government attempts to influence its decision-making.

Social market critics of selective intervention argue that it often degenerates into little more than a distribution of benefits to industries or localities that have some special political advantage. The formulation of detailed criteria, such as the 1976 Department of Industry criteria for assistance to industry, is one response to the problem of vested interests understandably preoccupied with their own immediate needs. However, apart from the fact that such criteria may themselves necessarily reflect short-run political considerations, there must be doubts about whether they offer a sufficiently strong basis from which to fight off interventions motivated by short-run political considerations. One former Labour Cabinet Minister has argued that errors of judgement in industrial policy are usually followed by 'attempts to buy out (the Minister's) error with even larger sums of public money'[49]. However, although 'This is an area of policy in which serious mistakes are relatively easy to make'[50], that is also true of many other policy areas. Considerable uncertainties always surround major industrial policy decisions, but one should be careful not to miss opportunities to stimulate the industrial economy merely because every signal along the whole route to be followed is not yet showing green. The real danger is that the economic indicators, such as future market trends, may be highly uncertain; whereas the political indicators, such as the distribution of marginal constituencies, are all too obvious.

The problem of gathering adequate information on which to base acts of selective intervention, and of monitoring those decisions once they have been implemented, manifests itself on two levels. First, there is the technical problem of ensuring that the government machine has the right expertise to enable it to gather and assess information; and of ensuring that the internal channels of communication work sufficiently well so that relevant information is transmitted to the appropriate decision-maker—and taken sufficiently seriously by him—before it is too late. Although the way in which government collects information in order to operate its industrial policies has been the subject of criticism (Ganz, 1977; Hogwood, 1979b), one must not underestimate the extent to which government has learnt from the experience of many years of operating interventionist policies. A second, and more difficult, problem is that of firms withholding vital information from government until it is too late for government to take appropriate action. Particularly when one is dealing with a transnational firm, significant decisions may be taken well beyond the range of any monitoring arrangements devised by the UK Government.

Socialist approaches to industrial policy

Industrial policy in Britain in the 1970s was dominated alternately by the social market (1970–72, 1979–) and selective intervention (1972–79) approaches. What both approaches have in common is an assumption that, given the right conditions and/or incentives, a form of capitalism can be made to work in Britain. It is true that the two approaches take a different view of the efficacy of market mechanisms as a means of achieving industrial policy objectives. Proponents of the social market approach regard the market as a generally efficient allocator of resources, with government intervention being permitted only where it can clearly be shown that the necessity of such intervention offsets the inevitable distortion of the market which will result. Thus, government intervention is tolerated to *facilitate* the operation of the market (e.g., by sponsoring or licensing appropriate regulatory mechanisms to avoid malpractice); to *correct* unavoidable market malfunctions (e.g., to inhibit monopoly through a competition policy and to regulate inherently unstable markets such as those for agricultural commodities); and to *offset* some of the grosser social inequalities produced by the operation of the market mechanism (e.g., those who have personally to accept the burden of industrial change through redundancy should be compensated).

Selective interventionists take a more sceptical (even agnostic) view of the efficacy of the market economy. They believe that quite extensive areas of economic activity have to be insulated from market forces either because the market is failing to work properly or because the social costs which would be imposed by market operation are perceived as being too great. The areas of market failure are not, in their view, confined to special types of market which are inherently unstable and cannot always be offset by a vigorous competition policy or by the use of taxation so that the price mechanism takes some account of social costs. Thus, one *replaces* the market where it is believed to have failed; in other areas, where there is some hope of resuscitation, there is a resort to financial inducements to *modify* the behaviour of market actors.

What unites both approaches is that they strive to avoid as far as possible the element of compulsion inherent in socialist approaches to industrial policy. Although selective interventionists are more willing to accept that capitalism has certain inherent flaws than are the supporters of the social market approach, they appear to believe that these can be overcome with the right mix of paragovernmental agencies, funding packages, networks of tripartite committees and the like. Socialists would argue that neither approach will work because capitalism is beset by internal contradictions which are now manifesting themselves in a terminal global crisis, the effects of which are especially apparent in Britain's weakened economy. However, it should be recognized that going beyond either of these models in the direction of a socialist solution (or, for that matter, a pure market solution) would involve creating a society fundamentally different from that in which British people have been used to living. Ultimate limits to the range of industrial policy options are set by a polity which accepts, on the one hand, certain responsibilities to care for its citizens and, on the other, limits to compulsion arising from a recognition of property rights and of certain basic individual liberties.

A number of accounts of what a socialist industrial policy might look like and how it could be attained are available. (Conference of Socialist

Economists, 1980; Holland, 1975; TUC–Labour Party Liaison Committee, 1980; Workers' Inquiry, 1980). Holland's book originated in a number of papers presented to the Labour Party's National Executive between 1971 and 1974 and is important if only for its influence on Labour Party thinking at that time. However, his call for 'revolutionary reforms'[51] suggests some confusion about ultimate objectives and, although he recognizes the importance of outlining the means for the transformation of capitalist society, he is rather optimistic about the difficulties that such a transformation would necessarily encounter.

The TUC–Labour Party document is a summary of the arguments for an expansionist industrial policy based on import controls and comprehensive planning. A greatly expanded role for the National Enterprise Board is envisaged and there is a call for the mobilization of funds from North Sea oil revenues and the financial institutions through a new National Investment Bank.

By way of contrast, the Workers' Inquiry has little faith in the value of working through the structures of the existing state which it sees as biased towards the private corporations. The report argues against those who believe that what is needed is the determination to carry through the policies abandoned by Labour in 1974 and calls for industrial policies 'which do not rely on the existing state power, but which instead help to build up workers' own political power from the base, the shop floor and the locality'[52].

The design for an alternative economic strategy produced by the Conference of Socialist Economists London Working Group is by far the most intellectually impressive of these accounts. It rejects a 'political strategy of "exposing" capitalism by mobilizing people around popular but non-realisable slogans'[53] and attempts to tackle some of the problems that would be encountered by a government trying to implement a socialist industrial policy. For example, the report recognizes that 'Nationalisation is in no sense panacea—rather it is the beginning of the real problem'[54]. The report is also one of the few documents to argue against the view 'which we suspect is common in the Labour movement, that manufacturing is in some sense "productive" while other sectors are not'[55].

One theme running through all these accounts is the importance of planning agreements, although the Workers' Inquiry doubts their value and calls for '"planning agreements" without management'[56]. This rather unusual demand does in fact touch on one of the central difficulties of planning agreements between governments and firms, that of persuading the management to agree. Reflecting on his experiences as an industry minister in the last Labour Government, Kaufman has pointed out, 'The trouble was, they were called *agreements*. How do you compel somebody to agree and still claim that they have agreed?'[57] Talk of *compulsory* planning *agreements* is clearly a nonsense.

There is also some uncertainty about what planning agreements are supposed to achieve, other than complementing government's control of the nationalized industries, which is not a happy example to emulate. It is all very well to argue, as Tony Benn does, that they 'were designed to secure the co-operation of leading companies with national economic priorities'[58], but that statement of broad objectives leaves a lot of questions unanswered. The Conference of Socialist Economists is honest enough to admit that 'it is not entirely clear what role profit is supposed to play in the whole process'[59], which is a rather important omission.

In the first fifteen months of the 1974 Labour Government, 'nobody seemed to have sat down and worked out what should actually go into a planning agreement'[60] and it is therefore not surprising that the Government only managed to conclude agreements with the ailing Chrysler company and the National Coal Board. This failure cannot be attributed to civil service obstruction. In fact, there were extensive discussions with companies and some interest from companies that depended on government for orders (Young, 1978). However, trade unionists 'did not want to touch planning agreements with a barge-pole'[61], being only too aware that they could be used as a framework for bringing about redundancies. In view of this experience, and the conceptual confusion about planning agreements, it is surprising that socialists still place so much faith in them as a centrepiece of socialist industrial policy.

One of the strengths of the Conference of Socialist Economists analysis is that it recognizes the strength of the domestic and international opposition that any socialist industrial strategy would have to overcome, although it is pointed out that the danger of such resistance is not an argument for rejecting such a strategy. Their cautious realism is preferable to Holland's breezy optimism which allows him to brush aside the problem of a Labour Government being reliant on a public sector management not itself committed to socialism and to deal with the risk of an army coup by recommending the unionization of the troops.

However, even Holland's vision is more realistic than that of the Workers' Inquiry with their faith in spontaneous, locally based workers' action, co-ordinated through shop stewards' combine committees which, nevertheless, 'cannot instruct plants to carry out decisions'[62]. Moreover, even the Workers' Inquiry is forced to recommend a strategy of proceeding through small gains and defensive victories. The problem with all the socialist strategies is that they assume, on the one hand, that private capital, in alliance with the state, has immense power; and, on the other hand, that this power can be curbed through some combination of centralized planning using the state machinery and industrial democracy relying on the socialist consciousness of the workers which, whatever the devotion of unionized workers to the pursuit of wage claims, is in practice conspicuous by its absence.

Socialist approaches: the lessons of foreign experience

Although most contemporary western socialists regard the debased state socialism of the eastern bloc countries as an example only of what is to be avoided, some attention must be paid to the lessons learnt from the experience of industrial planning in the state socialist countries. The western conception of industrial policy is one in which the state uses a variety of measures to influence the behaviour of legally autonomous enterprises. This is, of course, very different from the way in which the state approaches its relationship with enterprises in state socialist societies, particularly under the classic Soviet model of economic planning. As Stalin observed, 'our plans are not forecasts but instructions'. In the classic Soviet model, planning 'takes the form of instructions binding on participants in the economy' and 'the mark of "planning" is thought to be that economic activity proceeds in accordance with instructions from above'[63].

In practice, of course, the plan is often not implemented by subordinates as it is supposed to be, but what is of more interest for the analysis of industrial policy is the move towards more decentralized forms of planning in a number of socialist economies so that enterprises enjoy considerable legitimate autonomy. One consequence of this move away from 'the unique model of socialist planning'[64] is that some of the central problems of industrial policy in the west—such as what to do about failing enter-prises—start to appear on the decision-making agenda in a way that they would not have done under centralized planning. Nevertheless, it should be stressed that even the most market-oriented of the socialist economies, Yugoslavia, does not have an industrial policy in the full western sense. For example, although Yugoslavia has a regional policy, and allows joint ventures, no fiscal or other inducements are offered to foreign investors.

The Hungarian case is of particular interest because what started as a highly centralized, command economy on the classic Soviet model has been transformed since the 1968 reforms into a 'guided market' economy. One should not exaggerate the extent of the changes: the Hungarian model is closer to that of the Soviet Union than is that of Yugoslavia. Although the enterprises in Hungary now have more freedom in terms of the use of their own internally generated funds and the availability of credit, and although the sharing out of the responsibility for investment decisions between the state and the enterprises is a complex matter, the central authorities still have a substantial role in investment decisions.

What is of interest about the Hungarian case in the context of the present study is the question of what happens when an enterprise runs into financial difficulties and, in effect, requires what in the west would be called a 'rescue scheme'. What happens in political terms, as described by a Hungarian commentator, sounds very much like what happens in western countries: 'The firms sends delegates who complain and "cry". Lobbying begins: the firm tries to get support for its case in the political and social organizations and in the upper-level state offices. Personal connections are used.'[65] Bankruptcies are rare and the state 'can rescue the firm on the brink of ruin by various methods'[66] such as a special subsidy or an exceptional price increase.

1.5 The objectives of industrial policy

The maintenance of 'full' employment has often seemed to be the central objective (in effect, if not in intention) of industrial policy, particularly in Britain. It could be argued that the central goal should be the creation of an efficient, internationally competitive industrial economy. Without such an economy, it is difficult to see how fuller employment can be attained in the long run. On the other hand, the creation of such an economy may destroy jobs through a trend towards greater capital intensity in industry. Moreover, any attempt to 'pick winners' in the British case is handicapped by the fact that there are many evident losers and few potential winners (Stout, 1980).

Certainly, not just in Britain, there has been a 'growing disenchantment with selection born of the past failure of government officials to "pick winners", the recognition that powerful lobbies often lead to spending money on propping up losers instead, and the tendency of various governments to pick the same industries for special treatment . . . and so to cancel out each other's efforts'[67]. These concerns have led to an interest, particularly on the part of the OECD, in the notion of a 'positive adjustment policy'. According to this criterion, industrial policies are judged by whether over the long run they 'facilitate movement of labour and capital from the production of goods and services in declining demand to those whose demand is increasing, from less to more efficient forms and locations of production, and from production in which other countries are gaining a comparative advantage to new competitive lines of production'[68].

Critics of positive adjustment would argue that it amounts to little more than the latest fashion in 'Emperor's clothes', allowing a neat tick to be put against certain items on a list of industrial policy measures such as the ambitious French programme to make the country a world leader in products which combine the use of computers and telephones (*telematiques*). Indeed, even the OECD admits that 'most policy instruments can be construed as being "positive" in their intent or, at least, as having some "positive" features'[69]. For Britain, the risk of a positive adjustment strategy is that 'Britain's performance gap is now so great that faster adjustments to immediate market signals may lead to even greater losses of industrial markets than have already been incurred'[70].

Britain's ageing industrial economy often seems to be caught in a pincer movement between, on the one hand, the increasingly advanced technology and higher rates of capital investment of countries such as the United States and Japan, and, on the other hand, the cheap mass production of an increasingly wide range of goods by the 'new industrializing countries' such as Taiwan and South Korea with their reserves of cheap labour. Nevertheless, it should not be imagined that industrial failure, and the need to adapt to new technology, are peculiarly British problems. Even one of the most market-orientated of western countries, Switzerland, has been obliged to take measures directed at its ailing watch industry and to encourage the rapid diffusion of electronics technology.

Although the adversarial British political system apparently led to more frequent switches between social market and selective intervention strategies in the 1970s than happened elsewhere, those countries that have less adversarial political systems may simply be able to make the choices within government, rather than in open debate between the political parties. Thus, it could be argued that West Germany has drifted towards a selective intervention policy without much public debate of the alternatives. The highly political character of the industrial policy debate in Britain may often seem to stand in the way of the development of a more effective policy, but at least it focuses public attention on the difficult choices that have to be made between different industrial policy objectives and strategies.

Notes to Chapter One

1. P. Mottershead, 'Industrial Policy' in F. Blackaby (Ed.), *British Economic Policy 1960–74* (London: Cambridge University Press, 1978), pp.418–483, p.483
2. G. Ohlin, 'Subsidies and Other Industrial Aids' in S. J. Warnecke (Ed.), *International Trade and Industrial Policies* (London: Macmillan, 1978), pp.21–34, p.24
3. Organization for Economic Co-operation and Development, *The Aims and Instruments of Industrial Policy: a Comparative Study* (Paris: OECD, 1975), p.8
4. A F_1 hybrid is a plant raised from seeds produced by crossing two perfectly true parent strains. F_1 hybrids are vigorous and uniform
5. B. W. Hogwood, 'Analysing Industrial Policy: a multi-perspective approach', *Public Administration Bulletin*, No. 29, April 1979, pp.18–42, p.18
6. C. Freeman, 'Government Policy' in K. Pavitt (Ed.), *Technical Innovation and British Economic Performance* (London: Macmillan, 1980), pp.310–325, p.310
7. ibid., p.320
8. ibid., p.312
9. 'Orthodoxy' is used here in terms of the first two characteristics defined by Dearlove: 'they are widely shared and long-established' and 'because of this they are rarely questioned – or where they are questioned the critique comes from within the confines of the wider tradition emphasising currently neglected aspects of it'. J. Dearlove, *The Reorganisation of British Local Government* (London: Cambridge University Press, 1979), p.3
10. T. Smith, *The Politics of the Corporate Economy* (Oxford: Martin Robertson, 1979), p.100
11. ibid., p.99
12. *Transport Policy: a Consultation Document* (London: HMSO, 1976), p.1
13. Rogow's definition, quoted by Smith[10], p.99
14. Manifesto Group of the Parliamentary Labour Party, *What We Must Do: A Democratic Socialist Approach to Britain's Crisis* (London: Manifesto Group, 1977), p.10
15. S. Holland, *The Socialist Challenge* (London: Quartet Books, 1975), p.149
16. R. J. Ball, quoted in I. Gilmour, *Inside Right* (London: Quartet Books, 1978), p.233
17. The figure is derived from Commission of the European Communities, *European Economy, Annual Economic Report 1979–80*, p.66
18. L. Metcalfe and W. McQuillan, 'Corporatism or Industrial Democracy?', *Political Studies*, Vol. 27 (2), 1979, pp.266–282, p.268
19. *Politics and Industry – the Great Mismatch* (London: Hansard Society, 1979), p.10
20. Confederation of British Industry, *Britain Means Business 1978* (London: CBI, 1978), p.37
21. Confederation of British Industry, *The Road to Recovery* (London: CBI, 1976), p.9
22. *Politics and Industry*[19], p.60
23. D. K. Stout, 'De-industrialization and Industrial Policy' in F. Blackaby (Ed.), *Deindustrialization* (London: Heinemann, 1979), pp.171–196, p.173
24. ibid., p.173
25. R. Bacon and W. Eltis, *Britain's Economic Problem: Too Few Producers*, Second Edition (London: Macmillan, 1978), pp.24–25
26. ibid., p.28
27. F. Blackaby, 'Report of the Discussion' in Blackaby[23], pp.263–268, p. 268
28. ibid., p.268
29. Bacon and Eltis[25], p.17
30. ibid., p.13
31. J. Aylen, 'Britain's Economic Problem: No Simple Answers', *Public Enterprise*, Number 17, September/October 1979, pp.7–9, p.7
32. H. Wilson, *The New Britain: Labour's Plan* (Harmondsworth: Pelican Books, 1970), p.297
33. Quoted in Bacon and Eltis[25], p.117
34. J. R. Sargent, 'UK Performance in Services' in Blackaby[25], pp.102–123, p.108
35. F. Hirsch, *Social Limits to Growth* (London: Routledge and Kegan Paul, 1977), p.186
36. M. Friedman and R. Friedman, *Free to Choose: a Personal Statement* (London: Secker and Warburg, 1980), p.33

37. M. Friedman, *Capitalism and Freedom* (Chicago: Chicago University Press, 1962), pp.33–34
38. A. Maude (Ed.), *The Right Approach to the Economy* (London: Conservative Central Office, 1977), p.39
39. This aspect of the typology is influenced by the work of Stephen Young. *See* S. Young with A. V. Lowe, *Intervention in the Mixed Economy: the Evolution of British Industrial Policy 1964–72* (London: Croom Helm, 1974), p.18
40. CBI[40], p.9
41. ibid., p.55
42. ibid., p.55
43. Department of Industry, *Wool Textile Industry Scheme* (London: Department of Industry, 1978), p.60
44. J. Burton, *The Job Support Machine* (London: Centre for Policy Studies, 1979), p.28
45. ibid., p.31
46. ibid., p.31
47. E. Dell, *Political Responsibility and Industry* (London: Allen and Unwin, 1973), p.44
48. Young with Lowe[39], p.208
49. E. Dell 'Some Reflections on Cabinet Government by a Former Practitioner', *Public Administration Bulletin,* No. 32, April 1980, pp.17–33, p.21
50. ibid., p.21
51. Holland[15], p.154
52. Coventry, Liverpool, Newcastle and N. Tyneside Trades Councils, *State Intervention in Industry: a Workers' Inquiry* (Newcastle-upon-Tyne: Newcastle Trades Council, 1980), p.147
53. Conference of Socialist Economists London Working Group, *The Alternative Economic Strategy* (London: CSE Books, 1980), p.57
54. ibid., p.74
55. ibid., p.69
56. Workers' Inquiry[52], p.148
57. G. Kaufman, *How To Be A Minister* (London: Sidgwick and Jackson, 1980), p.53
58. T. Benn, *Arguments for Socialism* (Harmondsworth: Penguin Books, 1980), p.56
59. Conference of Socialist Economists[53], p.73
60. Kaufman[57], p.53
61. Kaufman[57], p.53
62. Workers' Inquiry[52], p.154
63. M. Ellman, *Socialist Planning* (London: Cambridge University Press, 1979), p.17
64. ibid., p.40
65. J. Kornai, 'The Dilemmas of a Socialist Economy: the Hungarian Experience', *Cambridge Journal of Economics,* Vol. 4 (2), 1980, pp.147–157, p.151
66. ibid., p.152
67. National Economic Development Council, 'Adjustment Policies in Europe: Memorandum by the Director General', typescript, NEDC(80)33
68. Organization for Economic Co-operation and Development, *The Case for Positive Adjustment Policies* (Paris: OECD, 1979), p.82
69. ibid., p.82
70. D. K. Stout, 'Comment' in W. Wallace (Ed.), *Britain in Europe* (London: Heinemann, 1980), pp.133–137, p.133

Chapter Two

The Industrial Policy Community

This chapter is not simply concerned with how central government in Britain is organized to deal with industrial policy, or how it shares its responsibilities with public agencies. Nor is it confined to the problems of co-ordination between the different departments and agencies concerned with industrial policy, although the difficulties that arise in this area are examined. A broader perspective is needed and Hogwood's concept of an 'industrial policy community' is used because, although it 'is clearly a much more dispersed and fragmented community than the expenditure community described by Heclo and Wildavsky'[1], the concept of such a community does help us to reach out beyond the remotest quango to the other non-governmental actors that make up the industrial policy community. The place of interest groups and firms in the industrial policy community must be considered, although clearly the core of the community is to be found in central government departments. Even in Whitehall, it is not so much a community bound together by common values as what one senior civil servant who was interviewed described as a 'community of regular meeting attenders'.

2.1 The role of central government departments

A cynical definition of British industrial policy might be 'what the Department of Industry does (or does not) do', but such a definition would not even be an accurate description of how the machinery of government works. The Department of Industry is, in fact, only responsible for some parts of British industry. Apart from its important responsibilities for commercial policy, the Department of Trade is the sponsoring department for the shipping and civil aviation industries; the newspaper, printing and publishing industries; tourism and the hotel and travel industries; and the distributive trades. The Department of Energy is the sponsoring ministry for some of the most important nationalized industries such as coal and electricity, whilst the Department of Transport deals with British Rail, the National Bus Company and the state-owned docks. The important food and drink industry is handled by the Ministry of Agriculture, Fisheries and

Food; the construction industry is dealt with by the Department of the Environment; the pharmaceutical industry and the medical supplies industry is handled at the Department of Health and Social Security. Perhaps most important of all, the Department of Industry is in some respects a Ministry of Industry for England alone; important responsibilities in industrial policy are delegated to the Scottish Office, the Welsh Office and to the Department of Commerce in Northern Ireland.

The Treasury

One of the changes introduced as part of a reorganization of the Treasury in 1975 was the creation of an Industrial Policy Group headed by an Under-Secretary. Ever since the demise of the Department of Economic Affairs, the Treasury had always had a small unit dealing with the agenda for the National Economic Development Council and during Mr Benn's tenure as Industry Secretary, the rise in spending in the Industry Department naturally led the Treasury to take an interest in developments there. However, the creation of the Industrial Policy Group, which survived the change of government in 1979, was a recognition of the increasing importance of industrial policy as an aspect of government activity. It also reflected Chancellor Healey's growing interest in the problems of the supply side of the economy.

The Treasury developed an effective working partnership with the Department of Industry under Mr Varley. The Department of Industry was pleased to have an alliance with the Treasury, even if it meant accepting that the Treasury was the senior partner on industrial policy questions. During the lifetime of the 1974–79 Labour Government, the Treasury chaired the Industrial Strategy Staff Group, which involved representatives of the CBI, TUC and NEDC as well as civil servants; it also took the lead in persuading non-industrial departments to think more seriously about the industrial implications of their policies, with a joint Treasury/Department of Industry secretariat looking after an official committee with very wide responsibilities for identifying aspects of departmental activities which might impinge on the success of industry.

Although the Department of Industry welcomed the Treasury's view that other policies should be subordinated to industrial requirements, questions remain about the Treasury's suitability as a central co-ordinator for industrial policy. It has a natural interest in cutting public expenditure and a tendency to seek fiscal solutions to industry's problems. Its links with the Bank of England are an advantage when it comes to discussing the problems of raising finance for industry but, even under a Labour Government, the Treasury seemed more eager to talk to industrialists and financiers than to trade unionists. Evidence given by the then head of the Industrial Policy Group to the Wilson Committee on Financial Institutions revealed that groups of industrialists were invited to the Treasury for informal discussions with senior officials on selected themes; asked how many trade union officials went to the Treasury for such discussions, the answer was, 'As of now I have to say none.'[2]

Under Mrs Thatcher's Government, the Treasury seems to be less in the driving seat on industrial policy than was the case under Labour. A civil servant in another department who was interviewed remarked that he thought the title 'Industrial Policy Group' was a bit of a misnomer. He commented, 'It isn't a central body dealing with industrial policy or anything like it. It's used for Treasury purposes.' In part, this changed state of affairs reflects Sir Geoffrey Howe's different interests and in part it reflects the different character of the policy, although it is interesting that some responsibilities that were discharged by the Treasury under Labour now appear to be discharged by the Cabinet Office.

The Department of Industry

The role of the Department of Industry in the formulation and implementation of industrial policy can only be properly understood in relation to the policy strategy favoured by the Government in office. Under a selective intervention policy, there is an active, energizing role for an Industry Department. Under a social market policy, its role is less clear. West German evidence to the OECD linked the absence of an active industrial policy in that country with the fact that there is no separate ministry for industry, although it could be argued that the Research and Technology ministry performs a similar function[3]. In Britain, Sir Keith Joseph has argued that 'My Department can do very little on its own'[4] and has expressed the hope that it will be possible to gradually reduce the Department's functions so that it could be merged with the Department of Trade.

The emergence of a single, if not comprehensive, Industry Department in Britain has been a long drawn out and tortuous process. Originally, such industrial policy as there was in Britain (regional policy or policy for the textile industry, for example) was the responsibility of the Board of Trade. In 1964, the new Labour Government created two new ministries with industrial policy responsibilities, the Department of Economic Affairs (which had an Industrial Policy division) and the Ministry of Technology. As the DEA's star waned following the demise of the National Plan, the Ministry of Technology's status rose as it became the main ministry responsible for conducting industrial policy. It gradually acquired additional powers, with the most important set of changes occurring in 1969 when it absorbed the Ministry of Power, together with many of the Board of Trade's functions and some of the DEA's responsibilities. For the first time, Britain had an Industry Ministry in fact if not in name. Indeed, its remit was wider than that of the present Industry Department as it had responsibility for the energy industries as well as a range of private sector industries and steel.

When the Conservatives came into office in 1970, they merged the Board of Trade and the Ministry of Technology to form the giant Department of Trade and Industry. For a variety of reasons, this arrangement did not work particularly well and shortly before the February 1974 general election, Edward Heath 'hived off' a new Energy Department. Harold Wilson took the process further, retaining the new Energy Department, but splitting Trade and Industry into two separate ministries, as well as giving some of its functions to a new Department of Prices and Consumer Protection. No doubt he was influenced by the heavy political workload that had been imposed under the Conservatives on the minister in charge of Trade and Industry, and also perhaps by a wish not to give too many important responsibilities to Tony Benn. The basic structure of separate Trade and Industry departments was retained by the 1979 Conservative Government.

Of the various divisions of the Department of Industry in existence in 1980, two of the most important are those dealing with Industrial and Commercial Policy. Among their responsibilities are the industrial implications of domestic economic policies, policies towards international investment and multinational enterprise, and European Community industrial policy matters. These divisions probably have the most contact, other than at the highest levels of the Department, with the Treasury and other key departments such as Trade.

Their role (apart from the fact that their organization and formal responsibilities were different) under the selective intervention policy of the Labour Government was more of an 'energizing' one, undertaking such tasks as briefing government representatives from other departments on NEDC Sector Working Parties on the Government's industrial policy. However, even if they no longer operate as a 'powerhouse' of industrial policy co-ordination in quite the same way, the role of the divisions is rather more than the residual one of handling issues that cannot be allocated elsewhere in the Department. As well as handling requests for information from other government departments about industrial problems, they deal with important 'horizontal' issues such as energy prices, assembling information from the sponsoring divisions that deal with particular industries and preparing a case for presentation (in that instance) to the Department of Energy. There is a necessary organizational tension between these divisions and the sponsoring divisions, with the sponsoring divisions acting almost like trade associations in making representations to the Industrial and Commercial Policy divisions, and the staff in those divisions, with their contacts in other parts of the government machine, having to explain what is and is not viable politically.

The sponsorship divisions, such as Chemicals and Textiles, offer a point of contact for the industries within government; the divisions act, to some extent, as spokesmen for the industries within government; and they also explain government policies to the industries. Once again, their role differs according to the policy strategy favoured by the Government of the day. Under a selective intervention policy, when government is trying to influence investment decisions taken by firms, the sponsoring divisions are likely to have an 'interactive' relationship with the firms for which they are responsible, initiating close contacts on such matters as selective aid schemes. Under a social market policy, when industry is expected to stand on its own feet, they are likely to have a 'responsive' role in relation to the firms, waiting for the firms to come to them with problems, although these contacts will in any case be supplemented by more or less formal liaison arrangements with trade associations. These contacts are necessary if only because gathering intelligence about the industry and its firms must always be an important part of the task of a sponsoring division. Government needs a reliable source of 'in house' information to which it can turn when necessary, e.g. when considering an application for selective financial assistance.

It should be stressed that the 'spokesman' aspect of the sponsorship function is not interpreted as the uncritical representation of the views of industry within government. It involves pooling the views of the industry and placing them in the context of government policy. A danger for an industry ministry is that, like agriculture, it will come to be seen within government as primarily a spokesman for a certain set of interests, with the attendant risk that its views may be discounted. A civil servant in another economic department who was interviewed saw the Department of Industry's job as 'to go out and put a case for industry as strongly as they can and to be a representative voice within government'. Another civil servant in frequent contact with the Industry Department commented, 'The great bulk of the Department of Industry is the industry divisions. That is the view I have of them.' (In fact, ten of the twenty-three Industry divisions in existence in October 1980 had sponsorship functions.) He added, 'There is a danger that an individual division in Industry dealing with nothing but a particular industry may become so enveloped in it, may involve themselves so heavily, that they do, unintentionally, become spokesmen for the industry.' However, he thought that the hierarchical structure of the civil service was a safeguard as the Under Secretary with responsibility for the division would have broader interests than the assistant secretaries and principals in it.

The Industry Department is responsible for a number of important nationalized industries, although it is in no sense a 'Ministry of Nationalized Industries'. The most important of the industries dealt with by the Department, at least in terms of the burden of decision-making it imposes on departmental staff, and the difficult decisions it presents for ministers, is British Steel. The Department also deals with the Post Office, which is being split into two separate corporations dealing with post and telecommunications; British Shipbuilders; British Leyland; Rolls-Royce; the National Enterprise Board; and the Government's stake in what was British Aerospace. The problems that some of these undertakings present hardly need emphasizing, and will be dealt with in Chapters 4 and 5. Another important area of the Department's work, the administration of schemes of selective financial assistance, is considered in depth in Chapter 4.

Another important area of the Department's work is scientific and technical assistance for industry. Around forty per cent of the net budget was accounted for in 1979–80 by Industrial Research and Development which covers a wide range of activities. The largest category of expenditure is the work supported by the nine Research Requirements Boards such as those for Electrical Technology and Mechanical Engineering and Machine Tools. The Boards were set up following the adoption of the Rothschild customer/contractor principle in 1972 and are chaired and manned mainly by senior industrialists, but also by officials and academics. Freeman argues that they have 'introduced an element of longterm strategic thinking and planning where it is most needed'[5].

In 1979–80, the Department also provided funding of £38 million for space technology, mainly through the European Space Agency, and £21 million for Aircraft and Aeroengine Research and Development. Last but not least, the Department runs a number of Industrial Research Establishments such as the National Engineering Laboratory. As well as carrying out programmes determined by the Requirement Boards, and undertaking contract work for industry, they provide the Department with a valuable source of technical advice.

Rapid institutional adaptation is particularly important in the area of high technology where new industries may emerge which are not catered for by traditional classifications. An example is information technology, which combines the technologies of computing and telecommunications and 'will perhaps be the most important area of application of microelectronics'[6]. There is a large and expanding world market for information technology products. A report by the Advisory Council for Applied Research and Development (ACARD), a body established in 1976 to advise ministers on applied Research and Development, found that government responsibilities for information technology were 'fragmented and organized in traditional sectors which do not correspond to the new technological possibilities'[7]. ACARD concluded that 'A single focus within Government is required in order to ensure that this subject is given adequate attention and that its development is not inhibited through conflicting responsibilities.'[8]

The Government responded to this call in 1980 by reshuffling ministerial responsibilities, giving a Minister of State at the Industry Department a special responsibility for information technology work and supporting him with a new information technology division, bringing together the former computer systems and electronics divisions and other sections dealing with matters such as office automation. Subsequent changes following a ministerial reshuffle placed even greater emphasis on the importance of information technology, and gave the responsible Minister of State charge of the related areas of telecommunications and micro-electronic applications.

However, these internal changes left unresolved the wider question of improving the co-ordination of information technology responsibilities discharged elsewhere in the government machine. For example, the radio frequency spectrum—the most important natural resource used in information technology—is regulated by the Home Office. Its regulatory concerns are rather different from those of the Department of Industry whose attention must be directed towards the most efficient use of the spectrum for industrial purposes. However, an internal reorganization of the Industry Department is one matter; transferring responsibilities from another department is more difficult because, ultimately, it touches on a minister's prestige and power. The official response to the interdepartmental co-ordination problem was to set up a committee of senior civil servants, chaired by an Industry Department Deputy Secretary, but working out of the Cabinet Office. The difficulty of its task is illustrated by the fact that it was necessary to involve fourteen government departments, each with a legitimate interest in some aspect of the use of information technology.

The 'merger mania' of the late 1960s has now been replaced by a fashionable belief that small firms are the key to economic revival and clearly the Department of Industry's responsibility for small firms is of considerable political importance. Since the appointment of a Minister with special responsibilities for small firms in the early 1970s, the role of the Department of Industry's Small Firms Division has been to monitor the wellbeing of small firms and to act as a focus within government for their interests. As well as lobbying other departments on behalf of small firms, the Department runs the Small Firms Service, established in 1972–73 as an information service for small businesses, working through a chain of regional centres. Some of the supporters of small firms consider that it is not sufficient to have a representative within government at the junior level of Parliamentary Under-Secretary of State and would like to see a Cabinet Minister with special responsibility for small firms.

The Department of Industry shares its economics and statistics staff (five divisions in 1980) with the Department of Trade. In their classic study of the British civil service, Heclo and Wildavsky note an attitude of 'professional scepticism' on the part of administrators towards economists, quoting a Treasury civil servant: 'You get the right technical people and they can do the quantification very precisely; they do it and we take due note, then disbelieve it.'[9] Undoubtedly, many administrative civil servants have a narrow definition (and perhaps a low view of) economics and this does sometimes make it difficult for economists to get to the heart of decision-making. The pressures on administrators to deal with the immediate problem makes it difficult for them to spare time to deal with the longer-term concerns of economists. However, it would be misleading to paint a picture of administrators who are insensitive to economic advice. Clearly, this cannot be the case in an economic department such as Industry.

However, the need for administrators to be receptive to economic advice must be balanced by the development of political sensitivity on the part of economists in the government service. Economists in the Industry Department appear to be aware of the need to draw a balance between research activities and the cultivation of a client group. If economic advice is not to be confined to the annexes which usually dwarf the crisply written memorandum at the beginning of internal government documents, economists need to act to some extent on their own initiative, at least in terms of creating a credibility among administrators One way of achieving this objective is for economists to use their analytical skills to give administrators bargaining counters they might not otherwise have.

The Scottish and Welsh Offices

The Scottish and Welsh Offices play important parts in the formulation and implementation of British industrial policy. They have their own voices in Cabinet and in official committees, they administer discretionary regional aid under Section 7 of the 1972 Industry Act and they have their own networks of regional agencies concerned with industrial development, most importantly the Scottish and Welsh Development Agencies.

However, all this does not mean that they are allowed to operate distinctive national policies. For example, the provision of Section 7 assistance is governed by United Kingdom rules, which the Industry Department endeavours to ensure are applied equitably throughout the country. Indeed, the separate section of the Scottish Economic Planning Department in Glasgow which deals with Section 7 assistance was formerly an Industry Department regional office and might be said to still see itself as much as an outpost of the Industry Department as part of the Scottish Office in Edinburgh. The development agencies have to operate within guidelines which reflect the Treasury's concern that different parts of the UK should not bid against each other for industrial investment. Industrial promotion has to be conducted within the UK framework provided by the Industry Department's Invest in Britain Bureau.

In addition, the regional ministries may feel cut off from the informal Whitehall information network which has at its apex the now almost legendary informal meeting of permanent secretaries in the Cabinet Office mess on Fridays. This is particularly true of the more junior of the two regional ministries, the Welsh Office. The Commons Welsh Affairs committee came to the conclusion that 'there are profound defects in the arrangements within Government for disseminating information to the Welsh Office'[10].

Nevertheless, one must not underestimate the considerable advantages that the regional ministries possess as lobbying organizations which are able to operate within government to protect the interests of Scotland and Wales. A classic example is the lobby mounted in the summer of 1980 by Scottish Office ministers worried about the possible consequences of the disposal of the National Enterprise Board's stake in Ferranti. It was feared that control of the company might pass to one of Ferranti's rivals, leading to a loss of jobs and local control. A compromise was reached whereby the sale of the shares was subject to the unusual provision that the purchasers should not dispose of them for two years without the NEB's consent. The success of the regional ministries in protecting the interests of their areas often leads to resentment in other regions such as the North East which have similar industrial problems to those of Scotland and Wales, but lack a distinctive institutional framework of departments able to act as spokesmen within government and agencies with public funds at their command.

The Department of Trade

The work of the Industry Department and that of the Department of Trade is closely related. Indeed, the two departments share a number of common services and a common establishment. The extent of overlap between their activities is reflected in the fact that the important Projects and Export Policy Division in Trade reports both to Industry Department and Trade Department ministers.

Opinion within government is favourable to a merger of the two departments. Certainly, the reduced scope of industrial policy under a social market strategy makes it difficult to justify the separate existence of the two departments. Even if a more interventionist policy was being followed, there would still be a case for merging the two departments, particularly if a future version of selective intervention policy involved the use of selective import controls. The fact that there would still be a separate Energy Department—which was not the case between 1970 and 1974—should prevent the workload of a merged department from becoming politically or administratively unmanageable.

However, there are some points of tension between the two departments which could make a merger difficult. The Trade Department, because of its responsibilities for commercial policy, tends to see itself as the guardian of free trade; the Department of Industry, because of its sponsorship responsibilities, tends to have a more protectionist outlook, pressing with Trade an industry's case for more vigorous anti-dumping measures. The Trade Department's interests in competition policy and consumer affairs are also potentially at odds with the interests of the Industry Department. One civil servant thought that in a merged department it would be 'very easy to work out an industrial policy which forgets about the consumer who will be deprived by blanket controls on imports'. Moreover, at present, most conflicts of interest between the two departments can be resolved through the use of the close and extensive bilateral contacts that exist between them. A merged department might face a more fundamental conflict of purpose which could only be resolved at ministerial level.

Sponsoring divisions in other departments

As has already been pointed out, a number of important industries have sponsoring divisions elsewhere than in the Department of Industry. In each case, there are special circumstances that can be pleaded in defence of these arrangements: food processing needs to have an institutional arrangement with agriculture because it is an important part of the 'food chain' and raw materials account for a significant proportion of the industry's costs; construction needs to be in the Department of the Environment because of its importance to housing policy; medical supplies and pharmaceuticals should be located at the Department of Health and Social Security because the National Health Service is the industry's principal customer. However, these particular justifications need to be balanced against the general desirability of promoting the overall co-ordination of government industrial policy, although such overall co-ordination is probably more important when one has a selective intervention policy than when a social market policy is being pursued.

It is difficult to generalize about the relationship between the Industry Department and sponsoring divisions in other departments. In some cases, the sponsoring divisions located elsewhere almost see themselves as outposts of Industry; in other cases, the relationship is more tenuous. Some of the sponsoring divisions in other departments do feel that they are rather left out of things, both in terms of their relationship with their own department and Industry. In some cases, it is felt that they have fewer manpower resources to cope with their industry than would be the case if they were running a sponsorship operation within the Industry Department. There has also been a tendency for selective assistance schemes in the past to be concentrated on industries sponsored by the Industry Department, although this could be justified in terms of the concentration of the last Labour Government's Industrial Strategy on the problems of the engineering industry.

Two questions need to be answered in any attempt to evaluate the desirability of transferring these sponsorship functions to the Industry Department. Would such a transfer enable anything to be done in the way of industrial policy which could not be achieved by interdepartmental co-ordination? Would the transfer make it more difficult to undertake initiatives which are facilitated by present arrangements, e.g. the efforts of Peter Walker as Agriculture Minister to build closer links between the three elements of the 'food chain': agriculture, the food processing industry and food distribution. It should also be remembered that any redistribution of functions would have to take place at the beginning of a new administration or as part of a major ministerial reshuffle, since taking away a major slice of a minister's work is a political as well as a machinery-of-government question.

2.2 Public agencies and industrial policy

The use of public agencies, or 'quangos' as they are often somewhat misleadingly called[11], for the discharge of particular policy functions acquired by central government has been transformed in recent years from a little ventilated machinery-of-government question to a quite highly charged political issue. However, despite the political passions which the existence of large numbers of such agencies arouse in some quarters, attempts at mass 'quangocide' have made less impact than might be supposed (Hood, 1980).

The debate about the general advantages and disadvantages of the public agency format will not be entered into here, except to point out that three questions need to be borne in mind when assessing the desirability of using a public agency to discharge a particular government function. Should the particular task be a responsibility of government? If so, is it best discharged by a government department or a public agency? If the task is given to a public agency, how can the tension between the agency's need for autonomy and demands for adequate accountability best be managed?

One striking fact about the agencies for which the Industry Department is responsible, compared with those handled by the other major economic departments, is their relatively capital-intensive character. In 1978–79, public bodies for which the Industry Department was accountable had a gross total expenditure per employee of just over £295 000; the comparable figures for Agriculture, Employment, Energy, Trade and Transport ranged between just under £15 000 and just over £18 000[12]. This difference largely reflects the activities of the NEB and the Board is of such central importance to the debate about recent British industrial policy that it will be considered separately in Chapter Five. Similarly, the Scottish, Welsh and Northern Ireland Development Agencies, and the National Research Development Corporation, whose work is related to that of the NEB, will also be considered in Chapter Five. There are a number of other public agencies which discharge important industrial policy tasks and which are considered below.

The National Economic Development Council

The tripartite National Economic Development Council (NEDC), with its representatives from government, employers and the unions (plus City and consumer representation), has played an important role in the development of British industrial policy. At the time of its formation in 1962 it was seen as being largely concerned with macro-economic questions and the promotion of economic growth, although it always had an Industrial Division. Under the 1964 Labour Government, and particularly after the National Plan was killed off by the 1966 deflationary package, the work of the Industrial Division and the Economic Development Committees (EDCs) dealing with the problems of particular industries, grew in importance (Leruez, 1975). The NEDC survived the threat of abolition by the Conservatives in 1970 and, after an uncertain phase at the start of the 1974 Labour Government's term of office, came to play a crucial role in the Government's Industrial Strategy (discussed more fully in Chapter Three). The dominance of micro-economic work at this stage of the NEDC's life is demonstrated by the fact that eighty-seven staff were employed by the Industry Division in 1979 compared with sixty-seven in all other operational divisions[13].

As under the 1970–74 Conservative Government, meetings of the Council remain important, if only as one of the few regular points of tripartite contact. NEDC has become more concerned once again with macro-economic questions, or at least cross-sectoral questions such as the prices paid by industry for energy. However, a number of important staff papers have been produced on such topics as the form and extent of industrial aid in other countries, particularly to high technology. These papers have undoubtedly made a significant contribution to the debate within government about the conduct of industrial policy.

Industrial development in rural areas

The Council for Small Industries in Rural Areas (CoSIRA) was set up in 1968 to support employment in small firms in rural parts of England. It is financed by the Government through the Development Commission, a body established to assist rural areas in 1909. Although CoSIRA is the most important aspect of the Commission's work, its wider responsibilities as a rural development agency mean that it reports to the Department of the Environment and not to the Industry Department.

Working in partnership with local authorities, the Commission devises programmes of small-scale factory building in rural areas which are executed by CoSIRA and the English Industrial Estates Corporation. CoSIRA also provides business management and technical advice, training facilities and a credit service to small manufacturing, servicing and some other businesses in rural areas. It did seem for a time that the Development Commission and CoSIRA might be disbanded by the 1979 Conservative Government. Although both bodies survived, the Commission has argued that if they and CoSIRA are 'to be really effective as a rural development agency for England, the Commission needs to be given greater freedom of action and an assurance of adequate long-term financing'[14].

Specialist bodies concerned with rural development also operate in Wales and Scotland. The Development Board for Rural Wales started work in 1977 and is able to acquire land, develop property and provide factories and offices to assist the development of Mid-Wales. The Commons Welsh Affairs Committee expressed its concern that the complete loss of assisted area status in parts of Mid-Wales will adversely affect the Development Board's operations[15].

The Highlands and Islands Development Board, established in 1965, has won considerable respect for its determined and imaginative efforts to tackle the very special problems of the remoter parts of Scotland. The problems encountered in this large but very sparsely populated region are very different from these found in rural England and, although the Board has clearly been helped by the advent of North Sea Oil, it must be able to claim some credit for a long-run reduction in unemployment relative to other parts of the country since 1966 and, within the Highlands and Islands, a relative improvement in the more remote areas[16].

In 1979 about one-third of the Board's expenditure on financial assistance went to manufacturing industry, crafts or non-tourist services. Assistance to manufacturing industry over the 1971–79 period totalled nearly £9 million with over 6000 jobs being created or retained. The Board's assistance mainly goes to small firms, for small projects. An analysis of the total value of grants and other financial incentives from 1971 to 1978 at 1978 prices showed that, of 3318 cases approved, forty-five per cent involved a 'grant equivalence' of less than £3000, while only 1.3 per cent involved a 'grant equivalence' of more than £100000[17]. Approval by the Scottish Economic Planning Department is required for assistance totalling more than £250000 for any one project, but only one case of this type occurred in 1979.

Co-operative Development Agency

The Co-operative Development Agency was established in 1978 with all-party support and an initial funding ceiling of £900000 to cover a three-year period. The role of the Agency is advisory and promotional, and it has no development funds to invest in co-operative projects. It has placed particular emphasis on assisting local authorities to develop co-operative projects in their areas. The continued existence of the Agency beyond the initial three-year period cannot be assured, particularly as it would be relatively easy to dissolve[18].

English Industrial Estates Corporation

The English Industrial Estates Corporation has a substantial budget for the construction of advance factories in the assisted areas, but its functions are not generally seen as politically controversial. The 1979 Conservative Government has stated that 'Factory building is a useful and relatively inexpensive instrument of regional industrial policy and will continue.'[19] The 1980 Industry Act provides for a greater degree of self-financing and the involvement of private sector finance and it is intended that the Corporation should become more commercially oriented.

2.3 Parliament and the making of industrial policy

There is considerable discussion of industrial policy questions in Parliament, but major industrial policy legislation has been little altered in its passage through Parliament. Control of secondary legislation which is often necessary to implement selective assistance schemes is even less satisfactory and there was no Parliamentary control over, or input into, Labour's industrial strategy (Coombes and Walkland, 1980). Edmund Dell had argued that Parliamentary control of the Executive is particularly weak over industrial policy decisions that discriminate between companies, industries or regions. In his view, governments often have to work harder to justify their industrial policy interventions internationally than they are ever likely to have to do to win Parliamentary support (Dell, 1973).

Even when the Labour Government lost its Commons majority during the lifetime of the 1974–79 Parliament, it can hardly be said that this represented a significant constraint on the Government's development of its industrial policies, although it might have sometimes offered a convenient excuse for the lack of progress towards socialism. Parliamentary Questions can, of course, sometimes extract significant nuggets of information from industry ministers, but given the quality and depth of the briefing given by civil servants, they are unlikely to lead to major revelations.

The main hope of a Parliamentary contribution to the making of industrial policy must lie in its committee system. It is here, particularly in the new specialist committees introduced in the 1979 Parliament, that the complex web of industrial policy can be unravelled through the cross-examination of ministers and civil servants. The Public Accounts Committee, with the services of the Comptroller and Auditor-General at its disposal, has made a significant contribution to the debate about the efficacy of various industrial policy measures, particularly through its investigations of regional policy. Of the new specialist committees, both the Scottish and Welsh Affairs committees chose industrial policy topics for their first reports, although the Government's subsequent rejection of the recommendations of the critical Welsh Affairs committee report emphasizes the limited powers of such committees.

The specialist Industry and Trade committee got off to a slower start with a rather long-winded investigation of imports which was not published until 1981 with some sensible but rather dull conclusions about such matters as EEC control of dumping (Industry and Trade Committee, 1980–81). Although almost every witness who gave evidence to the committee took up a position on the question of free trade and protectionism, the committee avoided delivering a verdict on this central issue of industrial policy, noting that 'The division of opinion goes deep in the country and finds a reflection within the Committee also.'[20] Very often, specialist committees have to avoid contentious issues or risk a split on party or other lines, which inevitably diminishes the impact of any report produced. Perhaps it is unrealistic to hope that specialist committees will do more than provide useful background information for discussions of policy in the way that the reports of the House of Lords Select Committee on the European Communities have helped to unveil some of the mysteries of Community industrial policy.

One must not forget the specialist backbench committees which exist within each Parliamentary Party. These are particularly important within the Conservative Party, where the annual elections for officers of these committees are often keenly contested. Ministers appear before the backbench committees from time to time to explain and defend their policies, particularly when new legislation is in prospect. They can also be a promotion route. In 1981, the chairman of the Conservative backbench Industry Committee, Kenneth Baker, was made Minister of State for Industry in a reshuffle. As well as the Industry Committee, the Conservatives also have specialist groups dealing with smaller businesses and with shipping and shipbuilding. Labour has groups dealing with industry, steel and shipping. The experience of the Lib–Lab pact encouraged the practice of consulting Labour subject groups about pending legislation so as to balance the consultations with the Liberals (Kaufman, 1980).

Apart from the general factors which limit the influence of Parliament such as the nature of the party system and insufficient staff resources, there are a number of special factors which apply in the industrial policy arena to limit Parliament's contribution to the development of policy. First, important decisions on industrial policy matters are taken by public agencies such as the NEB; the continuing debate about how the need for autonomy of these bodies can be reconciled with Parliamentary accountability is discussed in Chapter Five. Second, many of the decisions taken in the sphere of industrial policy, such as those to grant or refuse selective financial assistance, involve the proper use of discretion by civil servants in what are in effect negotiations with individual companies which are difficult to subject to systematic Parliamentary control. Third, whatever decisions are taken in the future about official secrecy, many matters which arise in the course of government's discussions with firms could not be disclosed without damaging consequences such as revealing commercial secrets to foreign competitors or making public the true extent of the difficulties of a particular company, thus pushing it into a liquidation which might otherwise have been avoided.

2.4 Interest groups

The single most important interest group in the industrial policy arena is the Confederation of British Industry (CBI). In part, this reflects the growing effectiveness of the CBI as an organization in recent years (Grant, 1980; 1981), and in particular the increasing attention which the CBI has given to industrial policy questions, culminating in the formation of a top level Industrial Policy committee within the organization in 1978. It also reflects a general willingness within government to listen to arguments advanced by the CBI. This attitude is well illustrated by a letter written in January 1970 by a Deputy Secretary at the Ministry of Technology to Campbell Adamson, then Director-General of the CBI. The letter reminded Campbell Adamson that the expanded Ministry of Technology had the task of 'advising the Minister on the main lines of industrial policy including such major topics as further work on the rationalization and restructuring of industry and the review of various forms of assistance to industry . . . in this work it would obviously be of great benefit to the department if we could have a regular opportunity of discussion with you on major questions on which we are working or which seem important to you in the development of Government thinking'[21]. The letter suggested a series of regular exchanges at monthly or two-monthly intervals, held alternately at the Ministry and CBI offices, supplemented by specialist groups on particular aspects of industry if necessary.

The implementation of these arrangements was overtaken by the 1970 general election and the subsequent dissolution of the Ministry of Technology, but the example does illustrate the generally close contacts which exist between government and the CBI on industrial policy matters. Indeed, Shirley Williams has suggested that the Department of Industry is 'very close to the CBI and to industrial interests'[22].

The work done on industrial policy by the CBI is supplemented by the contribution to the debate on industrial policy by the large number of specialist sector and product associations. Some of these, such as the Chemical Industries Association, command substantial resources and are widely respected as authoritative spokesmen for their industry. Organizations of this calibre will have regular contacts on both a formal and an informal level with civil servants, particularly those in the relevant sponsoring divisions. One arrangement, which operates in the aluminium industry, may be to invite the relevant civil servants to sit in at meetings of a committee of the trade association. However, there are also a large number of small associations with inadequate resources which do not command respect in government. Attempts to reform the system of industrial representation have met with little success, although sometimes government has itself played a significant role in stimulating a reorganization or rationalization in a particular sector.

The trade union movement

Even under a Labour Government, the trade union movement often complains about its lack of influence on industrial policy. It may be that civil servants are less used to developing close contacts with trade unionists than they are with industrialists, although good contacts have existed between individual trade union leaders and civil servants in sponsoring divisions. In any case, the blame for this state of affairs cannot simply be laid at the door of government. Although the TUC's Economic Committee has identified industrial policy as a growing area of its work, the fact that it talks about 'the *development* of a strong and coherent TUC industrial policy'[23] amounts to an admission that such a policy does not exist.

The trade union movement's organizational arrangements for dealing with industrial policy matters are not as effective as they might be, although this state of affairs is in part a reflection of a lack of resources and the weakness of the TUC compared to the individual unions (as distinct from the strength of the CBI compared with the individual industry associations). However, the TUC does not have a direct equivalent of the CBI's Industrial Policy Committee, although it does have a series of committees dealing with individual industries ranging from the steel industry to the hotel and catering industry. In part, these committees offer a forum where a number of (often rival) unions in a particular industry can be brought together to try to develop a common approach to problems. Although the committees are often understandably preoccupied with industrial relations questions, they have also concerned themselves with broader industrial policy issues. The TUC considers that the industry committees are 'working well'[24], although the fact that it has urged a 'wider circulation to documents' by member unions and pointed to the need for 'a systematic feed-back to the TUC on how unions are using industry committees' work'[25] suggests that relations between the industry committees and the unions represented on them are often tenuous. Moreover, the recommendation that 'industry committees should establish links with appropriate outside bodies (SWPs, industry advisory committees etc.) and should consider the work of such bodies at least once a year'[26] poses the question of why such an obvious step has not already been taken.

However, even when the trade union movement is presented with opportunities to exert influence on industrial policy, it does not necessarily take advantage of them. The attendance record of trade unionists at NEDC Sector Working Party and Economic Development Committee meetings has often been poor (although attendance at meetings of the Council itself have been taken seriously by the so-called 'Neddy Six' group of leading union leaders). Under a selective assistance scheme for the wool textile industry, companies were eligible for assistance only if they had consulted with the unions, but in some plants all that happened was that 'a headquarters union official signed the relevant document which indicated consultation had taken place'[27]. In some cases, 'one union official signed the consultation document before the other unions had been consulted', but, as the study of the scheme drily observes, 'this . . . appears to be a function of union organization'[28]. That might be said of a lot of the problems which the trade union movement encounters in attempting to exert influence on industrial policy.

The CBI's influence on industrial policy does not vary greatly between a Conservative Government and a Labour Government; indeed, it could be argued that the CBI had more influence on the 1974–79 Labour Government than it was able to exert in the first two years of the 1979 Conservative Government. The trade union movement, on the other hand, does enjoy better contacts with a Labour Government and its hopes of seeing the kind of industrial policy it wants implemented must rest with the return of a Labour Government. In December 1980 the Labour Party and the TUC set up a joint twelve-member committee to prepare a new kind of industrial strategy in which central planning and shopfloor worker democracy would be fused.

2.5 The firm

It should not be forgotten that the ultimate target of all the government activity in the arena of industrial policy, at least under a social market or selective intervention approach, is the individual firm. It is therefore disturbing to learn that firms often have a rather poor knowledge of the subsidies available to industry (Walker and Krist, 1980). Industry Department concern about lack of knowledge among firms of the range of financial assistance available was reflected in a letter written in 1980 by a Deputy Secretary to the *Sunday Times Business News* about aid for research and development which concluded, 'We should be grateful if you would publicise these facts, since there is some evidence that the availability of this support is not as widely known as we should wish.'[29]

Transnational companies

Academic analysis of the part played by individual firms in economic and industrial policy-making has concentrated on the study (which usually means the criticism) of the transnational corporation. Concern has been expressed about the ability of such firms to play the government of one country off against another to obtain the most favourable package of financial incentives; the skill that such companies display at minimizing their tax burden through the use of such devices as transfer pricing; their alleged propensity to deal with financial difficulties by closing branch factories, although whether they have a greater propensity to do this than domestic companies is not clear; and the weakness of attempts by international organizations to draw up and enforce codes of conduct, or of the efforts of trade unions to mobilize countervailing power.

It should be remembered that Britain has a large number of transnational companies of its own: the second largest number of companies and employees after the United States among the larger transnationals[30], and the second highest level of overseas production as a percentage of domestic output after Switzerland[31]. The consequent existence of an informal 'foreign lobby' in London with an interest in overseas investment is perhaps a more important constraint on British industrial policy than the activities of foreign-owned transnationals.

The relative weakness of nation states in dealing with transnationals is seen as being illustrated in the UK by the sequence of events in relation to what was originally the Rootes Motor Company. The Government was unable and unwilling to prevent the original acquisition of Rootes by Chrysler at its various stages, and simply obtained what turned out to be meaningless assurances. When Chrysler threatened to close its UK operation, the Government had to persuade them to stay by means of a financial package that was incompatible with its recently announced industrial strategy, despite the Prime Minister's subsequently declared distaste for what he referred to as "'blackmail'" and a pistol being held 'at the heads of the Government'[32]. Subsequently, the Government had to accept the transmutation of Chrysler UK into Talbot through its sale to Peugeot-Citroen despite complaints by a minister that Chrysler had been 'less than straightforward'[33] over the merger talks. On the other hand, it may be that if the Government had stood its ground in 1975, it would have been able to negotiate a much more favourable agreement with Chrysler (Wilks, 1980). Also, if all transnationals behaved in a similar way, political pressure for their stricter control would become irresistible.

Government relations departments

There is a substantial body of economic theory dealing with the firm and organization theorists have made their own distinctive contribution to a fuller understanding of the behaviour of firms. However, there have been very few attempts to develop a political science contribution to the study of firms (an exception is Tivey, 1978). One important topic that has been neglected in the United Kingdom, if not in the United States, is the development of a specialized political function within very large firms through the formation of government relations departments. Data on the distribution of such specialized units is incomplete, partly because they operate under a variety of titles, but it is clear that they are most common in the very largest firms. Seven of the ten largest industrial companies were known to have such units in 1980. The government relations director of one of those companies commented when interviewed: 'Any big company should have a government affairs function, particularly a major corporation with manufacturing plant in a number of countries—there is a need for a political input into investment decisions. Country X has good wage rates, good grants, but is it going to persist over ten years, will there be a breakdown in political cohesion?' A senior government relations executive with another of the 'top ten' companies commented, 'Our planning staff are doing the econometric guessing, but we also need an input on social and political guesses.'

The existence of such specialized units in very large companies is of little importance if they are merely upgraded public relations departments with little input into company decision-making. However, although the degree of integration varied from one company to another, many of the companies interviewed had elaborate arrangements for taking the views of the government relations unit into account in corporate planning and also for the development of a government relations strategy. Although government relations staff tend to be small (the largest unit had fourteen staff, including secretaries), the executives employed are generally of high calibre. In a typical department, a government relations executive might be responsible for managing an issue (e.g. impending legislation affecting the firm's activities), for monitoring an organization (e.g. the Conservative Party or the TUC), and for running a programme (e.g. senior management contacts with MPs). Considerable use is also made in many firms of 'bought in' information and expertise, e.g. from Parliamentary consultants or specialized research institutes.

Given the importance of very large firms in the UK economy, governments naturally tend to develop direct contacts with them, particularly on industrial policy issues. The emergence of government relations departments (largely over the 1970s) is in part a reflection of the importance of such contacts and allows firms to develop a more sophisticated approach to their relations with government. The attitude of civil servants to this development appears to vary in accordance with their responsibilities. Civil servants with a strategic policy function welcome the existence of a central point of contact with government in each firm, but those with more specific responsibilities for a particular industry or programme often feel that direct contacts with those in the firm with the relevant technical expertise are of more value and that routing such contacts through a government relations department can be a hindrance rather than a help.

2.6 Conclusions: the problem of co-ordination

The increasing centralization of the government relations function within firms stands in some contrast to the picture that emerged earlier in the chapter of the dispersal of government industrial policy functions around a number of locations, both within central government and a number of public agencies. One defence for this apparently chaotic arrangement is what might be termed the 'Whitehall view': it would not be subscribed to in its entirety by any one civil servant, although it emerged from the interviews conducted with civil servants as part of this study.

According to this viewpoint, the way in which the machinery of government is organized is not really very important and, in any case, it is easier to operate the system than to describe it. The machinery of government cannot be analysed in a mechanistic fashion, as there is a fluid network of contacts which is almost as important as the fixed network that could be explained in an organization chart. The links are so numerous and close—between ministers and their private offices, through Cabinet committees, interdepartmental official committees and bilateral links between civil servants with related responsibilities—that it doesn't really matter all that much where the functions are. In any case, it is argued, changes in the formal structure can follow from *ad hoc* groupings that acquire a permanent character. The interpretation is underpinned by certain widely held political values such as a belief in providing a number of points of access (and incorporation) for affected interests; a confidence in the value of the diversity of approaches to problems that can result from letting a hundred institutional flowers bloom; and a desire to prevent monolithic concentrations of institutional power.

Given the collegiate character of the civil service, there is no doubt that the system does work smoothly within the network of central departments. However, more problems can occur with the 'outer rim' of public agencies, who often feel that they face a choice between neglect and haphazard interference. As Hogwood points out, 'Links are often weakest where sectoral and regional concerns cross-cut; for example, links between regional development agencies and "industrial strategy" organizations such as the NEDC.'[34] Moreover, the complexity of government arrangements for dealing with industrial policy can foster institutional rivalries and confuse and frighten off the ultimate clients of the system, the industrialists. For example, an Industry Department Under-Secretary was asked in cross-examination at a session of the Commons Scottish Affairs Committee: 'Some written evidence we have had . . . indicated that American executives looking to the United Kingdom, and to Scotland in particular, were concerned about dealing with a plethora of energetic representatives lacking co-ordination. From what you have been saying you would accept that?' The Under-Secretary replied: 'That is a polite description of what happens, yes.'[35]

In such a fragmented system, co-ordination mechanisms are very important if policy formulation and its execution is to have any coherence. The importance of the Industrial and Commercial Policy divisions within the Industry Department and the Industrial Policy Group in the Treasury as a means of securing co-ordination have already been outlined, although the co-ordination function in the Scottish Office might benefit from further development. There is also an important role for interdepartmental committees such as that on Overseas Promotion set up 'to prevent clashes between promotional activities . . . to promote mutual trust and to discourage unnecessary secrecy and wasteful competition between agencies'[36], terms of reference which indicated that lack of trust, secrecy and wasteful competition were seen as problems.

The advantages of a merger of the Industry and Trade departments have also been outlined. Nevertheless, such a merger would still leave a number of important functions related to industrial policy being discharged elsewhere in government. Apart from the sponsoring divisions in other departments, the Department of Employment deals with manpower and training policy which undoubtedly has a crucial impact on the health of the industrial economy; the work of the Ministry of Defence has a considerable impact on some sectors of industry; and it could be argued that some of the functions discharged by the Department of Education and Science are highly relevant to the wellbeing of industry. However, there are limits to the extent to which the merger process could be taken without disrupting the discharge of other equally important policy responsibilities and creating a ministry of unwieldy size.

There might be a case for the creation of a strategic co-ordination function, discharged by a senior minister of Cabinet rank (holding some honorific title such as Paymaster-General) with responsibility for the co-ordination of all aspects of policy concerned with both the promotion of industrial efficiency and the social consequences of industrial change. Although the apparent fragmentation of the industrial policy community is offset by the informal links between policy-makers, the dispersal of functions can make the pursuit of a coherent industrial policy more difficult. The sense of shared purpose that arises from a genuine concern among policy-makers for the wellbeing of the industrial economy can all too easily be overriden by the disputes that arise as a result of the discharge of overlapping functions.

A co-ordinating minister could not prevent such disputes arising in the tangled web of industrial policy decision-making, but he might be able to help to resolve them more quickly and effectively. For example, such a minister could undertake the co-ordination of important individual issues which cut across the responsibilities of several departments through the chairmanship of cabinet committees. The job would not be an easy one, as the minister would be exposed to conflicting policy pressures and would lack executive authority. It could be argued that the unhappy precedent of the first Wilson Government's Department of Economic Affairs is relevant, but the DEA had broader functions, and it suffered from being seen as a potential rival to the Treasury. It could also be argued that it would be more sensible to centralize the discharge of industrial policy functions within government, rather than appoint a co-ordinating minister. However, the feasibility of that option is reduced by the likelihood of ministers resisting the transfer of any of the functions of their departments elsewhere; and the fact that the single most important complicating factor, the existence of special industrial policy-making and implementation arrangements for Scotland, Wales and Northern Ireland, cannot be tackled without offending highly sensitive regional bodies of public opinion. A co-ordinating minister could help to ensure that the best possible use was made of the range of policy instruments available to government and that the reactive, crisis management aspects of industrial policy—which will always be there—did not dwarf the pursuit of a longterm strategy unconfined by departmental boundaries.

The arguments presented in this chapter have rested on an assumption that the institutional arrangements for the conduct of industrial policy do matter. There has been an understandable reaction against the 'institutionitis' of the 1960s which involved the belief that the answer to every problem was the creation of a new public agency. However, this has perhaps developed into an overreaction, so that the assumption that organizational change is the answer to everything is replaced by the assumption that organizational arrangements do not really matter at all. Indeed, this scepticism about the importance of institutional arrangements is able to draw on the belief of some economists that 'the excellence or otherwise of administrative machinery can only be judged by its results'[37]. Although one can get good results with bad machinery and bad results with good machinery, the chances of getting the results one wants must be enhanced if the machinery of government is designed to facilitate the achievement of the central goals of policy.

Notes to Chapter Two

1. B. W. Hogwood, 'Analysing Industrial Policy: a multi-perspective approach'. *Public Administration Bulletin*, No. 29, April 1979, pp.18–42, p.37
2. *Committee to Review the Functioning of Financial Institutions, Evidence on the Financing of Industry and Trade*, Volume 1 (London: HMSO, 1977), p.84
3. Organization for Economic Co-operation and Development, *The Aims and Instruments of Industrial Policy* (Paris: OECD, 1975), p.10
4. House of Commons Industry and Trade Committee, Session 1979–80, Minutes of Evidence, 23rd January 1980, *Department of Industry*, Q.94
5. C. Freeman, 'Government Policy', in K. Pavitt (Ed.), *Technical Innovation and British Economic Performance* (London: Macmillan, 1980), pp.310-325, p.323
6. Cabinet Office/Advisory Council for Applied Research and Development, *Information Technology* (London: HMSO, 1980), p.7
7. ibid., p.49
8. ibid., p.7
9. H. Heclo and A. Wildavsky, *The Private Government of Public Money* (London: Macmillan, 1974), p.45
10. House of Commons Committee on Welsh Affairs, First Report, Session 1979–80, *The Role of the Welsh Office and Associated Bodies in Developing Employment Opportunities in Wales*, Vol. 1, p.xxxiii
11. The original academic literature on the subject distinguished between quasi-governmental organizations and quasi-non-governmental organizations ('quangos'). 'Quasis' are now popularly referred to as 'quangos'. *See* D. C. Hague, W. J. M. Mackenzie and A. Barker, *Public Policy and Private Interests* (London: Macmillan, 1975)
12. Figures derived from Cmnd.7797, *Report on Non-Departmental Bodies*
13. National Economic Development Council, *Annual Report, 1978–79*, p.24
14. *38th Report of the Development Commission, 1979–80*, p.vii
15. House of Commons Committee on Welsh Affairs, First Report[10], p.xxviii
16. *14th Annual Report of the Highlands and Islands Development Board, 1979*, p.8
17. Minute of Evidence taken before the Committee on Scottish Affairs, Inverness, 21st April 1980, p.89
18. *See* Cmnd.7797[12], p.94
19. House of Commons Industry and Trade Committee, p.68
20. First Report from the House of Commons Industry and Trade Committee, Session 1980–81, *Imports and Exports*, p.lxxxv
21. CBI Archive, Modern Records Centre, University of Warwick, Gough papers, TBN 7/2, Miscellaneous correspondence 1970 (January–February), letter from R. B. Marshall, Deputy Secretary, Ministry of Technology, to Campbell Adamson
22. S. Williams, 'The Decision Makers' in Royal Institute of Public Administration, *Policy and Practice: the Experience of Government* (London: RIPA, 1980), pp.79-102, p.93

23. Trades Union Congress, *The Organization, Structure and Services of the TUC*, TUC Consultative Document, December 1980, p.23
24. ibid., p.12
25. ibid., p.26
26. ibid., p.26
27. Department of Industry, *Wool Textile Industry Scheme* (London: Department of Industry, 1978), p.24
28. ibid., p.24
29. Letter from R. H. W. Bullock, published in the *Sunday Times Business News,* November 2nd, 1980
30. N. Hood and S. Young, *The Economics of Multinational Enterprise* (London: Longman, 1979), p.17
31. Conference of Socialist Economists, London Working Group, *The Alternative Economic Strategy* (London: CSE Books, 1980), p.28
32. H. Wilson, *Final Term* (London: Weidenfeld and Nicolson and Michael Joseph, 1979), p.197
33. Alan Williams, *H. C. Debs.,* Vol. 958, c.23
34. Hogwood[1], p.35
35. Second Report from the Committee on Scottish Affairs, 1979–80, *Inward Investment,* Vol. 2, Minutes of Evidence, Q.249
36. ibid., Q.1041
37. R. Pryke, *Public Enterprise in Practice* (London: MacGibbon and Kee, 1971), p.457

Chapter Three

Selective Intervention, 1972–1979

3.1 The continuity of policy

Although the period from 1972 to 1979 saw three different administrations in the United Kingdom, it was marked by a basic continuity in the conduct of industrial policy. Successive governments and ministers attempted to design and execute an industrial policy based on a belief in the efficacy of selective intervention. There was a short interregnum in this continuous process of policy development when Mr Benn, as Industry Minister from February 1974 to June 1975, attempted with little success to implement what he saw as a socialist industrial policy. However, Mr Benn faced considerable opposition within the Government, not least from the Prime Minister who personally took charge of the preparation of what was to become the 1975 Industry Act. Harold Wilson did not conceal his distaste for what was going on in the Department of Industry at the political level and subsequently described the Department's draft White Paper on industrial policy as 'a sloppy and half-baked document, polemical, indeed menacing in tone, redolent more of an NEC Home Policy Committee document than a Command Paper'[1]. All that Mr Benn left behind him was a few symbolic but highly controversial achievements such as the worker co-operatives at Meriden, Kirkby and the *Scottish Daily News* project, all eventually to collapse in their original form. Some commentators have placed much of the blame for the failure of Mr Benn's approach to industrial policy on civil service obstruction (Sedgemore, 1980), but it is clear that a more consensual approach to industrial policy was widely favoured within the Cabinet and the Parliamentary Labour Party, if not among the party in the country.

Benn's successor at Industry, Eric Varley, fitted more closely into the established pattern of ministers quietly administering with care and caution a gradually evolving set of policies. The maintenance of continuity in policy was assisted by the fact that many senior civil servants remained in the Industry department throughout the period. For example, John Lippitt, who had a particular concern with programmes of selective aid, was at the Department of Trade and Industry and subsequently the Department of Industry, ultimately as a Deputy Secretary, leaving to take up a senior post with GEC early in 1980. Mr Lippitt, who maintained a rather high profile even for a modern civil servant, frequently appeared before enquiries such as the Wilson Committee and Parliamentary Select Committees to explain and justify the Department's policies.

Labour's industrial policies were as much based on the Conservatives' 1972 Industry Act as they were on their own 1975 Act. The 1972 Act, one of the major changes of political direction introduced in the now almost legendary 'U turn' of that year, represented the most comprehensive and most interventionist piece of legislation concerning government assistance to the private sector ever to have been passed in Britain. Its corporatist philosophy, with potentially controversial initiatives under the Act being cleared by the Industrial Development Advisory Boards representing major industrial interests, fitted in well not only with Mr Heath's approach to industrial policy matters in his post-1972 phase, but also with the approaches of Mr Wilson and Mr Callaghan. The Act's provision of a detailed set of arrangements for industrial aid and its permissive character gave it sufficient flexibility to be used in a number of different ways by the three successive administrations, although use was also made of the 1965 Science and Technology Act, a measure forged in the white heat of Mr Wilson's scientific revolution. Nevertheless, the 1972 Act remained the principal piece of legislation in use throughout the period. As Mr Lippitt put it in 1978, 'It provides the necessary statutory cover for the policies.' Asked, 'Have you come across anything that you would have liked to do that the statute did not permit?', he replied, 'Not yet, to my knowledge.'[2]

Labour's 1975 Industry Act had its origins in the ideas generated by the Labour Party in opposition, with a particularly influential contribution being made by the socialist economist, Stuart Holland. In a lucid and well informed analysis, Hatfield has shown how the original radical proposals were watered down, first in opposition and then in government (Hatfield, 1978). In fact, the Act in its final form did contain some radical provisions, but, unlike the provisions of the 1972 Act, they were never used. Part II of the 1975 Act contained provisions to prevent the loss of important British manufacturing companies to foreign control through the prohibition of the acquisition of such undertakings by foreign firms. However, the Department of Industry was anxious to encourage foreign investment and in recognition of the importance of this function upgraded it through the creation of the Invest in Britain Bureau in 1977. Part IV of the Act gave the Government powers to require companies to disclose information to government and the unions on such matters as capital structure, sales and research and development. The need to secure Parliamentary approval and the fear of upsetting industry and losing its co-operation were enough to ensure that these powers were never used, and they were repealed in the 1980 Act. The Act also provided the legislative framework for negotiating planning agreements, but the relevant provisions were repealed in the 1980 Act. The main lasting achievement of the 1975 Act was the establishment of the National Enterprise Board, but the guidelines issued to the Board by the Industry Secretary and the philosophy espoused by the Board itself ensured that it did not resemble the instrument of socialist reconstruction envisaged by its progenitors but rather a state merchant bank.

3.2 The forms of selective aid

The period 1972–1979 in industrial policy was characterized by a complex series of selective assistance schemes, largely operated under the terms of the 1972 Act. The most important parts of the Act as far as selective assistance is concerned are Sections 7 and 8. Section 7 of the Act provides for discretionary government assistance to projects that create or safeguard employment in the assisted areas or regions. Such assistance has usually been provided in the form of interest relief grants to 'top up' the major form of regional assistance, the 'automatic' Regional Development Grant which has been given since 1972 to all qualifying assets in the assisted regions without any job creation or retention test being applied.

Assistance under Section 8 of the 1972 Act is not restricted to the assisted areas and is supposed to benefit the economy and serve the national interest. Section 8 has been used to assist capital-intensive projects in the regions, but its main use has been to support projects in the non-assisted areas. The Section 8 powers were used by the Labour Government in three main ways.

First, a number of schemes of aid were devised for individual industrial sectors. Lippitt described the purpose of these schemes as being 'to take a particular industry and over a reasonable period of time to jack it up into a modern, efficient competitive situation'[3]. The first two schemes were introduced by the Conservatives in 1973 covering wool textiles and offshore supplies to oil installations. The Labour Government introduced a further fourteen schemes covering such diverse industries as machine tools, paper and board, footwear and red meat slaughterhouses. Up to March 1980 £272 million of assistance had been offered under the sectoral schemes, with another £52 million of payments under the offshore supplies scheme.

Second, there were general schemes to encourage new industrial invest-ment. The first of these, Labour's Accelerated Projects Scheme (APS), was open for applications from April 1975 to June 1976 and was designed to have a counter-cyclical effect in the recession and to encourage companies to bring forward investment projects that might otherwise have been deferred. A total of 111 projects were assisted involving £72 million of assistance and £568 million in project costs. The Selective Investment Scheme (SIS) which succeeded APS was intended to encourage companies to go ahead with projects costing more than £500000, particularly in the engineering industry, which might otherwise have been abandoned, built abroad, or executed on a smaller scale. By the closing date in June 1979 742 applications had been received and by March 1980, grants totalling £106.5 million had been offered to 166 projects involving capital outlays of over £1000 million. The assistance offered varied between three per cent and twenty-one per cent of project costs, averaging at 10.5 per cent. The scheme was very successful in attracting inward investment projects to the UK, with thirty-five such projects being offered assistance up to March 1980 with eighty per cent of the resultant investment being located in the assisted areas[4].

Finally, Section 8 was also used for one-off rescues such as those of

British Leyland and Chrysler. At one stage, rescues accounted for about one-half of Section 8 payments, but they declined in relative importance in the latter part of Labour's term of office. Section 8 powers were also used by the Labour Government in 1978 to introduce a scheme designed to facilitate energy conservation by industry. Apart from small scale assistance towards consultancies, £12.2 million of assistance to capital projects had been offered by March 1980.

The Product and Process Development Scheme (PPDS) launched in 1977 consolidated a number of earlier aid schemes supporting research and/or development operated under the 1965 Science and Technology Act such as the Pre-Production Order Scheme. PPDS was designed to assist firms in bearing the cost of product and/or process development from the design stage up to the point of commercial production, special attention being given to new products and processes.

The Microprocessor Application Project (MAP) was launched as a crash programme in 1978 under the 1965 Act against a background of concern at the UK's slow rate of takeup of this key technology compared with major competitors. The objectives of MAP were to raise significantly national awareness of the potential of micro-electronics at all levels in UK industry; to increase substantially the supply of people retrained in micro-electronics skills; to help firms to establish the relevance of micro-electronics to their business; and to improve the rate of application of micro-electronics in firms' products and processes, particularly by first-time users. The Government also launched in 1978 the Micro-electronics Industry Support Programme (MISP), funded through the 1965 Act and Section 8. The scheme particularly emphasized assistance for the design and manufacture of silicon integrated circuits and the infrastructure companies supplying goods and services to the industry.

The administration of these various schemes will be discussed in Chapter Four. The general point that needs to be noted here is that the overall total of state aid to the private sector of industry declined in the last two years of the Labour Government's term of office. Even after allowance has been made for the nationalization of the aerospace and shipbuilding industries, one can still detect a downward trend (*See Table 3.1*). Moreover, in 1978–79, expenditure on regional and industrial support was about twenty-five per cent below the level planned. In part, this was due to changes in the NEB's requirements, but official blame was also placed 'on the difficulties of estimating the demand for assistance'[5]. It is true that the problem of shortfalls in demand for assistance is a complex one. Partly, demand is a function of the overall level of investment which may be overestimated at the forecast stage. There is also the common problem in estimating public expenditure programmes—namely that forecasters make inadequate allowance for the extent to which projects are cancelled or deferred or delayed in the execution stage. Nevertheless, the problem is more than simply a technical one. The fact is that individual firms have, in many cases, been reluctant to take up the funds available, leaving money unspent. As Sir Peter Carey, the Department of Industry's Permanent Secretary from 1976, has stated, 'On the whole, where selective assistance is concerned, we have been response constrained, not resource constrained.'[6] This apparent reluctance on the part of industrialists to take up available funds has implications for the whole rationale of a selective intervention approach to industrial policy which will be returned to later in the chapter.

TABLE 3.1 Industrial assistance to the private sector, 1972–79 (£ million at 1979 survey prices)

Form of assistance	Year						
	72–73	73–74	74–75	75–76	76–77	77–78	78–79
RDGs, provision for land and buildings and Investment Grants.	610	560	500	450	420	340	350
Sections 7 and 8 of the 1972 Act, Local Authority Act 1972, and NEB funding.	50	80	120	550	330	480	360
Shipbuilding, Aerospace, Research and Development, and miscellaneous support.	520	600	630	500	290	30	70
TOTAL	1180	1240	1250	1500	1040	850	780

Source: *Written Answer,* 1st February, 1980

One other important general point needs to be stressed. The basic incentive offered by successive governments to encourage industrial investment has taken the form of accelerated depreciation allowances against taxation rather than discretionary assistance to selected firms. The thousand million pounds or so a year spent by government on regional and general industrial support has been dwarfed by the sums allowed in the form of tax relief. The United Kingdom does, in fact, have a relatively generous, if complicated tax regime by international standards, although whether this approach to company taxation has helped to stimulate industrial investment is open to question.

3.3 The politics of regional policy

Regional policy, as the oldest form of industrial policy, has attracted more academic attention than any other aspect of the subject. Most of the writing about regional policy has been by economists who generally give only cursory attention to political considerations[7]. Despite the fact that this is a policy arena in which purely political factors play an important role in influencing policy outcomes, there has been little interest in the systematic examination of the political forces surrounding the formation of regional policy. An attempt will be made to develop such a systematic examination of the politics of regional policy by examining the sharing out of resources between regional policy and other forms of industrial policy, and the use of public funds allocated to regional policy. Thus, Section 3.3 will examine why location-specific aid has generally been preferred to aid to industrial sectors and also why the balance started to change in favour of sectoral aid and against regional aid towards the end of the 1970s. Section 3.4 will seek an explanation for the difficulty that has been experienced in securing cost-effectiveness in regional policy, particularly in terms of cost per job.

The political preference for regional policy

In the seven-year period from 1971/2 to 1977/8 inclusive, total direct expenditure on regional policy was just under £5000 million pounds at 1978/79 prices[8]. The principal form of regional aid throughout this period was the non-discretionary Regional Development Grant introduced in 1972 and given to all qualifying assets in the assisted areas. Even allowing for expensive rescue cases like British Leyland, the amount spent on regional aid over the 1972–79 period exceeded the amount spent on aid to individual industrial sectors, particularly in the earlier part of the period.

It might seem that governments favour regional policies simply because they are necessary and efficacious. Certainly, there is a great deal of evidence and argument that can be adduced to support such a view. Governments throughout the world support regional policies because gross imbalances between regions are regarded as socially undesirable, politically intolerable, and injurious to national economic efficiency, although as McCallum observes, 'The problem of the trade-off between regional welfare distribution and national economic efficiency has generally been ignored, or at least heavily downplayed.'[9]

Regional imbalances manifest themselves in a number of ways: net outward migration, an ageing population, run-down public amenities, derelict land, out-of-date factories and industrial plant, incomes below the national average, and a vicious cycle of collective despondency and low economic growth. However, despite the importance of all these indicators, 'unemployment discrepancies have always been the basic, almost exclusive, dynamic of regional policy'[10]. As long as a person has a significantly higher chance of being unemployed because he or she has the misfortune to live in, say, Strabane, Greenock or Penzance rather than Croydon, Reading or Chelmsford, there will be political pressure, and a social need, for a regional policy. Even if one is not prepared to accept arguments based on a notion of approximate equity of treatment of persons living in different locations in terms of their chances of obtaining employment, it must be accepted that it is not in the interests of those living in the more prosperous regions to be subject to a continual influx of seekers after work, leaving the rest of the country as the haunt of the unskilled, the disabled, the retired-on-state-pensions and other socially-disadvantaged groups.

However, the necessity of having some kind of regional policy does not resolve questions about the relative shares of public funds that should be devoted to location-specific policies and general aid schemes. In so far as there is evidence that industrialists seem more responsive to regional aid schemes, this may simply reflect the fact that such schemes have been in operation longer, are more familiar, and are thought more likely to continue. Moreover, a study by Political and Economic Planning of new factories in Special Development Areas found that financial incentives were not an overriding reason for the choice of location; among main reasons, the availability of incentives ranked third after the availability of a factory or site and the availability of suitable labour[11].

General aid schemes may, of course, themselves provide aid to regions in difficulty. Almost ninety per cent of the aid provided under the Wool Textile Scheme went to plants in assisted areas, and most of the applications under the Clothing Scheme emanated from assisted area plants[12].

Forty-nine per cent of the funds provided under APS and seventy-one per cent of SIS offers went to projects in assisted areas up to March 1980. However, an industrial policy that emphasizes schemes designed to promote the development of high technology is likely to lead to the more prosperous regions receiving a disproportionate share of the available aid. Of 271 applications for grant approved under the microprocessor application scheme to June 1980, 164 were located in the South East of England. The next highest numbers of applications were also from relatively prosperous regions: the South West (23), the West Midlands (16) and the East Midlands (17)[13]. These figures do not reflect a lack of willingness on the part of government to give such aid to the regions, but rather the concentration of workers with the relevant skills in the more prosperous regions. Recent research suggests that 'the South East possesses an environment external to the enterprise and establishment which is conducive amongst other things to invention and innovation'[14], a finding which has disturbing implications for the efficacy of conventional forms of regional policy.

The efficacy of regional policy

The assessment of the efficacy of British regional policy is not an easy task, given the range of variables involved, the lack of reliable regional statistics in relation to many relevant indicators, and the discontinuities in government policy. Nevertheless, official figures do suggest that 'differences in regional economics have narrowed over the past decade but there are signs that the trend may have been reversed in the last couple of years'[15]. This reversal at the end of the 1970s coincides, of course, with the rundown in regional policy, although undoubtedly other factors have played their part. The general picture over the decade is one of incomes becoming more equal, unemployment differences reducing, and spending patterns becoming more alike. In part, however, this is because formerly prosperous regions have become less prosperous; where formerly less prosperous regions have started to catch up, this has often been the result of fortuitous factors such as North Sea oil rather than government assistance. The harsh fact remains that 'the areas with highest unemployment are those which had highest unemployment at the inception of regional policy some fifty years ago'[16].

Nevertheless, regional policy does seem to have had some beneficial impacts. Manufacturing output in Scotland, Wales and Northern Ireland appears to have been significantly higher in 1976 compared with 1958 'than would have been expected in the absence of regional policy . . . by far the major part of the increase appears to have occurred in the period of strong regional policy since 1965'[17]. However, the case for regional policy often seems to rest on an argument that, although things are bad, they would have been far worse without it. Minimizing one's losses is sometimes the best available strategy, but what is particularly worrying is that the outlook for the future, at least in terms of the efficacy of conventional policy measures, looks bleak. Fewer firms are moving and 'whilst regional incentives may still have some influence on the location of expansions and new openings, the influence appears to be much weaker than formerly'[18].

Although economists disagree about the precise impact of regional policy[19], it is clear that it has ameliorated the basic problem of regional imbalance rather than gone very far towards solving it, despite the quite considerable share of industrial policy funds which has been devoted to regional policy. The continuing attachment of politicians of all parties to regional policy, until recently in preference to other forms of industrial policy, cannot simply be explained in terms of socio-economic necessity and efficacy. Moreover, the problem could have been tackled in other ways than the relatively indiscriminate provision of location-specific aid for industrial development.

Towards a political explanation

It has been suggested that the contribution of political scientists to the explanation of such industrial policy preference problems should be to develop models of politicians as vote maximizers (Hogwood, 1979a). It is argued that a model which simply treats the individual politician as a utility maximizer (or even aggregates of individual politicians) is inadequate. Nevertheless, such a model is not totally unhelpful, provided that it is suitably modified. The first modification must be to treat politicians as vote satisficers rather than vote maximizers, i.e. their objective is to obtain a 'good enough' number of votes rather than obtaining all the votes available.

This modification would seem to be sensible when considered in the light of experience. When one considers the strategy of political parties in the UK as competitors for votes, it can be seen that they do not seek to annihilate their opponents, but rather try to secure a comfortable majority in the House of Commons, a majority not so small that it makes the passage of legislation difficult or can be eroded by by-election defeats, but not so large that it increases the risk of frequent backbench revolts. As far as the individual candidate is concerned, he or she will want, as a minimum, to secure a plurality of one vote over his or her nearest rival. However, although 'one is enough' to secure election, most candidates will want to have a larger majority, if only to diminish the need to spend excessive amounts of time nursing the constituency and to make their political future less insecure. Moreover, it is argued that politicians want to do at least as well as their party colleagues elsewhere in the country, as measured by the national swing, so as to enhance—or at least maintain—their standing in the party[20].

However, piling up a large majority brings diminishing returns. A majority of 5000 is psychologically more reassuring than one of 500; one of 10000 is somewhat better than 5000; but does a majority of 20000 give more reassurance than one of 10000? The conclusion drawn, then, is that politicians are vote satisficers rather than maximizers, but that their vote satisficing activity is affected by the competitive environment in which it takes place. Partly because they are operating in an environment in which outcomes are relatively uncertain, politicians tend to err on the side of caution, and aim for an electoral outcome rather more favourable to them than would be minimally necessary to secure re-election or, from the aggregate viewpoint, to secure a comfortable working majority in the Commons.

The relevance of this discussion to regional policy is that elections in Britain are fought entirely in geographical constituencies and that regional aid is a highly visible form of location-specific benefit. However, such evidence as is available suggests that regional aid is a relatively unpopular form of policy with the general electorate. A poll carried out by Market and Opinion Research International for the *Sunday Times* after the 1980 Conservative Budget showed that grants for regional development were the *least* popular form of government spending after social security benefits, with thirty-seven per cent of respondents favouring cuts in spending on regional aid and only nine per cent favouring an increase (although the fact that over half of all respondents did not select regional aid as one of the six policies on which they could express a view suggests that its political salience is relatively low among the electorate)[21].

Nevertheless, the provision of regional aid may affect, or be thought to affect, electoral outcomes in particular constituencies. Hogwood maintains that 'political scientists have no idea what effect rescuing a yard or factory has on the votes of employees or others in the affected constituencies or whether there is a "spillover" effect to other constituencies'[22]. Certainly, there is a technical problem if analysis is confined to the constituency level, as eligibility for regional aid is determined on the basis of travel-to-work areas and employment office areas, and not by reference to the boundaries of individual constituencies.

However, there is a case for looking at the political effects of regional policy at a regional level. In the 1979 general election, there was a much lower swing to the Conservatives in the northern half of the country (a mean 4.2% in 'North Britain' as against a mean 7.7% in 'South Britain'). The variation was a genuinely regional one and could not be accounted for 'by differences in urbanisation or any other compositional characteristics'[23]. North Britain, defined in terms of a line drawn just south of the Humber to the Mersey, contained most of the areas receiving regional assistance, although Wales did swing strongly to the Conservatives. Fifty-three per cent of Labour candidates had mentioned industrial policy in their election addresses, whereas 'Conservatives made little reference to their party's promised cuts in industrial subsidies'[24], presumably because they regarded them as an electoral liability.

One should not, of course, place too much reliance on aggregate statistics that show that a few voters out of every hundred voted differently in most of the assisted areas from electors in more prosperous regions. What is really important is whether politicians perceive that a useful net gain (or, minimally, reduction in net loss) of votes can be gained from regional assistance, even if such a perception can be shown to be based on a false understanding of the forces influencing electoral behaviour. The important question, then, is not whether electors do in fact reward in the ballot box MPs who 'deliver' a specific regional policy benefit or punish those who fail to 'deliver' a desired benefit, but whether politicians, particularly when they are in a position to influence decisions, seek to secure or protect benefits for particular localities.

Apart from any electoral calculations, politicians are likely to promote the cause of their own constituencies as recipients of regional aid because of their highly developed sense of the importance of the constituency role. Of course, some Members of Parliament attach more importance to this role than do others, but none of them seem to regard it as 'anything less than very important'[25]. Moreover, electors would seem to regard this aspect of the MP's job as very important. The Granada survey found that the three aspects of the MP's job considered most important by electors 'all emphasised the Member's local rather than national role'[26].

Crossman's account of Cabinet discussions on the future of Bristol Docks offers an illuminating example of the way in which constituency loyalties can be a factor in decision-making at the highest level. Crossman notes that Tony Benn 'made his constituency case' and claims that Harold Wilson 'knew that there were five Labour constituencies in Bristol'[27]. Nevertheless, the scheme was eventually defeated by what Crossman calls 'Welsh regional self-interest' with Callaghan supposedly arguing that 'we couldn't have a port at Bristol because Newport and Cardiff wouldn't like it'[28]. Similarly, Crossman claims that discussions about the fate of the Central Wales Railway were influenced by the fact that 'three seats were in danger in Central Wales'[29].

Calculations about the possible electoral consequences of regional policy decisions assume a particular significance when regionally based (Nationalist) parties are doing well. Richard Marsh argues, 'If the Welsh and Scottish Nationalists achieve nothing else they can claim to be responsible for the retention of some of the most uneconomic and socially unnecessary railway services in the country.'[30] Certainly, the Cabinet's decision to bail out the ailing Chrysler company's British operations in December 1975 was influenced by the fear of giving a propaganda boost to the Scottish Nationalists.

The three regions which have received the largest amounts of regional aid—Scotland, Wales and Northern Ireland—each have their own minister in Cabinet to argue their case if necessary. Regardless of the strength of any regional parties, the regional ministers will always be there in Cabinet and Cabinet committees to defend the interests of their regions. Perhaps even more important, their civil servants will also be safeguarding regional interests in the network of official committees which honeycomb Whitehall. It is not easy for the Industry Department to ride roughshod over the interests of the politically represented regions.

There are also important external interests that are prepared to defend regional policy. Perhaps the most important of these is the CBI, which, despite its distaste for government intervention in industry, has always taken a relatively benevolent attitude towards regional aid, if only because many of its members have benefitted from it. The CBI's own regional councils in the depressed regions always take a close interest in regional aid questions and have influenced the CBI on occasions to take a more favourable attitude towards regional aid'[31].

Last but not least, regional policy attracts support simply because it has been around for a long time. One should never underestimate the importance of inertia in the policy-making process. Moreover, because the policy has been in existence a long time, it has attracted its own group of supporters. There are undoubtedly many civil servants who favour regional aid as a form of industrial assistance, if only because it is familiar. There are also many academics who are interested in the study of regional policy and are prepared to come to its defence when it is threatened, whatever criticisms they may have of specific policies.

The decline of regional aid

The analysis so far has been a static one and does not explain why, after a long period of popularity, regional aid started to decline in the late 1970s. Total expenditure on regional industrial policy in Great Britain (at 1978/79 prices) declined from a peak of £903 million in 1975/76 to £854 million in 1976/77 and £530 million in 1977/78[32]. The budget of July 1976 saw the first cutbacks in regional policy with Regional Employment Premium (REP) payments reduced and delayed, RDG (Regional Development Grant) payments delayed, and mining and construction projects excluded from the RDG scheme. The December mini-budget saw even bigger reductions in regional aid with the termination of the labour subsidy provided by REP. As McCallum points out, 'This constituted the most drastic single cut in regional expenditures ever.'[33] In 1977, North Yorkshire and Aberdeen were downgraded to Intermediate Area status. A change of this kind may not seem to be a particularly significant development, but it was the first downgrading since 1966. The fact that these changes were not isolated incidents, but represented a shift in the balance of policy priorities, is emphasized in the Government's 1977 White Paper on expenditure which stated that 'The Government intend to move towards putting emphasis on selective, as against general, assistance to industry.'[34]

An important reason for these changes was the pressure for public expenditure cuts generated by the international financial community, particularly the International Monetary Fund (IMF). However, that does not explain why regional policy should receive relatively severe treatment compared with its favoured past, particularly given that the NEB was receiving additional resources as regional policy was being cut back. No doubt the need for resources for the NEB and the selective aid schemes meant that regional policy faced more competition for public funds than had been the case in the past. As Eric Varley told a meeting of Midlands MPs and industrialists in Coventry in November 1976, the emphasis in regional development was now being placed firmly on aid to industry on an industry-by-industry basis.

One major reason for this change of emphasis in policy was that the economic recession was starting to adversely affect parts of the country which had hitherto been immune to the effects of economic downturns. The Government was facing pressure from areas in difficulty, particularly the West Midlands, which were requesting regional assistance. However, some forty-three per cent of the employed population was already living in areas eligible for one of the three categories of regional industrial aid. If significant parts of the West Midlands were added in, over half the working population would have been classified as living in areas in need of regional assistance—a difficult situation for the Government to defend politically. It should also be remembered that all this was happening against the background of the devolution debate which was having the effect of intensifying regional rivalries in the struggle for resources (Guthrie and McLean, 1978). Clearly, a halt had to be called before regional policy became both an insupportable economic burden and the focus of dangerous interregional tensions. When one also takes account of increasing doubts about the cost-effectiveness of regional aid, the shift away from regional policy becomes more understandable.

3.4 The cost-effectiveness of regional policy

One of the main difficulties that arises in any attempt to assess the cost-effectiveness of regional policy is that the objectives of the policy are ambiguous. The UK's 1977 submission to the European Regional Development Fund states, 'The primary objective of United Kingdom regional policy is to bring the supply and demand for labour in the Assisted Areas . . . more closely into balance by safeguarding existing employment and creating new jobs in those Areas.' Despite this statement, 'most regional incentives have been associated directly with investment, only indirectly with employment, and still more indirectly with unemployment'[35]. The old REP was the only form of regional assistance specifically linked to the provision of jobs. Regional selective assistance is linked to the safeguarding or creation of employment, but over the period to the end of March 1978 this amounted to little more than one-eighth of total payments on regional incentives[36].

Concern about the cost-effectiveness of regional policy has centred on the question of the cost per job created. The average figures do not look too bad, particularly when one considers that a job, once created, should last for many years, although some factories opened with regional aid have subsequently closed. In addition, the number of jobs created does not always match the original forecasts with the average degree of attainment between 1972 and 1976 being seventy per cent[37].

As far as discretionary Section 7 assistance is concerned, Sir Peter Carey told the Public Accounts Committee in 1978, 'The published figure of the cost of each job to be created or maintained averaged in 1977 £1200 . . (which) compares with flat rate unemployment benefit alone of £1446 per annum for a married man with two children, to which have to be added other benefits and the loss of tax and national insurance contributions.'[38] However, in some capital-intensive projects, the cost per job of the non-discretionary RDGs was very high. In 1976-77, the Public Accounts Committee examined four oil industry projects which had received, or appeared likely to receive, substantial RDGs. Three of the cases were examined by the committee in particular detail. In the case of the Seal Sands Terminal on Teesside, RDG paid out in 1975-76 was provided at a cost of £36398 for all jobs, but nearly £60000 for each job which actually qualified for RDG.

These rather high figures nevertheless compare favourably with the other two cases considered in detail by the committee. Rhosgoch Tank Farm in Anglesey is primarily a staging post for the movement of oil and, as such, would not normally qualify for regional aid. However, the flexible hose which was used to bring oil ashore from tankers was being kept filled with sea water when it was not in use to prevent environmental damage resulting from oil spillage. The need to remove the sea water qualified the plant as a processing rather than a storage facility. Twenty-eight new jobs were created, with sixteen employees engaged on qualifying activities. Given that it was estimated that grants might amount to £3 million, this represents a cost of £187500 per qualifying job and £107142 for all jobs. The figures for Flotta Terminal, Orkney, indicated a likely RDG cost of £140339 per job created, and a staggering figure of not far short of quarter of a million pounds for each qualifying job created. These figures do not, of course, take account of temporary jobs created during construction or of additional jobs created in the external local economy as a result of the presence of the plants. However, given the small numbers employed at the plants, this effect was not likely to be significant except at Seal Sands, where it was estimated that one and a half extra jobs would be created outside the basic industries concerned for every one within them.

During discussion in the committee, the Chairman commented, 'you are paying the oil companies some pretty big sums to construct terminals for North Sea oil where they had to put them anyway for reasons of geography and economics'[39]. The Department of Industry accepted that on three of the four oil terminal projects considered by the committee, there was no evidence that the large grants provided affected the location of the projects. The Public Accounts Committee came to the conclusion that it was not 'cost effective to pay large regional development grants on projects which would be located in the assisted areas anyway'[40].

The Department of Industry pointed out in its evidence that 'from the first it has been part of the concept of the regional grant scheme that the aim is the regeneration of industry in these areas rather than the stimulation of specific employment, and that is one reason why there is no cost per job test in this scheme'[41]. In the Department's view, it was important for the success of the RDG scheme that it should be simple, assured and predictable, although they accepted that a simple scheme might result in some large projects attracting grants which might have been thought unnecessary under a discretionary scheme. A strong argument for the scheme's continuance in the Department's view was that its effectiveness was closely linked with its stability. Apart from some minor rule changes, the Labour Government refused to modify the scheme, stressing 'the importance to the scheme of simple, objective criteria and continuity in the incentive offered'[42].

It should not be supposed that the oil industry projects considered by the Public Accounts Committee were isolated examples. The Callaghan Government provided the Swiss pharmaceutical group, Hoffman La Roche, with grants of £45.6 million (made up of RDG and Section 8 assistance) to build a Vitamin C plant in Ayrshire. With 450 permanent jobs being created, the cost per job figure worked out at £100000[43]. In 1980, the Conservatives gave Hoffman La Roche an additional £1.2 million under the 1974 Railways Act to meet half the cost of a railway siding. In 1979, the new Conservative Government gave the US-owned silicones manufacturer, Dow Corning, £34 million in RDG and Section 8 assistance to enable them to go ahead with an expansion of their Barry plant. It was estimated that 125 permanent jobs would be created, giving a cost per job of £272000.

Defenders of these decisions would argue that RDG and Section 8 should not be aggregated in this way, as Section 8 assistance is not concerned with employment objectives, but with broader economic considerations such as balance of payments effects and the introduction of new technology. They would also argue that RDG should be assessed in terms of its overall impact in regional industrial structure. Nevertheless, the contribution that regional aid makes to the fulfillment of employment objectives must be one major criterion by which the effectiveness of regional policy is assessed.

There is evidence that regional aid may have a deleterious impact on local industrial structures. Cleveland has been a major recipient of regional aid, and a report commissioned by Cleveland County Council suggests that regional development grants may actually have contributed to job losses by subsidizing the efforts of local chemical and metal manufacturers to become more capital-intensive (Robinson and Storey, 1980). In terms of job loss, decline in existing plants has been a more important factor in Cleveland than employment decline resulting from plant closures. On the other hand, the report also stresses that if no grants had been paid at all, companies might have been encouraged to invest abroad. Cleveland thus faces a 'major dilemma' which also faces other assisted regions: 'regional aid is encouraging firms to accommodate to broader trends which result in labour-shedding but a failure to accommodate to those trends would leave Cleveland's basic industries uncompetitive in world markets and so undermine the security of the remaining jobs in those industries'[44].

An industrial policy without a regional aid programme as a major element is inconceivable. However, as Marquand emphasizes, 'To argue that regional investment incentives . . . appear to emerge reasonably well from comparisons of the effectiveness of different macro-economic measures, does not absolve us from the need to look closely at regional costs and benefits, and to look critically at the structure of the incentives themselves.'[45] It might be beneficial, as the Cleveland study suggests, 'to separate assistance for industrial restructuring from regional policy designed to bring diversification and employment growth'[46]. There is also a case for imposing an upper cost per job limit on regional aid which could only be breached if the particular project brought exceptional benefits to the national economy.

3.5 Labour's industrial strategy

As has been pointed out, the Labour Government shifted the emphasis of its industrial policy away from regional aid to selective schemes of aid for particular industries. This shift of emphasis was carried out within the framework of the Government's industrial strategy which was formally launched at a special NEDC meeting at Chequers in November 1975. This meeting approved a White Paper on what was described, perhaps significantly, as 'An Approach to Industrial Strategy' (Author's italics).

The industrial strategy had its origins in a paper presented by a Deputy Secretary at the Department of Industry (Alan Lord) to Tony Benn early in 1975[47]. The immediate political background to the adoption of the strategy was the symbolic defeat of the left in the Common Market referendum, the subsequent removal of Tony Benn from the Industry Department, and the introduction of an incomes policy. There was a clear need to fill the policy vacuum left by the virtual abandonment of the industrial policy that Labour had developed in opposition, complemented by a growing interest by the Chancellor and others in supply-side economics. The approach adopted in the industrial strategy was essentially one of persuading management and unions, sometimes with the help of financial incentives for firms, that it was in their interests, as well as the interests of the nation as a whole, to modify their behaviour so as to move towards a high output/high wage economy. As one senior civil servant who was interviewed put it, 'The main purpose was to get industry to put its own house in order.'

Mindful of the failures of the past, the White Paper which launched the strategy recognized the need for a completely new approach to industrial planning. It was recognized that the National Plan of 1965 had failed because it made over-optimistic assumptions about economic growth and allocated the components of growth arbitrarily among various industries. In 1975 it was agreed not to impose a strategy on industry from above, but to develop an agreed approach by feeding information upwards from the various sectors of industry into macro-economic planning.

In fact, this never happened as it was supposed to. A 1979 government memorandum discussed the aggregation of the objectives of the Sector Working Parties set up under the strategy and commented: 'SWP objectives are not designed to be aggregated since they are not related to a common set of assumptions about economic prospects or to a common base year or target year, they are not all expressed in common terms—some indeed are not quantitative at all—and they do not necessarily take account of the objectives of other, related SWPs '[48] Where the findings of the SWPs were aggregated, the results were not very impressive. For example, they implied an annual growth in the volume of imports between 1975 and 1980 of just under one per cent.

Right from the beginning, it was clearly envisaged that the burden of implementation would rest largely with management and the unions. The White Paper stated: 'The government must take the initiative in developing the industrial strategy, but the main task of seeing that it brings higher productivity in British industry must fall on unions and management.'[49] It was also hoped that the development of priorities through the strategy at a sector level would guide the provision of assistance by government and by public agencies such as the NEB and the Manpower Services Commission.

The institutional framework

The centrepiece of the industrial strategy was what the Director-General of the National Economic Development Office called 'its basic mechanism—the sector working party, an extension into more clearly defined manufacturing sectors of the previously existing pattern of tripartite organisation'[50]. A total of thirty-nine tripartite committees were created or involved with over one thousand members covering about forty per cent of manufacturing industry's output, principally in engineering, textiles and chemicals. In some cases, industrial strategy work was taken on by an existing Economic Development Committee, but in the majority of cases the coverage of the EDC was too wide for the purposes of the strategy and the work was taken on by a new Sector Working Party.

The first task that each SWP faced was 'to form a coherent unit out of a disparate group from management, trade unions and Government'[51]. The official view is that 'It is to their credit that so many achieved a mutual understanding and a sense of common purpose so quickly.'[52] Certainly, there was only one conspicuous failure in the sense of an inability to agree about problems and prospects—the working party covering the drop-forging industry.

However, the real problem was not to get men and women who were in some sense representative of what were defined as industries to sit around a table in London and talk about their problems, but rather to apply the results of the discussions at the level of the individual firm (or plant). As the National Economic Development Office put it: 'EDCs and SWPs have drawn up recommendations addressed to the companies on whose response and action implementation depends and also to the Government and the institutions wherever changes in the operating environment within their control have been seen as necessary. Only exceptionally have EDCs or SWPs been able to turn their conclusions and recommendations into direct action.'[53] The working parties were not themselves generally directly involved in policy implementation; their task as far as policy implementation was concerned was to communicate 'the results of their work and their recommendations to *those who can implement them*'[54] (Author's italics).

Implementation through government

The more successful part of the exercise was the attempt to ensure that government departments not directly concerned with industry gave a higher priority to industry's needs. Implementation within government was made easier by the authoritative backing given to this aspect of the strategy by the political support of the Prime Minister and Chancellor and by the institutional backing given by special co-ordinating arrangements within the Treasury. An important expression of the high level Government commitment to the industrial strategy was the practice which developed of bringing ministers from a wide variety of departments to meetings of the NEDC to discuss the implications of particular areas of Government policy for industry. A number of initiatives were taken in other policy arenas such as education and planning as a result of these meetings. Taken individually, these policy changes were not very dramatic, including such matters as the setting up of the first competition for national engineering scholarships and the transmission of a circular encouraging local authorities to speed up industrial planning applications. However, taken together, they did represent a systematic attempt by government to give a higher priority to industrial needs in other policy arenas.

Rather more difficulties were encountered in securing the co-operation of public agencies. The Electronic Components SWP rebuked the NEB for its lack of co-operation. Members of the SWP were particularly annoyed when the NEB went ahead with its INMOS micro-electronics venture without apparently consulting the SWP. The working party argued in a progress report, 'The National Enterprise Board, when preparing its plans should co-operate with the SWP at least to the same extent as do private companies in this sector'. One member of the SWP complained, 'Since the working party was set up by the Government to co-ordinate strategy, we would expect an outline of what the NEB intended to do before we read about it in the newspapers.'[55]

The NEB replied to these criticisms by claiming that it was impossible for the NEB to be represented on all the SWPs, although, given the NEB's interests, one might have thought that it would have been particularly important for it to be represented on the SWP dealing with electronic components. The NEB also argued that a consideration when disclosing information to SWPs was that members included representatives of competitors. Like any other company, the NEB was reluctant to give too much advance warning to competitors. There were also complaints from some SWPs about a lack of responsiveness on the part of the Health and Safety Executive to their requests. The more general problem that these examples reveal is the fragmented nature of the industrial policy-making community and the often conflicting conceptions that different organizations have of their tasks.

One way in which the SWPs could indirectly implement policies which they thought desirable was to persuade the Government to introduce new Section 8 selective aid schemes. This was, of course, a three-stage process: the SWP had first to identify a problem which it thought could be tackled through selective government assistance; the Government had to be persuaded that selective financial assistance would help in the particular case; and the individual firms in the sector had to respond by taking up the money available. In devising and administering aid schemes, the Government was willing to take account of views put to it by SWPs. As Sir Peter Carey put it, 'If out of the sector working parties on the strategy . . . we find there are sectors which require some assistance, whether perhaps another selective investment scheme is required at some stage, then it is open to us to go back, and we are fully prepared to do so.'[56] Projects assisted under SIS and PPDS to some extent reflected priorities accepted by the Government through participation in the industrial strategy exercise. The Electronics Components and other SWPs contributed to the discussions out of which emerged the enlarged micro-electronics support programme announced in 1978.

Implementation through management and unions

In their efforts to stimulate improvements in marketing and product development and to improve productivity and industrial efficiency, the SWPs ultimately relied on the co-operation of management and unions in the individual firms. Securing the attendance of management representatives at SWP meetings was not a problem. Indeed, it has been suggested that meetings tended to be 'dominated by company representatives'[57]. One reason for management participation was that organizations like the CBI welcomed the strategy meetings as an additional opportunity for business to seek to influence government policies. However, there were limits to the extent to which managers were prepared to work towards common solutions with competitors. In the case of the industrial strategy it was found that 'Companies treasure their autonomy and while they may be prepared in sector working parties to discuss common problems, especially on competing abroad, they are not prepared to blur competition at home for the sake of any industrial strategy. As one managing director put it: "It's one thing to gang up on beating the Japanese but you don't want all this mateyness with your competitors at home all the while."[58]

When working parties moved beyond the restatement of the obvious, conflicts between the management side and the trade union side started to surface. For example, chemical industry trade unions accused multinational petrochemical companies of sabotaging attempts to develop an industrial strategy for the plastic materials sector where there were substantial imports. Some trade unionists quickly lost confidence in the industrial strategy. In 1978, the then TUC chairman, David Basnett of the GMWU, wrote an article arguing that the Government's industrial strategy had progressed at a disappointing rate and lacked the 'drive, energy and enthusiasm it needs to succeed'. However, he also admitted that the TUC had 'never really thought out what it wanted from the sector working parties and how they should fit in with other aspects of planning. As a result, our influence has not been as effective as it might have been.'[59]

The communications exercise

Initially, press statements and items in company and trade union journals were used to publicize the objectives of the industrial strategy, but during 1978 there was an increasing realization that written material was likely to have only a limited effect in motivating change and a new emphasis was placed on face-to-face communication. Accordingly, more use was made of meetings at plant level for management and workers and eight conferences for trade unionists were organized by the TUC. The clothing industry working party appointed retired executives as 'ambassadors' to spread the word in the country and this idea was taken up by other SWPs.

However, it should be stressed that the problem was not simply one of developing a more sophisticated approach to communications or of making more money available for communications than the quarter of a million pounds spent in 1978. A more fundamental problem was the views of management and unions about what could permissibly be discussed at plant level. A number of SWPs reported that 'companies have not given written material the hoped-for circulation, are reluctant to involve trade unionists in company-level discussions of the SWP's work and findings, dislike the idea of in-company "presentations" to management and union representatives jointly or wish to see them held within the existing communications network of the company'[60].

In 1977, there was an attempt by the Government to introduce formalized planning discussions at the company level as a watered-down substitute for planning agreements. The idea was that there should be tripartite discussions at company level about how the SWP reports would affect individual companies, but it was not pursued in the face of strong opposition from the CBI. Thus, the industrial strategy continued to face 'the inherent difficulty of translating analysis into action at the level of the company'[61].

Assessment of the industrial strategy

In view of the various difficulties that have been outlined, it is not surprising that the achievements of the industrial strategy were somewhat limited. One commentator dismissed it as 'not so much a strategy, more an empty slogan' which produced nothing more than 'talking shops and pious declarations'[62]. As has been pointed out, the strategy did have some impact on the priority attached to industrial needs within government, although one civil servant who was interviewed argued that the general atmosphere within government had started to change in this respect before the strategy was initiated. There were some specific achievements as a result of the efforts of the SWPs: for example, discussions in the domestic appliance working party encouraged two firms to make freezers and washing machines for each other instead of importing them from abroad. However, these rather small scale achievements are offset by the fact that, of the sectors covered by the working parties, twenty-three experienced a rise in import penetration up to the beginning of 1979 and more than half witnessed a continued decline in employment[63]. There was no sign of any significant improvement in Britain's poor industrial performance which had led to the strategy in the first place.

One member of the Labour Cabinet subsequently remarked of the strategy, 'the unreality of the exercise was demonstrated above all by its lack of contact with anything important that actually happened in industry'[64]. The Director-General of NEDO admitted, 'SWPs have inherent limitations in what they can do. They are not executive bodies; they operate at sectoral, not company level; management members are often, if not always, in competition with each other in the market place.'[65]

Five general defences have been advanced by supporters of the industrial strategy. First, there has been a justifiable view that the use of the strategy as a public relations exercise by government created excessive expectations, and that a more modest, low key strategy would have produced a better balance between expectations and results. Second, it has been argued that it was unreasonable to expect a hundred years or so of general economic decline to be reversed in a few years. Third, the deterioration of the world economic and trading environment after 1975 did not help, and it is possible that things might have been even worse without the industrial strategy. Fourth, although the climate of opinion generated by the strategy might influence decisions at company level, such decisions would not be clearly attributable to the industrial strategy or be acknowledged as being influenced by it.

A fifth and central argument advanced by supporters of the industrial strategy was that 'the very fact of tripartite discussion of sectoral matters'[66] should be counted as a positive gain. Ultimately, the success of the industrial strategy was 'based on an assumption that people will respond if shown a better way'[67]. Undoubtedly, participants in tripartite discussions do benefit from gaining a broader view of the problems of their industry and of the constraints faced by decision-makers in the other two corners of the tripartite triangle. However, the experience of tripartite negotiation is only one of many influences operating on the participants and it will only be a worthwhile influence if they can carry their 'constituencies' with them to the extent of persuading them to modify their behaviour. The crucial test of tripartite arrangements like the industrial strategy is not in their ability to create forums in which government, management and unions can discuss their common problems in a constructive atmosphere, but is rather in the difficulty of ensuring that decisions arrived at are actually implemented at the level of the firm. However, as has been pointed out, it was in policy implementation through management and the unions at the company level that the industrial strategy was at its weakest.

Should a future government decide to resurrect the industrial strategy in some form, it must pay particular attention to the need to secure more effective implementation mechanisms for the solutions arrived at by the various SWPs. It would have to rely less on simple persuasion, and a faith in the responsiveness of decision-makers in companies to reasoned argument, and more on the modification of the behaviour of key actors through the use of incentives and penalties. However, in pursuing such a course, one would quickly come up against the constraint that too much use of compulsion would place at risk the whole tripartite approach on which such a strategy rests.

If government thinks that tripartite arrangements really are worthwhile, it should be prepared to take even more account of the views that emerge from such discussions than the last Labour Government did. Some changes were secured in the Government's policies as a result of views expressed in the industrial strategy exercise, but in some problem areas identified by the SWPs, there was little or no action. For example, a major problem identified by the SWPs was, not surprisingly, that of import penetration. Several SWP reports drew attention to concern at the apparently uneconomic prices quoted for imports or emphasized the importance of the effective monitoring of import control arrangements or of changing EEC policies.

However, it is clear that the solutions that could emerge from the strategy were limited by an insistence, stemming from the Government's opposition to import controls, that 'The basic approach is that sectors should aim to compete with imports by identifying the vulnerable product areas and the reasons for importing, and not to seek to limit or regulate imports.'[68] The lesson to be learnt here is not the desirability of import controls or that a government favouring a tripartite industrial strategy must respond to every instance of special pleading by industries suffering over-capacity. The general point that emerges is that a government that really believes in a tripartite strategy should not attempt to set limits to the solutions that can be suggested, but should be prepared to consider modifying its policies to implement solutions which have broad management and trade union support. If this looks suspiciously like government surrendering its authority to functional interests, that is one of the inherent limits of tripartism.

3.6 The lessons of Irish experience

The British experience with selective intervention policies has in many respects been an unhappy one, but the Republic of Ireland has for many years been pursuing a selective intervention policy with considerable success. The policy pursued has been a classic selective intervention policy in the sense that it has relied on inducing firms to behave differently, i.e. to locate their plants in the Republic, through a package of incentives rather than through compulsion or even the use of state shareholdings. The incentives, and their application to individual cases, are related to an industrial strategy which aims 'to shift our industry into products with higher added value based on good quality and design, aimed at specialist market niches using well planned professional marketing'[69]. General responsibility for the execution of industrial development policy rests with a single agency, the Industrial Development Authority (IDA).

In the three years to 1978 manufacturing industry in Ireland expanded faster than in any other country in the EEC and 1979 proved to be a record year for new industrial investment in the Republic. The Republic is Britain's main competitor for inward investment and has been particularly successful in attracting foreign investment. The Northern Ireland Department of Commerce has commented: 'In terms of all industrial promotions in the British Isles (i.e., UK and RoI), it appears that the RoI share increased from about five to six per cent in the late 1960s to about thirty per cent in the late 1970s; a level of increase that could not be accounted for by the decline in Northern Ireland's rate of success.'[70] The Republic has rapidly become the leading European location for Japanese investment, a trend symbolized by the decision of Fujitsu, Japan's leading computer company, to establish a £42 million plant to manufacture integrated circuits near Dublin. The average grant cost in real terms per job approved was around I£7000 in 1979, but the IDA's approach is highly flexible and it is prepared to bid high for plants it really wants. Thus, it saw Mostek, a leader in the technology of memory chips, as so important to its strategy that it was prepared to pay I£19 000 for each job created.

The example of the Irish Republic may seem to suggest that a successful selective intervention strategy is possible, given a clear long-run strategy, flexibility in its implementation, the provision of sufficiently generous incentives, and a streamlined institutional structure. However, one consequence of such a strategy would appear to be the acceptance of an industrial economy which is substantially dependent on foreign entrepreneurs. Moreover, it is doubtful whether the Irish solution can be readily exported to other countries, least of all to Britain. The Republic enjoys a special advantage that does not apply in the case of Britain, that of 'complete independence of policy-making, in an economy sufficiently small not to provoke retaliation if its policies broke international trading rules and conventions'[71]. The EEC has intervened to end a generous 'tax holiday' concession on profits on exports, but the Republic is allowed under EEC rules to give very high levels of regional grant assistance throughout its territory. The Irish solution could not be applied to Britain, or parts of Britain within the present United Kingdom framework; hence it is most politically attractive to Nationalists and radical devolutionists.

3.7 The limits of selective intervention

It is possible to estimate the effectiveness of the policies favoured by selective interventionists either through the use of questionnaires to the recipients of aid or through the use of modelling techniques, but in either case methodological difficulties arise (Meeks and Meeks, 1979). Question-naires require the investor to make a guess about what his behaviour might have been in the absence of assistance and, if the questionnaire comes from the government department providing assistance, respondents may be reluctant to state that the aid had no impact on their investment decisions for fear of undermining the case for future assistance schemes. The source of the evidence for Chapman's claim that the experience of the APS and SIS 'demonstrates that offers of relatively small amounts of selective financial assistance can bring forward major investment projects with substantial benefits for the economy'[72] is unclear. However, if as seems likely, the source was departmental contacts with industrialists, it must be treated with as much, if not more, scepticism than questionnaire-based studies.

Similarly, modelling techniques face the problem of isolating other influences from the impact of government incentives. In any case, the available econometric evidence which suggests that government aid schemes have stimulated investment (Lund, 1976) does not represent a surprising conclusion. It would be very surprising if the schemes had actually led to a decline in investment or had been neutral in their impact. The interesting question is not whether they had any positive impact, but the actual magnitude of that impact in relation to the resources deployed. Only with such information can one start to make judgements about the opportunity cost of selective aid schemes. Such information is, of course, unobtainable because one does not know what would have happened in the absence of incentives or, indeed, what alternative uses the resources would have been put to if they had not been diverted into selective aid schemes. One can, of course, make all kinds of more or less realistic simplifying assumptions to enable a modelling exercise to take place which can at least suggest a range of outcomes and thus enhance the discussion of alternative policy scenarios. Exercises of this kind can add to the stock of useful information available to the decision-maker, but it should not be supposed that they can provide us with a definitive ordering of the efficacy of alternative policy measures. However, the difficulty of reliably estimating the effects of government selective incentives is not, by itself, a reason for rejecting them as a set of policy measures, as similar difficulties will arise in any attempt to evaluate alternative policy strategies.

If selective intervention policies are going to be effective, two minimal conditions have to be met before one even considers the question of the yield from the investment to which the incentive has been applied: firms need to know about the incentives available, and the incentives need to influence their investment decisions. Firms, especially smaller firms, often know remarkably little about the range of incentives available. For example, in one study of British firms twenty-five per cent of the panel had not heard of selective financial assistance and less than half of the companies felt completely confident that they had full knowledge and understanding of incentives. Only a minority of medium-sized and larger firms who had received or were applying for selective financial assistance incorporated it into their investment appraisal (Walker and Krist, 1980). A study of a Section 8 scheme in the wool textile industry found that ten firms said that they would have carried out the investment project started under the scheme in any case; twelve would have carried out the project piecemeal, on a smaller scale and over a longer period; four would have undertaken the same project over a longer period; and two would have deferred the start of work. Only three firms would not have started the project at all (Department of Industry, 1978).

The fact that there are sometimes failures (e.g., plants which close during the anticipated lifetime of the investment) is not an argument against selective intervention. By its very nature, selective intervention involves influencing investment decisions which, on normal commercial criteria, are marginal and might not go ahead without aid. When such risks are taken for broader economic or social reasons, some failures are inevitable. What is more worrying about the British experience of selective intervention is the reluctance of industrialists to take up all the money that has been made available under the approach. However, this problem could not be overcome simply by ensuring, for example, that industrialists were more aware of the range of incentives available. Advocates of selective intervention policies often talk in terms of 'a need for groups of companies in the same business to develop a sector identity: to stop having eyes only for their nearest British rival and see themselves competing on a world stage; and to achieve a greater degree of inter-firm co-operation in world markets'[73]. The basic philosophical flaw of such an approach is that it really amounts to asking companies to stop behaving like firms in a capitalist economy while the basic structure of such an economy is retained.

The sums of money made available for industrial assistance as part of the selective intervention strategy pursued by successive governments from 1972 to 1979 were relatively small compared both to the scale of Britain's industrial problems and to the tax reliefs given to industry. One cannot be confident that larger sums of money would necessarily be used by industrialists, or at any rate used in a way that promoted the attainment of the goals of national industrial policy. As has been pointed out, the strategy is essentially response-constrained and the constraint can only be overcome by changing the strategy in such a way as to alter the nature of the relationship between government and the firm. However, the strategy would then cease to be one of selective intervention and would be likely to become instead one of discriminatory compulsion.

Notes to Chapter Three

1. H. Wilson, *Final Term* (London: Weidenfeld and Nicolson and Michael Joseph, 1979), p.33
2. Eighth Report from the Expenditure Committee, 1977–78, *Regional and Selective Assistance to Industry*, Qs.6 and 7
3. ibid., Q.86
4. *Industry Act 1972, Annual Report for the year ended 31 March 1980*, p.86
5. Cmnd. 7841, p.41
6. Eighth Report from the Expenditure Committee[2], Q.153
7. *See*, for example, the treatment given to political questions in two classic works on the subject by economists: G. McCrone, *Regional Policy in Britain* (London: Allen and Unwin, 1969), who discusses 'the political issues on pp.26–27; and S. Holland, *The Regional Problem* (London: Macmillan, 1976) who discusses 'politics and the regional problem' on pp.15–19

8. J. Marquand, *Measuring the Effects and Costs of Regional Incentives,* Government Economic Service Working Paper No.32, (London: Department of Industry, 1980), p.87
9. J. D. McCallum, 'The Development of British Regional Policy' in D. Maclennan and J. B. Parr (Eds.), *Regional Policy: Past Experience and New Directions* (Oxford: Martin Robertson, 1979), pp.3–41, p.35
10. ibid., p.35
11. J. Northcott, *Industry in the Development Areas,* Political and Economic Planning Broadsheet No. 573, (London: PEP, 1977), p.43
12. G. C. Cameron, 'The National Industrial Strategy and Regional Policy' in D. Maclennan and J. B. Parr, (Eds.), *Regional Policy: Past Experience and New Directions* (Oxford: Martin Robertson, 1979), pp.297–322, p.304
13. Information supplied by the Department of Industry to D. Wigley, MP, reported in the *Financial Times,* 20th June 1980
14. R. P. Oakey, A. T. Thwaites and P. A. Nash, 'Regional Distribution of Innovative Manufacturing Establishments', *Regional Studies,* Vol. 14 (3), 1980, pp.235–252, p.251
15. 'Differences in regional economies narrow in past decade', *British Business,* 22nd February 1980, pp.252–54
16. Marquand[8], p.iii
17. ibid., p.vii
18. ibid., p.109
19. For a useful review of the evaluative literature see B. Ashcroft, *The Evaluation of Regional Economic Policy: the Case of the United Kingdom,* University of Strathclyde Centre for the Study of Public Policy, Studies in Public Policy Number 12
20. The author is grateful to Shirley Williams for making this point to him. Personal communication, 20th March 1981
21. *Sunday Times,* March 30th 1980. The survey was conducted by MORI among an interlocking quota sample of 1077 electors in 54 constituencies throughout Great Britain on March 27th and 28th.
22. B. W. Hogwood, *Government and Shipbuilding: The Politics of Industrial Change* (Farnborough: Saxon House, 1979), p.280
23. J. Curtice and M. Steed, 'An Analysis of the Voting' in D. Butler and D. Kavanagh, *The British General Election of 1979.* (London: Macmillan, 1980), pp.390–431, p.395
24. D. Butler and D. Kavanagh, *The British General Election of 1979,* (London: Macmillan, 1980), p.302
25. A. King, *British Members of Parliament: a Self-Portrait* (London: Macmillan, 1974), p.26
26. I. Crewe, 'Electoral Reform and the Local MP' in S.E. Finer (Ed.), *Adversary Politics and Electoral Reform* (London: Anthony Wigram, 1975), pp.317–342, pp.320–21
27. Richard Crossman, *The Diaries of a Cabinet Minister, Volume Three* (London: Hamish Hamilton and Jonathan Cape, 1977), p.86
28. ibid., p.118
29. ibid., p.604
30. Sir R. Marsh, *Off the Rails* (London: Weidenfeld and Nicolson, 1978), p.167
31. W. Grant and D. Marsh, *The CBI* (London: Hodder and Stoughton, 1977), p.96
32. Marquand[8], p.88
33. McCallum[9], p.29
34. Cmnd. 6721, Vol. 2, p.23
35. Marquand[8], p.4
36. ibid., p.3
37. ibid., p.2
38. *Tenth Report from the Committee of Public Accounts, 1977–78,* Q.3681
38. *Tenth Report from the Committee of Public Accounts, 1976–77,* Q.2990
40. ibid., p.xi
41. ibid., Q.2987
42. Parliamentary Question, 27th February 1978
43. Parliamentary Question, 12th December 1979
44. J. F. F. Robinson and D. J. Storey, *Employment Change in Manufacturing Industry in Cleveland,* County of Cleveland Planning Department Report No. 176, May 1980, p.17
45. Marquand[8], p.107
46. Robinson and Storey[44], p.17
47. S. R. M. Wilks, 'Government and the Motor Industry with Particular Reference to Chrysler UK Ltd.', University of Manchester Ph.D., 1979, p.99

48. 'Industrial Strategy: Analysis of Sector Working Party Reports', Memorandum by the Chairman of the Industrial Strategy Staff Group, typescript, February 1979, p.6
49. Cmnd.6315, *An Approach to Industrial Strategy*, pp.6–7
50. 'The State and Progress of the Industrial Strategy', Memorandum by the Director-General of the National Economic Development Office, 25 January 1979, typescript, p.1
51. Memorandum by the Chancellor of the Exchequer and the Secretary of State for Industry, 25th January 1978, typescript, p.2
52. ibid., p.2
53. National Economic Development Office, *Annual Report 1978–79*, p.10
54. ibid., p.10
55. *Financial Times*, 1st February 1979
56. Eighth Report from the Expenditure Committee[2], Q.149
57. *Financial Times*, February 2nd, 1977
58. John Elliott, 'Seeking Credibility for the Industrial Strategy', *Financial Times*, January 18th, 1978
59. *Financial Times*, April 18th, 1978
60. 'Industrial Strategy: Analysis of Sector Working Party Reports'[48], p.45
61. G. Chandler, 'The Reindustrialization of Britain', *CBI Review*, Autumn/Winter, 1978/79, pp.2–8, p.6
62. T. Forester, 'Neutralizing the Industrial Strategy' in K. Coates (Ed.), *What Went Wrong* (London: Spokesman Books, 1979), pp.74–94, p.88
63. Adrian Hamilton, 'Big ambition, small means', *The Observer*, 4th February 1979
64. E. Dell, 'Some Reflections on Cabinet Government by a Former Practitioner', *Public Administration Bulletin*, No. 32 (April 1980), pp.17–33, p.20
65. 'The State and Progress of the Industrial Strategy'[50], p.3
66. ibid., p.3
67. Chandler[61], p.8
68. 'Industrial Strategy: Analysis of Sector Working Party Reports'[48], p.10
69. *IDA Industrial Plan 1978–82* (Dublin: Industrial Development Authority, 1979), p.5
70. Minutes of Evidence taken before the Committee on Scottish Affairs, Edinburgh, 13 May 1980, p.240
71. B. Moore, J. Rhodes and R. Tarling, 'Industrial policy and economic development: the experience of Northern Ireland and the Republic of Ireland', *Cambridge Journal of Economics*, Vol. 2 (1), 1978, pp.99–114, p.100
72. J. H. Chapman, 'The Department of Industry's Accelerated Projects Scheme and Selective Investment Scheme', *National Westminster Bank Quarterly Review*, May 1978, pp.27–37, p.36
73. Cabinet Office/Advisory Council for Applied Research and Development, *Industrial Innovation* (London: HMSO, 1978), p.17. This quotation is representative of a more general attitude

Chapter Four

A Social Market Approach?

4.1 Industrial policy in West Germany's 'social market economy'

Advocates of a social market approach to industrial policy usually support their case by referring to economies elsewhere in the world which they see as having benefitted from freedom from the constraints imposed by excessive state intervention. However, the fact that the weaker economies tend to have more interventionist policies does not mean that the interventionist policies have weakened the economy: very often, the interventionist policies are effect rather than cause, a response to a long history of industrial failure. Indeed, one of the most successful industrial countries in the world, Japan, does not follow a social market approach to industrial problems, although so many facets of the Japanese culture, society and economy are different from the economic and social systems in other OECD countries that it is difficult to make useful comparisons.

Even in social market economies such as that of the Federal Republic of Germany (Bundesrepublik Deutschland, BRD) there is more government intervention in the industrial economy than is often realized, although this does not mean that the West German approach to industrial policy has been the same as would be found in a 'selective intervention' country. The philosophy underlying intervention in the BRD has been very different from that which has prevailed in Britain and there has been no co-ordinated industrial policy similar to that attempted in the UK between 1972 and 1979.

Two alternative interpretations of the state of the West German 'social market economy', particularly in relation to the nature of BRD industrial policy, are possible at the beginning of the 1980s. One interpretation (the 'convergence interpretation') would be that the BRD's approach to industrial policy, although presented differently, is fundamentally similar to the approaches of other western countries; or, at any rate, is likely to become very similar in the near future in response to the economic and social pressures arising from world recession which even the BRD has not been able to escape. An alternative interpretation (the 'miracle interpretation') would be that the BRD approach to industrial policy has differed, in particular from that of the UK, in so far as it has been more limited in scope and more oriented to promoting a general industrial climate in which successful industries can flourish compared with the apparent emphasis in the UK on helping firms in difficulty to survive. The general position taken here is that the second interpretation·is the more correct one, but that there are indications that, given the appearance of economic stresses such as higher unemployment, the BRD might move towards policies which are more like those pursued by governments favouring a selective intervention strategy. Indeed, a start in that direction has already taken place, albeit gradually and undramatically.

Supporters of the 'convergence' interpretation of BRD industrial policy might first point to the fact that total government expenditure in the BRD as a percentage of GDP is around the European Community average, and above the level for the UK, even before the 1979 Conservative Government's public expenditure cuts took effect[1]. What is perhaps more significant than the overall level of government expenditure is the steady growth of direct aid to industry since the passage of the Promotion of Economic Growth and Stability Act in 1967. The 1967 Stabilitätsgesetz was, of course, preceded by earlier measures such as the 1952 Investition-shilfegesetz, but as Donges points out, 'during the 1950s and 1960s industrial policies were rather complementary to the market mechanism. It is only since the early 1970s that they have become more interventionistic and distorting'[2]. Moreover, there was a considerable acceleration of Federal aid to industry from 1977 to 1980 as *Table 4.1* shows, particularly through classic forms of selective intervention such as 'help for certain sections of industry'. Apart from the fact that total aid increased by just

TABLE 4.1 Bundesrepublik Deutschland: Development of Federal financial aid and tax advantages, 1977–80. Industrial economy (excluding transport). (Millions of DM)

Category	1977			1980		
	Grants and loans	Tax relief	Total	Grants and loans	Tax relief	Total
Mining	977	110	1087	1913	106	2019
Energy and raw materials	209	Nil	209	388	Nil	388
Promotion of innovation	17	Nil	17	388	Nil	338
Subsidization of measures in the context of special technology programmes	83	Nil	83	100	Nil	100
Help for certain sections of industry	179	Nil	179	821	Nil	821
Regional structural measures	228	3024	3252	269	3642	3911
Banking	Nil	155	155	Nil	207	207
General industrial economy	224	535	759	178	661	839
Totals	1917	3824	5741	4007	4616	8623

Source: *Deutscher Bundestag*, 8. Wahlperiode, Siebter Subventionsbericht, pp.24–25

over fifty per cent over the three year period, the share of aid provided in the form of grants and loans, as distinct from tax concessions, increased from thirty-three per cent in 1977 to forty-seven per cent in 1980. If, as suggested in Chapter One, one of the hallmarks of a social market industrial policy is a preference for the use of tax concessions to industry rather than direct aid, then the balance in the BRD by 1980 was a very fine one.

However, one important difference in the conduct of industrial policy between the UK and the BRD is that nationalization as a solution to the problems of declining industries has generally been avoided in the BRD. For example, the Federal Government did not respond to the crisis in coal mining in the late 1960s by nationalizing the industry, but instead preferred to create what is in effect a state-sponsored cartel. The postal and telecommunications service is in state hands, as are the Federal Railways, whose losses accounted for some 6½ per cent of the Federal budget, on average, for the years 1977–79[3]. Of the other major public utilities, electricity is not nationalized, but is generated by a variety of private companies, companies with state shareholdings and municipalities. In total, there are about 1200 supply undertakings, although the three largest are responsible for about forty-five per cent of production (Bayliss and Butt Philip, 1980).

There are also a number of companies which are not public utility concerns in which the state has shareholdings, the most important being a forty-four per cent share in VEBA AG, a holding company with interests in electricity, chemicals and transport which ranked in 1979–80 as Europe's fourth largest industrial group[4]. However, these shareholdings are not used to influence company policy in the ways that they might be used as instruments of an interventionist industrial policy in other countries. Indeed, a merger between VEBA and Gelsenberg AG which would have promoted state energy policy objectives was eventually blocked by the Monopolies Commission, after an earlier intervention by the Cartels Office, a sequence of events that one cannot visualize happening in Britain (Owen-Smith, 1979).

An important element in BRD industrial aid is expenditure on research and development which is seen as contributing to securing an adequate industrial base for the future. Although over eighty per cent of the cost of industrial research and development is still met by industry itself, it should be noted that total Federal Ministry for Research and Technology (BMFT) expenditure on the promotion of industrial research doubled between 1972 and 1977. Moreover, in 1979, DM300 million was set aside to provide additional assistance to small and medium-sized firms by awarding grants for R and D staff expenditure[5].

An important element in the 'miracle' interpretation of BRD industrial policy is that it has been 'stout hearted' in the face of industrial failure, refusing to bail out enterprises that are not viable. Thus, one can cite the contrast between the UK Government's treatment of British Leyland with the Federal Government's treatment of Volkswagen when it ran into difficulties as a consequence of the 1974/75 recession. The West German Government offered regional aid for the afflicted areas, rather than attempting to prevent plant closures and redundancies from going ahead

(Anglo-German Foundation, 1980). It could be argued, however, that such an approach is possible in a relatively buoyant economy, but is politically more difficult in an economy like that of the UK where displaced labour is unlikely to be rapidly absorbed into alternative employment.

Most of the BRD's industries have been successful, but in cases where an important industry has suffered chronic difficulties, the BRD's response does not seem to have been so very different from that of those countries which have a number of such industries. For example, in the case of shipbuilding it has been found that 'of the twelve methods of intervention used in the eleven most important shipbuilding nations, seven are used in the Federal Republic'[6]. It could be argued that shipbuilding is a special case, but it does show that the principles of a social market approach can be modified in the BRD when the national interest appears to demand it.

Perhaps the real difference to emerge between the BRD and the UK is not in the divergent character of their industrial policies, but simply the contrast between a country with a successful economy and political system and a country whose economic and political system is running into increasing difficulties. Because the BRD has a more successful economy, it has less need to resort to 'ad hoc' acts of intervention which exacerbate problems, or at least postpone their solution; because muddled acts of intervention in circumstances of crisis are less common, the economy continues to prosper. In such a relatively prosperous environment, it is perhaps easier to foster a pervasive feeling among employers, trade unionists and politicians that there is no way round becoming and remaining economically competitive.

However, there has been a shift away from the purer social market strategy of the past and one possible BRD response to the continuing global recession and the growing structural problems of its own economy is a shift to a selective intervention strategy, even if the Government continues to maintain that it is adhering to the tenets of social market ideology. As Donges points out, 'although officially the Federal Ministry of Economics still assigns to the market mechanism the task of steering structural changes in industry, it also recognises that the Government has become increasingly involved in the process'[7].

4.2 The disengagement experiment

The Conservative Government elected in Britain in 1970 attempted to reverse the development of a selective intervention policy begun under the Wilson Government of 1964–70. The Industrial Reorganization Corporation was abolished; investment grants were ended; and a rather unsuccessful attempt was made to sell off parts of the nationalized industries, leading to the disposal of the state-owned public houses in Carlisle and Scotland and the sale of the state-owned travel agents, Thomas Cook and Lunn-Poly, plus eleven BSC brick-making works. It is not intended to consider here the detailed history of the events of 1970 to 1972 in relation to industrial policy. This has already been done more than adequately elsewhere (Bruce-Gardyne, 1974; Young with Lowe, 1974).

However, it is important to consider the alternative interpretations of what happened, because the different ways in which politicians perceived the events of 1970 to 1972 affected their subsequent approaches to industrial policy. For members of the Labour Party, the collapse of Mr Heath's disengagement experiment in 1972 demonstrated the political impossibility of pursuing a social market industrial policy in Britain. Even moderates like Dell drew the lesson from what he termed 'the educative experience of Mr Heath' that 'Although it is easy to see the dangers that intervention can have, this in no way relieves government of the pressure to deal with specific problems as they are presented to them.'[8] Hence, after the return of a Conservative Government in 1979, Labour MPs were constantly scanning the heavens for the Second Coming of the U Turn. Indeed, the tendency of the Labour Party to greet every minor adjustment to industrial policy as evidence of the long awaited swerve in policy made it politically more difficult for the Government to adjust its industrial policies.

The Conservative reaction to the events of 1970 to 1972 comes in two forms: the 'apologetic' and the 'repentant'. The apologetic version, whose supporters are to be found on the moderate wing of the party, seeks to establish that 'the apparent shift to the Right of the new Conservative Government in 1970 was largely rhetorical'[9]. Peter Walker has maintained that there was never a properly worked out policy of disengagement anyway and that the non-intervention position was adopted almost accidentally as a result of the famous 'lame ducks' speech by John Davies to the Conservative Party Conference in 1970. Indeed, Davies never said in that speech that he would not intervene, only that he would not bail out companies in trouble because of their own mistakes and with no hope of recovery (Open University, 1976).

The 'repentants', on the other hand, see the experience of 1970 to 1972 as an object lesson in the importance of adhering to what they interpret as genuinely Conservative policies, however unpopular such policies may be in the short run. It is not clear why those 'repentants' who were in the Cabinet in 1972 did not object more vigorously to the introduction of interventionist policies at the time, although Sir Keith Joseph experienced what amounted to a 'road to Damascus' conversion after losing office. Sir Keith has revealed that 'it was only in April 1974 that I was converted to Conservatism. I had thought that I was a Conservative but now I see that I was not one at all.'[10] The broader significance of Sir Keith's re-emergence as a 'born again' Conservative was that, following his decision not to contest the party leadership and Mrs Thatcher's election, the 'repentant' interpretation of the events of 1970 to 1972 became the orthodox one among the Conservative Party leadership. Mrs Thatcher was certainly in no doubt about what the lessons of 1972 were with her declarations that 'the lady is not for turning'.

4.3 Selective financial assistance after 1979

A Government that was totally committed to non-intervention would have repealed the 1972 Industry Act and abolished all regional and selective financial assistance. In fact, the Conservatives retained the system of regional and selective financial assistance they had inherited, although in a reduced and changed form. As far as regional aid was concerned, the Government retained the three-tier structure of assisted areas which had been in existence throughout the 1970s, although it is intended to reduce the total area eligible for assistance from over forty per cent of the employed population to around twenty-five per cent over a three year period from 1979. This change means that large areas of the country, particularly in the north, will lose their assisted area status, although some small areas (such as parts of South Devon) were added to the assisted areas or upgraded to a higher level of assistance.

One of the characteristics of British regional policy has always been the significance of the incremental adjustments to policy which take place between the regular changes of policy characteristic of the policy arena. There has been a tendency for the area eligible for assistance to be enlarged in a series of small steps in response to particular local employment crises, whatever the general policy intentions of the Government of the day. The 1979 Government was no exception to the pattern of a general cutback, followed by a 'creep back' in hard hit localities. In December 1979, the Government designated the Corby employment office area as a development area (the nearest one to London) and the Shotton travel-to-work area as a special development area in response to the closure of BSC plants at Corby and Shotton. Further cutbacks in the steel industry led the Government in July 1980 to designate the Port Talbot travel-to-work area as a special development area; at the same time, the Scunthorpe and Newport travel-to-work areas and the Cwmbran employment office areas were designated as development areas.

The 'automatic' Regional Development Grant has been and remains the principal means of providing regional aid, although it should be stressed that it is only 'automatic' in the sense that it is given to qualifying assets in assisted areas at predetermined levels of payment. The Conservative Government decided to maintain Regional Development Grant at twenty-two per cent in the Special Development Areas which are the areas of greatest need. In Development Areas, the rate of grant on buildings, plant and machinery was reduced from twenty per cent to fifteen per cent, which was one way of dealing with the criticism that the gap between the level of RDG paid in Special Development Areas and Development Areas was too small to make a significant difference to firms' location decisions. The least favoured of the regional assistance categories, the Intermediate Areas, lost their twenty per cent RDG on buildings. The only advantages given to Intermediate Areas were a new freedom from Industrial Development Certificate Controls (which were being applied much less rigorously in any case) and an eligibility for selective regional assistance. The Government also introduced a four month deferment on the payment of approved RDGs, a measure which was criticized by the CBI because of its impact on company cash flows.

When the Conservatives came into office, they decided to allow the energy conservation scheme and the two remaining schemes for particular industrial sectors, those for footwear and red meat slaughterhouses, to run their course. The Labour Government's Selective Investment Scheme closed in June 1979 and, although outstanding applications were processed against the existing criteria, Sir Keith Joseph made it clear that 'we shall interpret these criteria somewhat more stringently than in the past, so that marginal projects will not in future be assisted'[11]. PPDS, MISP and MAP were kept open and their use is discussed later in the chapter in the section on 'high technology'.

Sections 7 and 8 of the 1972 Industry Act

The Government continued to make use of its powers to provide selective financial assistance to industry under Sections 7 and 8 of the 1972 Act, although in a rather different way from its predecessor. Section 7 assistance for sound projects providing employment opportunities in the assisted areas, continued to be available, although under a new set of criteria. Section 8 assistance continued to be available, although at a lower level than previously, to attract internationally mobile projects or projects leading to substantial improvements in performance or the introduction of new products.

Decisions relating to the provision of Section 7 and 8 assistance have an interest which goes beyond industrial policy as such. They offer an example of civil servants exercising considerable discretion in the use of public funds. In effect, civil servants are placed in a position where they have to negotiate with companies and, although the teams who carry out this work include accountants and others with commercial experience on secondment from the private sector, the task requires the development of special skills which take time to acquire. Decisions about the provision of selective financial assistance are, of course, ultimately the responsibility of the Secretary of State concerned, although in practice relatively few decisions have to be referred to ministers for detailed consideration. This reflects both the skill with which the sifting process is carried out and the availability of the advice of the statutory Industrial Development Advisory Board which can, and does, recommend that assistance should not be given in particular cases. Moreover, discretion is exercised within the context of the criteria laid down by ministers, although, as should be apparent from the discussion of 'additionality' below, the application of these criteria to particular cases is not always easy and requires the exercise of careful judgement.

Section 7 assistance in Scotland and Wales has been the responsibility of the Secretaries of State for Scotland and Wales, respectively, since 1975, although the Department of Industry retains a co-ordinating responsibility and the Industry Secretary deals with projects with implications for the whole of Great Britain. For example, a proposal by a company which provided for investment in a number of different parts of the country might merit Industry Department involvement. As far as Section 7 assistance within England is concerned, regional offices of the Department of Industry, with the assistance of their (non-statutory) regional Industrial Development Boards, have delegated authority to deal with smaller projects. In the case of the northern regions, the regional office can authorize a maximum grant of £2 million for a project of up to £10 million; the other regions have lower limits.

The grant of Section 7 assistance has always involved an assessment of the viability of the project and of the undertaking seeking assistance. This task involves examination of the company's accounts for the past three years and, more difficult but equally important, reaching a judgement about the company's management. As far as the project itself is concerned, information has to be gathered about the relevant product, forecasts of market share, etc. These tasks will generally involve consultation with the relevant sponsoring division in the Industry Department or elsewhere, although the amount of relevant information that the sponsoring division is able to provide may vary in quantity and quality.

Section 8 projects also have to be viable, but Section 7 projects differ in that they are employment-linked. Assistance is only provided where there is a benefit to employment. Projects should lead to the creation of additional employment (Category A) or the safeguarding of existing employment through modernization or rationalization (Category B) in the assisted areas. The amount of assistance offered is related to the number of jobs involved through the imposition of confidential cost-per-job limits.

Under the Labour Government, Section 7 assistance had to meet the employment link criterion, as well as the viability criterion and a requirement that the greater part of the cost of projects should be met from sources outside the public sector. However, the 1979 Conservative Government added two new criteria. First, assistance is provided only for projects which seem likely to strengthen the regional and national economy and thereby provide more productive and secure jobs, e.g. by improving efficiency or the introduction of new technology or products. The introduction of this criterion reflects the concern of the Conservative Government that the policies of its predecessors were not cost-effective. Where a company already has a business and wishes to modernize, extend or transfer it, an attempt can be made to compare the added value per employee before and after the project. In the case of an entirely new project, the national resource costs and benefits resulting from the project can be analysed to see what it adds to net UK output.

The second new criterion states that the Secretary of State must be satisfied that the project will not take place either at all or on the basis proposed without assistance, i.e. the provision of assistance must be shown to lead to a significant change in the nature and scale of the project or to a significant advance in time or to a desirable change in location. One consequence of this requirement is that assistance will not normally be provided for projects on which a start has been made before assistance has been offered. A similar provision applies to Section 8 assistance and to the remaining cases arising under the Selective Investment Scheme. Assistance will only be considered under Section 8 for projects which would not be undertaken on the basis proposed (in relation to their timing, scale and nature) without it. This means that there must be a genuine and significant enhancement of the project, as a result of the assistance—for example a genuine and substantial acceleration of the project; a substantial increase in the scale of the project, other additional features such as a desirable extension of product range.

This requirement that there must be a genuine and significant enhancement of the project as a result of the aid is known as 'additionality'. Additionality is new to Section 7 projects, but was introduced for Section 8 projects by the Labour Government. It was applied to the APS and SIS, although the wording used in the latter scheme under the Labour adminis- tration seemed to be more permissive with the words 'This might be demonstrated by' being used in relation to the examples of additionality rather than the wording 'This means there must be' employed by the Conservatives.

Additionality raises a number of complex conceptual and difficult practical questions. It should be remembered that it is concerned not with a judgement about whether the company could or should go ahead with a project without assistance, but whether they *would* go ahead without assistance. Civil servants only know that they are right when they turn down an application and the project goes ahead; when assistance is given, they never know for certain if they were right or not. One could only test the genuineness of company results for assistance by refusing every application and seeing how many projects still went ahead; in other words by testing the system to destruction!

Perhaps the most straightforward cases to deal with under this criterion are those where a transnational company has a choice between a number of national locations and would not undertake the investment in the UK without assistance. At the other end of the scale of difficulty are those cases where the applicant is subsidiary of a large group. Such large groups usually have a better understanding of how selective assistance can be used to enhance their investment programme and therefore start with something of an advantage in the negotiating process. To take a hypothetical example: supposing a large company acquires a company made up of a number of medium-sized plants in an assisted area. It then provides the Industry Department with a list of alternatives: without assistance, it would have to close all the plants except one; with a certain level of assistance, it could retain and modernize half the plants, and so on. In a sense, civil servants then almost find themselves faced with a series of 'call my bluff' negotiations. They will certainly examine the background of the company: does it have extensive cash reserves? What is its style of operation—does it tend to modernize plants it buys, regardless of whether or not it is given assistance? A crucial if intangible piece of evidence can often be the personal feel of the appraisal team for the choices facing the company, and their assessment of individual members of the applicant company's man- agement. However, the new, tighter criteria mean that it is unlikely that companies will be given the benefit of the doubt in marginal cases.

Of course, the outcome does not depend just on the additionality criterion being met, although that is a necessary condition of assistance being granted. The other criteria which apply to Section 7 applications have already been discussed. Section 8 assistance is considered for commercially viable projects which are internationally mobile or will lead to substantial improvements in performance—usually productivity— although other improvements, e.g. in quality or reliability of products, can be considered. In determining the most appropriate measure of improve- ment, regard will be paid to the nature of the project and the industry. The resulting productivity of assisted products is normally expected to be significantly better than the average for the industry. Assistance is also considered for projects that lead to the introduction of new products by the plant or company. In the case of new products the Industry Department has to be satisfied that appropriate up-to-date and efficient manufacturing methods are to be used.

In addition, it has to be demonstrated that the project will produce a substantial net contribution to UK output or will introduce a significant degree of innovation to the UK, although a significant degree of innovation would not in itself usually override the absence of a substantial net contribution to UK output. A contribution to net UK output may arise from additional exports, or import substitution, or the meeting of increased (or new) domestic demand. The Department's economists will usually be brought in to help to establish the UK resource impact of the project. Clearly, one of the considerations that the Department has to take into account is whether the project will damage an existing UK company. The purpose of assistance is not to bring about the destruction of existing companies, although the balance is a difficult one to draw when it can be established that the new company would introduce new technology and bring about substantially increased exports. Assistance is negotiated as the minimum necessary to bring about the enhanced project, although clearly it is difficult to attain such a target with precision, and in many respects this aspect of the criteria represents a politically reassuring statement of good intentions.

It should be remembered that the Industry Department's Industrial Development Unit can be involved in discussions about assistance at a very early stage of company planning. Very often the Unit goes into a company which is at a crossroads and facing a number of difficult strategic decisions. Civil servants do not just look at the particular project as a discrete problem which has to be processed through a particular set of procedures. Instead, they try to adopt a creative approach, talking through the problem with the company and pointing out other forms of assistance if they seem to be more appropriate in the particular case. In this respect, the Industrial Development Unit's blend of access to technical skills, acquired experience, mixture of private sector and governmental backgrounds, when combined with the information resources of the government machine, represents a unique approach to an aspect of government activity where what are really commercial judgements have to be made within a framework of public accountability.

4.4 Assisting high technology

In 1980 the phrase 'constructive intervention' started to be used by ministers to describe their industrial policies. In so far as the phrase meant anything, it appeared to represent a growing commitment to assisting high technology industries and to stimulating the application of new technologies to the production processes of older industries. Expenditure on general industrial research and development increased from £66 million (at 1980 survey prices) in 1978–79, the last year of the Labour Government, to £82 million in 1979–80 and £108 million in 1980–81. It was projected to increase to £124 million (at 1980 prices) in 1981–82, representing an increase of eighty-nine per cent since the Labour Government's last full year in office[12]. In particular, expenditure on micro-electronics and its applications was more than doubled between 1978–79 and 1979–80, as was expenditure on the development of new products and processes[13]. Of a £50 million additional allocation of funds for industrial aid announced by the Chancellor in November 1980, £16 million was set aside for the PPDS and two micro-electronic aid schemes.

Reference was made in Chapter Two to Government efforts to develop a better framework for dealing with information technology. These efforts were given a new impetus in Mrs Thatcher's January 1981 reshuffle when the two Ministers of State at the Industry Department were replaced. One of the main tasks of Kenneth Baker, brought in from the back benches where he was Chairman of the Conservative Industry Committee to be Minister of State, was stated to be the further development of information technology policy. Indeed, Mr Baker, a moderate Conservative with experience of the computer industry, was given a general responsibility for a number of high technology industries including telecommunications, computer systems, micro-electronic applications, robotics, the information technology aspects of space, and the Post Office including British Telecom. He was not, however, simply a Minister for High Technology, also being given responsibility for a number of troubled private sector areas such as textiles and mechanical engineering. Moreover, too much political signifi-cance should not be read into Mr Baker's appointment. He replaced a moderate minister, Adam Butler, and the other new Minister of State, Norman Tebbit, with responsibility for the main state-owned problem industries such as British Steel and British Leyland and for Section 7 and Section 8 assistance, was an original member of Mrs Thatcher's so-called 'Gang of Four' of tough minded right-wingers.

Product and process development scheme

The survival and further development of Labour's Product and Process Development Scheme under the Conservatives represents an interesting aspect of the Thatcher Government's industrial policies. Clearly, PPDS was seen as less politically controversial than the sector aid schemes sponsored by Labour under Section 8 of the 1972 Industry Act. As mentioned in Chapter Three, the scheme was introduced in 1977 with the aim of encouraging UK companies to invest more of their resources in development work to launch new or significantly improved products and processes more quickly and more effectively.

Assistance under the scheme usually takes the form of a twenty five per cent grant towards development costs, though in exceptional cases a fifty-fifty shared-cost contract, with the Department contribution recover-able through a levy on sales, may be offered. Although shared-cost contracts may be appropriate if a company badly needs an injection of cash, they require a greater monitoring effort by civil servants. The Department may also place pre-production orders for machines for user trials where there is evidence of user resistance. If the equipment meets the users' requirements and performs to specification, the user is expected to purchase it from the Department. If it is not purchased by the user, the manufacturer is required to buy the equipment back from the Department.

After a slow start, PPDS applications increased, and by the end of

December 1980, 1073 applications had been received. Of these, 531 had been approved, involving a government contribution of £64 million towards projects costing £205 million. 450 applications had been withdrawn or rejected and the remaining ninety-two were still under consideration. The appraisal process normally starts with a visit to the applicant company by a project officer who is a specialist with a technical background in most cases. Where he is not himself a specialist, such advice will always be taken. Many of the companies concerned, particularly in the instruments and automation area, are relatively small, although often their senior staff have previously worked for larger companies. One problem frequently encountered is that the idea may be at a relatively advanced stage of technical development, but may not have been costed properly; project officers may be able to help companies to clarify their financial thinking.

Applications are judged against four criteria. The Department must be satisfied that the company has the financial and technical resources to carry through the project to commercial exploitation. The Department's accountants look at the company's recent financial performance and at the details of finance for the particular project. A judgement also has to be made about the management capability of the company. Second, the project must offer good prospects of success and must be likely to lead to a significant improvement in the company's performance, for example by widening its product range. Application of this criterion involves the Department in assessing the market prospects for the project, the place of the company in the industry and the strategic significance of the project to the industry, a process that would normally involve the sponsoring division. Third, there is the additionality criterion which requires that the project or programme would not be undertaken in the form proposed or within a reasonable time scale without government aid. The application of the additionality criterion to PPDS cases is different from Section 7 and Section 8 cases. Account is taken not only of the degree of technical risk involved, but also of the fact that even a short acceleration in timescale which might be achieved with support may be significant, for example in terms of achieving a particular window in the market. For Section 8 cases, however, an acceleration of some two years is normally sought. Finally, the total qualifying cost must normally not be less than £25 000 or more than £2 million, although consideration is given to projects of less than £25 000 from small firms.

Britain has suffered not so much from a lack of research into basic technology, but rather a neglect of commercial product development and market considerations. PPDS goes a long way to fill that gap. The projects supported include a compact microfilm reader which can produce hard copies from the image displayed; a new range of industrial rotary fans which will compete with imports which account for seventy per cent of the UK market; and an inexpensive but reliable personal radio distress beacon for use on land and at sea. However, one must not be too complacent about what has been achieved. Ireland's Industrial Development Authority started its Product and Process Development Scheme in 1970 and in 1977 1363 grants were approved. Moreover, whereas the British scheme is essentially reactive and depends on companies making applications to the

Industry Department, the IDA is setting up a Project Identification Programme which will provide a bank of product possibilities to be availed of by Irish firms[14]. The IDA's Project Identification Unit picks out project opportunities through company visits and research and in 1979 twenty-five new enterprises were set up as a result of the activities of the Unit. A product research facility which collates import statistics, information on technology transfer opportunities and market information on successful products in other countries, was established by the Unit in 1979 and is used by about twenty entrepreneurs every month researching opportunities[15]. PPDS project officers in Britain have a heavy case-load and additional staff resources would allow more visits to firms to take place and hence an improvement in the quality of the information exchange between firms and the Industry Department.

Micro-electronics

The launch of MISP and MAP in 1978 has already been referred to in Chapter Three. By the end of March 1980, offers of support under MISP to a total of £23.9 million had been made, mainly for standard products such as micro-processors and memories. However, a new emphasis was being placed on support for devices required for specific types of application[16]. After a certain amount of dithering, the Government also agreed to finance a second tranche of money to the NEB's microchip manufacturer, INMOS, a saga discussed more fully in Chapter Five.

However, perhaps more important than supporting the micro-electronics industry itself is ensuring that companies in other industries adopt micro-electronics in their own production and processes. In some ways this is a more difficult task, as it involves overcoming ignorance, a lack of relevant skills and a reluctance to apply new technology. In 1977, a survey carried out for the Industry Department found that only five per cent of companies were aware of, and active in, micro-electronics applications; a new survey in December 1979 found the position much improved among the 'aware' fifty per cent, although 'around fifty per cent still did not fully appreciate the importance of micro-electronics and were not doing anything to adopt it'. Moreover, about fifty per cent of companies did not have any electronics (much less micro-electronics) expertise in top or middle management. The Department concluded: 'Even though the general level of awareness has improved, our impression is that companies tend not to appreciate the relevance of micro-electronics to their own activities and this includes some large companies.'[17]

Of the £55 million allocated for MAP, expenditure of some £28 million had been committed by February 1981. The largest sum has been spent on project support, with 405 new development projects underway ranging from mining machinery to consumer products. Companies applying for project support have tended to have had previous micro-electronics experience. Although over half of all projects have been undertaken by small firms, the Department's research shows that raising funds for micro-electronics applications is a major problem for over a third of smaller companies and it is intended that project support should be more heavily biased towards smaller companies in future. Grants are, however, limited to twenty-five per cent of project cost and smaller companies often have difficulty in finding their seventy-five per cent. Moreover, there appears to have been a communication gap between smaller companies and venture capital. The smaller entrepreneurs may not know how to present their project in the right form while financiers lack access to technical expertise to assess micro-electronic projects at their development stage. In April 1981, the Industry Department launched a scheme in partnership with sixteen banks and insurance companies under which the technical appraisal of a MAP project will be made available, with the applicant company's permission, to a financial institution chosen by the company from among those participating in the scheme. However, one of the participants commented that the Department might have to approach an average five participants on behalf of a particular company before finance was arranged, and another participant indicated that it was interested in larger projects by established companies and not in new or relatively young companies[18].

Over 133000 people have attended MAP 'Awareness Seminars' and over 34000 extra training places have been created on short-term courses. Now that the general level of awareness has improved, follow-up action is being tailored to the needs of sectors or even individual companies. A sectoral campaign covering the plastics industry was launched in February 1981. Given the programme's limited resources, emphasis has been placed on self help by companies backed up by material generated by MAP. Gaps in the geographical coverage of training courses arc to be filled and more advanced courses encouraged. In March 1980, the DES announced a £9 million micro-electronics programme mainly for curriculum development and development of software.

Consultancy grants are seen as a cost-effective way of encouraging firms to consider the specific application of micro-electronics. By February 1981, 1863 studies of the feasibility of applying micro-electronics had been approved. Grants of £2000 are paid towards the cost of initial studies undertaken for a UK manufacturing company by an authorized consultant on the feasibility of applying micro-electronics in its products and processes. However, this aspect of MAP has been so well received by industry that it has been necessary to tighten the criteria so that individual companies or distinct operating units within a group do not normally receive support for more than one study.

The general picture that emerges in this area of assistance to promote the effective commercial use of new technologies by British companies is, indeed, one of 'constructive intervention'. However, competitor countries have often been earlier in the field or more willing to commit substantial funds. A really effective high technology policy might involve spending more public money than the Conservative Government was prepared to countenance in its first two years of office.

4.5 Policy innovations

It might seem from the discussion so far that the Conservative Government's private sector industrial policy during its first two years of office consisted either of running down schemes started by its predecessor or continuing them in much the same way. Indeed, asked what the Government meant by 'constructive intervention', Sir Keith Joseph said in April 1981 that, in general, what the Government was doing was 'modifying the inheritance' received from the Labour Government in relation to industry[19]. However, the Thatcher Government did introduce three important policy innovations in its first two years of office.

Enterprise zones

In recent years, local authorities have become increasingly involved in industrial promotion and development (Muller and Bruce, 1981; Storey and Robinson, 1981). The Inner Urban Areas Act 1978 gave increased powers to inner city local authorities to assist industry. For example, once an Improvement Area had been approved by the Secretary of State, the Act authorized them to give grants for the improvement of industrial buildings up to fifty per cent of the cost of works. In addition, some thirty local authorities took supplementary powers to assist industry in private bills between 1963 and 1973[20]. A few authorities actually took shareholdings in companies in difficulty (Minns and Thornley, 1978).

The widespread belief that 'local authorities could and should play a more active role in the local economy'[21] was underpinned by a fashionable and increasingly widespead political belief in the virtues of decentralization, coupled with the frequent assertion that 'small is beautiful'. It is difficult to see how the problems of the national industrial economy (and ultimately the global economy) dealt with in this book can be adequately tackled at the local level. Although there are attractions in allowing a hundred flowers bloom in small-scale industrial experiments, locally conceived and controlled, the risk is that only one or two of these experiments will survive to adorn the industrial wasteland with their blooms.

It is questionable whether local government units, even the larger Scottish regions, are appropriate ones for handling industrial problems. There is a danger of replicating the competitive bidding for industrial investment between nation states within a country. It may be also the case that industrial promotion efforts by local authorities lacking in expertise may hinder more professional efforts by public agencies operating on a regional or national basis. For example, the former Chief Executive of the Scottish Development Agency has criticized 'the sudden departure from a small town in, shall we say, Angus of a totally unprepared mission to Dusseldorf which achieved nothing except bad publicity'[22].

The Conservative Government in its first two years of office did not, of course, encourage the trend towards more local government intervention in industrial affairs, nor, for that matter, did it increase local autonomy—rather the reverse. However, it did introduce the idea of enterprise zones—inner city and other depressed areas where red tape, taxes and rates are to be cut to a minimum to encourage business. A total of eleven zones were named by 1981, including Speke on Merseyside; the Isle of Dogs in London's dockland; Clydebank; and the Midlands steel town of Corby. The zones will benefit from such advantages as a ten year 'rates holiday'; a 100 per cent capital allowance on commercial and industrial buildings; a relaxed planning regime and streamlined administration of the controls that remain; priority treatment for customs concessions; and exemption from the requirements of industrial training boards.

Critics of the zones have argued that they will be competing against one another for a shrinking pool of investment and job opportunities. Jobs would be displaced from other locations, rather than new jobs created. It is too early to form an opinion about the likely success of the zones (or of the urban development corporations which have been charged with rejuvenating the London and Merseyside docklands). They are an unusual innovation, although it could be argued that they simply represent a diversion from the real problems of industrial decline.

Public purchasing

Nearly £10 million of the extra £50 million allocated to industrial aid in November 1980 was set aside for a new public purchasing policy developed by the Department of Industry. The basic idea is to encourage the public sector to use its orders, totalling £22 billion a year, to improve the technological development and international competitiveness of UK products. The aid will mainly be used for development projects and to assist customers who provide 'shop windows' in which new products can be shown in use to potential foreign buyers. For example, assistance is being given to a 'peoplemover' which will operate on a magnetically levitated track at Birmingham Airport.

One of the difficulties that the initiative faces is that it requires a change in the attitude of public purchasing officers who have been used to making their decisions within a set of rules which have stressed 'value for money' above everything else. It should be stressed that it is not intended to substitute a crude 'buy British' policy for existing arrangements, but rather to draw the attention of purchasing officers to the need to take account of longer-term costs and broader implications when making their decisions. However, as one civil servant has been quoted as saying, 'It's one thing to do all this for computers where we've always had a pro-British policy and all know where we stand; but it's quite another thing to write down what to do about, say, floor tiles.'[23]

Donges notes that the Deutsche Bundesbahn and the Deutsche Bundespost 'frequently use their monopolistic market power to discriminate among domestic industries to the benefit of established manufacturers or of those firms which are located in structurally weak regions'[24]. The General Agreement on Tariffs and Trade organization (GATT) is, of course, attempting to restrain the use of public procurement as a non-tariff barrier to trade, but GATT rules need not prove too serious an obstacle. As one civil servant has stated, 'GATT is really enforced by its Contracting Parties to the extent that they wish to do this . . . For example, the United Kingdom – I would not particularly want this recorded – has breached the GATT on a number of occasions.'[25]

Small firms

The historically high Minimum Lending Rate maintained for much of the

Conservative Government's first two years in office did not fit well with its pledges to help small businessmen. However, one of the more important elements in an 'enterprise package' introduced in the 1981 Budget was a bank loan guarantee scheme for small businessmen. The scheme, which will be funded through Section 8 of the 1972 Act, will provide government guarantees for bank loans to small businessmen unable to provide sufficient personal security, provided that the project is considered to be viable. It was intended that the loans would range up to £75000 for periods of two to seven years. How the scheme will work remains to be seen but, if it leads to high risk bank customers being helped by government, the Exchequer costs could be considerable.

4.6 Privatization

Although this book is principally concerned with Government policy towards the private sector, it is not possible to give a balanced account of the Thatcher Government's industrial policies without referring to its policy of 'privatization' of the nationalized industries. Expectations of a 'sale of the century' of publicly owned assets were raised before the 1979 general election and the disposals that took place in the first two years of the Government's term of office greatly exceeded anything achieved by the Heath Government in its four year term. However, some of the proposed disposals encountered greater difficulties or greater resistance than had been anticipated and the future of a number of state-owned industries remained uncertain at the end of the Government's first two years in office. The disposals were, of course, of profitable assets and 'lame duck' industries like British Steel raised different problems that will be discussed later.

In some areas, the Government was able to make rapid progress in its programme of 'privatization'. British Aerospace, the aircraft and missile corporation formed by the preceding Labour Government, became a public company on January 1st, 1981. A successful sale of half the shares followed in February, the Government stating that it would not use its rights as a shareholder to intervene in the company's commercial decisions, although it would be prepared to use its voting rights to prevent foreign acquisition of the company.

The National Freight Corporation, Britain's largest road haulage operator, was denationalized in October 1980 with the first sale of shares planned for 1981. The Government was to be issued with a number of fully paid-up ordinary shares to wipe out capital debts. The Government's Civil Aviation Act provided for the sale of forty-nine per cent of the shares in a new limited company controlling British Airways to the private sector. The Government's Telecommunications Bill provided for the sale of nearly half the shares in Cable and Wireless, the profitable telephone and telegraph company that operates in seventy countries, to the private sector. The Atomic Energy (Miscellaneous Provisions) Bill sought to enable the Government to sell up to one hundred per cent of the shares in the Radiochemical Centre (TRC), a world leader in the manufacturing and marketing of radioactive isotopes. Plans were also made for the sale of up to forty nine per cent of shares in the British Transport Docks Board by 1982.

The Government was persuaded to modify a plan to sell off British Rail's non-rail subsidiaries in their entirety to the private sector. Instead, a new holding company was to be set up to take over British Rail's hotel, shipping, hovercraft and property interests. The holding company would be wholly owned by the BR Board, but the understanding was that it would sell shares in its subsidiaries in the stock market. In the case of Sealink, it was expected that British Rail would sell a majority holding to the private sector.

In the case of the postal and telecommunications services a rather different, although ideologically compatible, approach was adopted. The Government decided to divide the Post Office into two separate corporations dealing with postal and telecommunications services and relaxed the state monopoly hitherto exercised in relation to these services. In the case of the Post Office's mail business, the relaxation was largely symbolic, affecting only one to two per cent of the postal business through such changes as allowing document exchanges to transport mail in bulk between centres. However, the Industry Secretary was given powers to remove the monopoly completely in the event of a strike or a deterioration of service. On the telecommunications side, the changes were more substantial and worried some British manufacturers who feared that the home market would be penetrated by foreign manufacturers. Under the changed arrangements, although British Telecommunications were to remain responsible for the installation and maintenance of each subscriber's first telephone and the maintenance of private branch exchanges, subscribers would be able to attach ancillary equipment (such as 'custom phones') made by the private sector.

However, in some other industries, the Government found it more difficult to put its principles into practice. Much of the shipbuilding industry belonged to the 'lame duck' category, but there were hopes that the Conservatives would sell back the profitable warship yards to their former owners. However, these plans were shelved, although not dropped altogether, against a background of threats of resignation from the British Shipbuilders' board and warnings that the industry needed a breathing space. Similarly, British Gas resisted suggestions that its North Sea oil fields and important onshore field in Dorset should be sold off. A report from the Monopolies and Mergers Commission suggesting that the one thousand High Street gas appliance showrooms should be sold off attracted support within the Government, but practical problems involved in such an operation delayed a decision.

The Government's first substantial sale of assets was of a 5.1 per cent holding in British Petroleum in October 1979 for £290 million, but its policy on the British National Oil Corporation was characterized by uncertainty. BNOC is perhaps the most attractive state-owned asset for private investors. However, an early proposal to sell £400 million of assets was dropped. When the Government introduced its Petroleum and Continental Shelf Bill in Parliament in 1981, the Energy Secretary said that 'it would be premature to say in what form the eventual (privatization) scheme will be brought forward'[26]. Any scheme, whether in the form of equity bonds or the disposal of shares, would probably only affect the exploration and development side of BNOC's activities. The oil trading arm would remain state-owned. One of the obstacles in the way of privatization has been the large number of partnerships built up by BNOC in oilfields in production or under development. These would have to be unravelled and modified in the event of any disposal of assets. More generally, progress on privatization plans was slow, partly because BNOC profits made a welcome contribution to the Exchequer and partly because it was argued that a state stake in North Sea oil could be defended on security grounds at a time of energy uncertainty.

In part, the Government's disposals were motivated by a need to raise funds without increasing taxes or borrowing. However, ideological considerations played an important role in shaping their privatization policy. This fact is clearly illustrated by the Government's stated intention to end the seventy-one-year-old state monopoly in the supply of electricity, a move that would entail amending the 1909 Electric Lighting Act and other complex changes in legislation. Admittedly, private generation does already account for around six per cent of British output, but only as an adjunct of industrial activities. The practical consequences of changing the law would probably be slight, as it is unlikely that the private sector would want to build its own power stations. Companies can already sell excess production to private customers or the national grid, provided it is not their main business. All that might happen is the establishment of small stations on industrial estates (perhaps in enterprise zones?). In short, the whole plan was little more than a political genuflection to fashionable dogma.

Of more significance is the creation of a whole new breed of mixed public-private companies. Such companies are not uncommon in other countries such as the BRD, but there is relatively little experience of this format in Britain. They raise a whole series of problems about ministerial control and public accountability which were only starting to be discussed when this book was written and which will no doubt preoccupy students of the nationalized industries for years to come.

4.7 The problem sectors: steel and motor vehicles

Much of the time that the Conservative Government spent on industrial policy in its first two years of office was taken up with the same two sectors whose problems had bedevilled its predecessors—steel and motor vehicles. Indeed, the fortunes of the two industries were closely interrelated. One might add to this group of 'lame duck' industries, British Shipbuilders, but the shipbuilding industry is less central to the economy, has fewer employees—and, on the whole, was treated relatively generously by the Conservatives.

Steel

The Conservative Government inherited a nationalized steel industry that was chasing a declining market downwards. An excellent account of nationalization and its aftermath is already available (Ovenden, 1978) and only a brief account of events will be provided here. Arguments about whether it was desirable to nationalize the British steel industry or whether some other device such as a state-sponsored cartel should have been used to bring about rationalization and modernization will no doubt continue among historians of the industry. What is clear is that the industry suffered a long period of uncertainty. First, the Labour Government was unable to carry through its nationalization plan until it had an adequate Commons majority after 1966, and by the time the newly nationalized industry had started to sort itself out, the Conservatives had returned to power. There was a long delay while the Conservatives reflected on the future of the industry, until an ambitious investment programme was announced in a White Paper in February 1973.

However, the 1973 oil crisis was followed by a sharp slump in UK steel demand which fell from 19½ million tonnes in 1973–74 to 15 million tonnes in 1975–76 and has never recovered. A principal cause of this slump in demand was the loss of UK market share by major steel-consuming industries, particularly motor vehicles. In addition, there was a sharp increase in the proportion of the UK steel market met by imports from just over five per cent in 1970–71 to sixteen per cent in 1974–75 and nearly a fifth by 1976–77. As Dudley points out, the new Labour Government faced 'a conflict of interest and values which was endemic to Labour's relationship with the nationalized British steel industry. The inevitable closure of older steelmaking plants to make way for the development of large coastal works highlighted the Labour Party dilemma of how to preserve the BSC strategy, while at the same time protecting the interests of workers threatened with redundancy.'[27] The Beswick review of proposed steel closures set up by Tony Benn was, in effect, about stopping plants being closed. In terms of jobs lost, only a quarter of the proposed closures went ahead[28].

It was expected that demand would pick up again and, to be fair, no one realized how abysmal the situation would be by the beginning of the 1980s. However, by the second half of 1977, BSC realized how desperate their plight was and Eric Varley's so-called *The Road to Viability* White Paper published in 1978 cut back investment and led to an acceleration in the closure of older plants. However, the Government rejected the idea of a target for reductions in the BSC workforce and the total reduction in the labour force between 1974 and 1979 amounted to some 44000.

The Conservatives inherited an industry which had been making losses for years. In 1979–80, following the steel strike, BSC lost £545 million, after taxation and interest, but before extraordinary items. In December 1979, BSC announced plans for a cutback in liquid steel capacity from 21½ million tonnes to 15 million liquid tonnes by the end of 1980, and a corresponding reduction in the workforce of 52000. Extraordinary items associated with write-down of fixed assets, closures and redundancies in 1979–80 amounted to £1.24 billion.

The Government's policy was based on trying to keep BSC within a cash limit of £450 million, but the steel strike defeated the achievement of this objective, if indeed it was ever possible. On June 6th 1980, the BSC Chairman wrote to Sir Keith Joseph informing him that the Corporation would need another £400 million in 1980–81 and, unless it was provided, BSC could not carry on trading and would have to recommend the liquidation of the business. Sir Keith knew that the economic disruption and social costs resulting from the collapse of the Corporation would be considerable and he agreed that, in the last resort, the Government would have to meet the claims of creditors of BSC in full. The cash limit was increased by £400 million in September 1980 and in November Sir Keith had to make use of the contingencies fund to provide BSC with another £110 million. The subsequent cut of another 20 000 jobs and 600 000 tonnes of liquid steelmaking capacity recommended by the new chairman, Mr Ian MacGregor, appeared to reflect a carefully drawn balance between financial necessity and the imposition of intolerable social costs.

In February 1981, the Government committed another £880 million to the BSC. This decision meant that BSC should receive £2551 million from the Government by March 1982, making it the largest single recipient of government industrial aid. The 1981 Iron and Steel Bill provides for some £3500 million of BSC's capital to be written off, with power to write off a further £1000 million later. Sir Keith Joseph emphasized that if Mr MacGregor's optimistic assertion that it would be possible to sustain a manned capacity of 14.4 million tonnes of liquid steel annually was not justified, further closures and redundancies might be necessary. Fears have been expressed about the longterm future of the Ravenscraig works in Scotland.

A further area of difficulty has been what Sir Keith Joseph has termed 'the problem of competition' between BSC and the private sector'[29]. The privately owned steel sector produces around a quarter of total UK steel production, although weighted towards the finished end of the product spectrum. The private sector was also hit by the depressed steel market in 1980 and was worried that the BSC under Mr MacGregor might try to increase the Corporation's concentration on higher value products, leading it into direct competition with the private sector. Moreover, the Industry Department's Phoenix project to rationalize production between BSC and the private sector split the latter. Sheerness Steel, one of the largest independent producers, resigned in protest from the British Independent Steel Producers' Association because of these plans, arguing that it would be bad for the private sector if some kind of semi-state sector was set up alongside BSC.

Phoenix 1 reached a successful conclusion with the formation of Allied Steel and Wire in February 1981, a joint venture between BSC and GKN which will rationalize the production of wire rod and bar. Phoenix 2 represented an ambitious attempt to rationalize production in engineering steels which encountered more difficulties. In a tragic way, rationalization was made easier by the reduction of capacity brought about by substantial cutbacks in steelmaking by two of the original four private sector partici- pants in the talks, Duport and Hadfields. In February 1981, Duport announced the closure of its Llanelli works which contained some of the newest electric-arc equipment in Britain. In April, Hadfields announced that most of its Sheffield workforce would be made redundant, the company concentrating in future on specialized steelmaking on a much reduced scale. These closures meant that BSC only had to find agreement with Round Oak, already jointly owned by BSC with Tube Investments, and, most important of all, with GKN. Nevertheless, much bitterness remains in the private sector at what has been portrayed as the judge, jury and hangman attitude of the Government and BSC and the fact that workers at plants like Hadfields will only get a fraction of the generous redundancy payments awarded to BSC workers.

No one can take very much pleasure from the recent history of the British steel industry, least of all the steel workers who have lost their jobs, particularly in towns like Consett, heavily dependent on the steel industry and already having high unemployment, where a marginally profitable plant with a good operating record had to be sacrificed to the requirements of overall strategy. On the other hand, it is all too easy to produce 'throw it all in' cost-benefit analyses with which one can demonstrate that no plant should ever be closed because the social costs are too high. There is an upper limit to the amount of aid that can be provided to the steel industry which is set by the needs of other industries and the ability of taxpayers to provide the necessary funds. It is hard to argue that the thousands of millions contributed to the industry by taxpayers have been well used, but it is not easy to apportion blame. BSC management is open to criticism, for having operated in the past an over-centralized system with a lack of information reported centrally. The steel unions have been slow to settle their differences and to realize the seriousness of the situation facing the industry. In the summer of 1980, the Iron and Steel Trades Confederation still felt confident enough to argue that 'BSC's current closure programme is totally unnecessary, that British Steel *can* cut prices, halt closures, make profits and grow'[30].

In the search for a scapegoat, it is all too easy to blame 'nationalization' and the decisions taken within the framework of public ownership such as Peter Walker's ambitious expansion plan and the Labour Government's reluctance to cut capacity. However, even the 1979 Conservative Government was unable to refrain from producing what amounted to a neo-corporatist solution for helping the ailing private sector. More generally, the example of steel casts doubt on two much favoured panaceas for the problems of British industry: massive investment programmes can create as many problems as they solve, although it is arguable that BSC's problems would be less serious if domestic demand was boosted; and the long-running experiment of having workers on the BSC Board, seems to have done little to help either the workers or the industry.

Motor vehicles

Even in opposition, the Conservatives made it clear that they were prepared to give further assistance to British Leyland, a pledge which probably contributed to their victories in such constituencies as Birmingham (Northfield), Oxford and Coventry South-West in the 1979 election. At times during the first two years of the Conservative Government, it seemed as if BL might succumb either to cash flow difficulties while the Metro was awaited or to strikes which brought management and unions to the very edge of the brink. Certainly, overall productivity trends were not encouraging, with a slow decline from 4.4 vehicle units per employee per annum in 1975 to 3.9 in 1979 and 1980[31]. However, the Metro was a marketing success and in January 1981, Sir Keith Joseph announced that

BL was to receive an additional £990 million of government aid over the following two financial years. In March, BL reported a record net loss of £535 million, largely because assumptions about sterling had gone astray. BL is probably the UK's largest net earner of foreign currency, but it lost 880 million on its export sales in 1980. Future financial performance is highly dependent on the level of sterling.

One Conservative backbencher complained when Sir Keith announced the latest BL aid package, 'We feel that BL has satisfied no criterion, save of exerting social and political blackmail, to justify such an enormous diversion of funds from the private sector.'[32] However, an important factor in the Government's thinking on BL must have been awareness of the impact that the collapse of a major car producer would have on Britain's important motor components industry. Hitherto successful, the motor components industry has been hit in recent years by a number of problems which would be compounded by the closure of a major vehicle producer. The British motor components industry has been stronger than that of other European countries, and has made a major contribution to the balance of payments, but it has been hit by the fall in home market demand for original equipment and replacement parts, the increased use of imported components sourced from the continent as part of a trend towards international rationalization of production by transnationals, and a growth in protection by developing countries to allow their own motor component industries to build up their strength to compete in world markets.

British Leyland offers grounds for some optimism, at any rate in comparison with the dismal picture in steel, although the Government's role has largely been an indirect, though supportive, one. However, there are a number of difficulties which could arise in the future. The management's industrial relations style, although successful in the short run, and a succession of low pay settlements, could lead to trouble in the future, particularly at the Longbridge plant. It is not going to be easy for a medium-sized car producer to survive on the international market, nor is the option of pulling out of volume car production an attractive one. Apart from the job losses that would result, there would certainly be higher component costs for quality cars and trucks (Bhaskar, 1979) and these markets are no less competitive than those for volume cars. BL was also concerned about Nissan's plans to build a large car plant in Britain, backed by government money. If BL does eventually fail, Britain's role in the international motor vehicle industry could be that of the major European production platform for Japanese cars.

4.8 The trimming of industrial policy

Policy outputs cannot be measured simply in terms of public expenditure on particular programmes. Nevertheless, the industrial policy arena is one in which the provision of funds for the implementation of policy by quasi-governmental or non-governmental actors is a very important aspect of government activity. Although year-to-year variations in expenditure on particular programmes may reflect the timing of payments in respect of commitments made several years earlier, a comparison of programme totals over the medium term has some validity. The Government had originally intended that the total Industry Department budget should decline rapidly after 1980–81. In fact, the projected figures for 1981–82 (at 1980 survey prices) increased to £1554 million, the highest level since 1975–76, and representing a real increase of forty-two per cent on 1979–80 and twenty-three per cent on 1980–81. Admittedly, most of the projected increase for 1981–82 was accounted for by the additional funding of British Leyland, but these figures do not generally take account of nationalized industries' financial needs. As well as the huge additional amount required for BSC, overspenders in 1980–81 included British Airways, British Shipbuilders and British Rail. British Telecom obtained a substantial revision of its external financing limit from £78 million to £223 million less than a month before the end of the financial year. The Government is providing industrial support and assistance in Northern Ireland at a higher level than originally envisaged, with £48 million being added to the Northern Ireland programme in 1980–81 mainly for industrial needs.

Although spending on industrial policy by the Conservative Government has increased, it is intended that spending should taper off sharply in 1982–83 and 1983–84, although this was supposed to have happened in 1981–82. There has been a change in the pattern of spending within the overall total. As was noted earlier, spending on general industrial research and development has been substantially increased, whereas spending on selective assistance to individual industries and firms, much favoured by the Labour Government, has declined from £107 million in 1978–79 to £47 million (projected) in 1981–82 (1980 survey prices). No doubt this balance of priorities reflected the Prime Minister's preference for constructive intervention, defined by her as 'stimulating industries which do have a future, rather than shoring up lost causes; helping to create tomorrow's world rather than to preserve yesterday's'[33].

The Government's first two years in office did not see a dramatic reversal in its overall industrial policy, although the availability of the 1972 Act for any interventionist measures thought necessary made a dramatic reversal less likely anyway. Thus, for example, in January 1980 the Government quietly introduced an order into the House of Commons to increase the statutory limit for Section 8 assistance by £250 million. Unlike the Heath Government in its first two years of office, the Government did not acquire any new burdens for the public sector on the scale of Rolls-Royce. However, there were a number of important modifications to the Government's industrial policy which amounted to a 'trimming' of policy, 'trimming' being defined by Sir Ian Gilmour as an aspect of the Conservative tradition which seeks to 'achieve balance'[34]. As Sir Keith Joseph explained in a speech that attempted to put the events of the first two years in context, 'We have not changed our diagnosis of the aims. Some unprecedented factors have made the transitional stage more difficult.'[35]

A number of important policy modifications occurred in the summer of 1980. In June, faced with the imminent collapse of the state steel industry, Sir Keith Joseph had to abandon his original financial targets and provide additional funds. A few days later the Government mounted a £66.5

million rescue operation for the Belfast shipyard of Harland and Wolff despite warning the previous year that no more support would be provided unless productivity was improved. It worsened, but the Government could not face the prospect of an extra 7000 out of work in Belfast. Later in July, Mrs Thatcher used a 'no confidence' debate to announce that £25 million was to be provided for the NEB to establish the first microchip production plant in the UK and also that £6 million would be provided for Dunlop to modernize its tyre factories. The November financial package provided an additional £50 million for industrial aid, a modest but significant addition to the budget.

The reduced level of provision for selective financial assistance has to be seen against a background of a decline in the level of assistance which had begun under the Labour Government. Indeed, Mrs Thatcher's Government seems to have made less radical changes in the provision of assistance to private industry or in the provision for mixed public-private enterprises than the Heath Government did in its first two years of office. The NEB survived, whereas the Industrial Reorganization Corporation was abolished. Moreover, although the term 'Industrial Strategy' was dropped from official parlance, most of the EDCs and SWPs continued working at NEDO, albeit on a 'self help' basis. However, the Thatcher Government went much further than the Heath Government in its privatization programme in its first two years of office.

Some of the most difficult industrial policy problems are presented by the collapse or imminent collapse of a major company, or closure or threatened closure of a major plant. Early on in the Government's life, Sir Keith stated that 'the receivership system is a way of preserving production and service processes that consumers still want'[36]. When Bowater announced in 1980 that it was going to close its Ellesmere Port newsprint mill with a loss of 1600 jobs in an area of high unemployment, the Government tried to avert the closure by putting together an aid package. Lack of success in this case was not for want of trying. Even more significantly, in March 1981 the Government guaranteed a £200 million loan from banks for the ailing British computer firm ICL. Sir Keith argued that the guarantee under Section 8 of the 1972 Act would not lead to any public expenditure unless it was called, although he did not explain why, if the company was so sound that the Government would never have to pay the £200 million, a guarantee was necessary at all. The aid for ICL must rank as the most significant policy modification in relation to the private sector by the Government in its first two years of office.

Just as it is difficult to argue against the frequent calls for consistency in industrial policy, because the alternative is apparently inconsistency, so it is difficult to argue against constructive intervention and thus to favour its opposite, destructive intervention. However, although investing in the industries of the future might seem to be obviously preferable to investing in those of the past, it is not always easy to identify the successful industries—or, more important, products—of the future. It is easy to be dazzled by technical innovations and to end up with a series of 'mini Concordes' which attract little scrutiny because the sum committed to each project is small and the technical processes involved are difficult for the layman to understand. Moreover, the tendency of social marketeers to become preoccupied with new industries, and the tendency of those who favour a selective intervention approach to devote much of their efforts to reinvigorating declining industries, may lead to an absence of industrial policy directed toward important industries which are neither technologically glamorous nor declining dramatically such as food processing. Slogans such as 'constructive intervention' may be useful for labelling a shift of approach, but they are not a substitute for a strategy which is as necessary for social marketeers as it is for selective interventionists.

In a critical speech on the Government's industrial policy delivered in April 1981, the Director-General of NEDO argued that in fact some sixty to seventy per cent of government assistance to industry in 1980–81 went to declining sectors such as steel and shipbuilding. It is not always easy to pick out growth sectors and declining sectors. For example, only commentators benefitting from hindsight will really be able to say whether BL was a company of the past or of the future. Nevertheless, there is much truth in the Director-General's observation: 'Britain is said to have acquired an empire in a fit of absence of mind, that is, by a series of ad hoc responses to short-term stimuli. We are in danger of acquiring an industrial policy in the same way.'[37] Moreover, even if the Government's industrial policy was characterized by a more moderate pragmatism than some of the statements of Sir Keith Joseph would lead one to expect, it could well be argued that its modest efforts in industrial policy were overshadowed by the impact on industry of its general economic policies.

Notes to Chapter Four

1. Commission of the European Communities, *European Economy: Annual Economic Report 1979–80*, p 66
2. J. B. Donges, 'Industrial Policies in West Germany's Not so Market-oriented Economy', *World Economy*, Vol. 3 (2), 1980, pp.185–204, p.189
3. K. Done, 'The Bundesbahn's dismal track record', *Financial Times*, April 16th, 1981
4. *The Times 1,000, 1979–80* (London: Times Books, 1979), p.5
5. J. Rembser, 'Promotion of Technology Transfer for Small and Medium-Sized Enterprises in the Federal Republic of Germany', address to the International Licensing Conference, Sydney, April 1979, p.23 (typescript)
6. E. Owen-Smith, 'Government Intervention in the Economy of the Federal Republic of Germany' in P. Maunder (Ed.), *Government Intervention in the Developed Economy* (London: Croom Helm, 1979), pp.160–189, pp.172–173
7. Donges[2], pp.193–194
8. E. Dell, *Political Responsibility and Industry* (London: Allan and Unwin, 1973), p.44
9. I. Gilmour, *Inside Right* (London: Quartet Books, 1978) p. 129
10. Sir K. Joseph, *Reversing the Trend* (London: Barry Rose, 1975), p.4
11. H. C. Debs., Vol.970, column 1307
12. Cmnd.8175, pp.46–47
13. Department of Industry, *Research and Development Requirements and Programmes Report, 1979–80*, p.4
14. *IDA Industrial Plan, 1978–82* (Dublin: Industrial Development Authority, 1979), p.28
15. Industrial Development Authority, *Annual Report 1979*, p.14
16. *Industry Act 1972, Annual Report for the year ended 31 March 1980, 1979–80*, p.11
17. Department of Industry, Micro-electronics Application Division, Background Paper on MAP, typescript, 6th October 1980. (Not pagenated)
18. *Financial Times*, April 1st 1981
19. Report on *Weekend World* interview, *Financial Times*, April 5th, 1981
20. Report from the Committee to Review the Functioning of Financial Institutions (Wilson Committee) Appendices, p. 544

21. R. Muller and A. Bruce, 'Local Government in Pursuit of an Industrial Strategy', *Local Government Studies,* Vol. 7 (1), pp.3–18, p.3
22. Second Report from the Committee on Scottish Affairs, 1979–80, *Inward Investment,* Vol. 2, Minutes of Evidence, Q.134
23. John Elliott, 'Sir Keith looks for winners', *Financial Times,* January 6th, 1981
24. Donges[2], p.193
25. First Report from the House of Commons Industry and Trade Committee, Session 1980–81, *Imports and Exports,* Q.193
26. *Financial Times,* February 14th, 1981
27. G. Dudley, 'Pluralism, Policy Making and Implementation: the Evolution of the British Steel Corporation's Development Strategy', *Public Administration,* Vol. 57 (4), 1979, pp.253–270, p.264
28. A. Cockerill, 'Steel' in P. S. Johnson (Ed.), *The Structure of British Industry* (St. Albans: Granada, 1980), pp.131–153, p.139
29. *Weekly Hansard,* issue 1197, column 745
30. Iron and Steel Trades Confederation, *New Deal for Steel,* 1980, p.9
31. Figures derived from answer to Parliamentary Question, 12th February 1981. 1980 employees figure is an estimate
32. Alan Clark, *Weekly Hansard,* issue 1193, column 640
33. Speech made in December 1980 and quoted in J. Elliott, 'Sir Keith looks for winners', *Financial Times,* January 6th, 1981
34. I. Gilmour, *Inside Right,* (London: Quartet Books, 1978), p.109
35. Report on speech to the Bow Group in *Financial Times,* April 3rd, 1981
36. First Report from the Industry and Trade Committee, Session 1980–81[25], Q.102
37. *Financial Times,* 8th April, 1981

Chapter Five

The National Enterprise Board

5.1 The state holding company model

The importance of the National Enterprise Board (NEB) lies not so much in the activities of the Board itself, which apart from the special case of British Leyland where the Board was essentially an intermediary, have had a marginal impact on the industrial economy, but rather in the way in which its history illustrates both the limits of what can be achieved through an industrial policy and the ambiguous political context in which industrial policies often evolve. The NEB was the product of disillusionment with what could be achieved through the conventional form of nationalization. The concept of a state holding company attracted support from all sides of the political spectrum: economic liberals were at least prepared to concede that the state holding company formula offered the possibility of more decisions being taken in accordance with commercial criteria than would be the case in a public corporation; social democrats saw it as a new mechanism for attaining greater state participation in the running of the mixed economy without wholesale nationalization; socialists saw it as a potential instrument of socialist transformation which would be able to acquire shareholdings without being hindered by the necessity of passing legislation through Parliament.

The emergence of the state holding company as a fashionable political option in Britain owed a great deal to the lessons of foreign experience, in contrast to the expansion of nationalization under the 1945–1951 Labour Government which drew on earlier British experience with such organizations as the London Passenger Transport Board. A Fabian pamphlet published in 1966 discussed the idea of the state holding company with reference to Italian experience (Posner and Pryke, 1966) and in the same year the liberal Institute of Economic Affairs published a not unsympathetic account of the Italian state holding company, IRI (Deaglio, 1966). The same year saw the establishment of the Industrial Reorganization Corporation (IRC), later disbanded by the Heath Government. Although preoccupied with the promotion of mergers as a means of improving industrial efficiency, the IRC blazed a trail for the NEB. It showed that the state holding company was a foreign concept which could be transplanted to

Britain and, in particular, it showed that such an organization could take its place in the mixed economy and build good relations with the centres of power such as the City and private industry.

The lessons of foreign experience

The foreign state holding companies which were quoted as examples of the success of the formula in the British debate have been conspicuously less successful in recent years. A number of countries (e.g. Spain under Franco) have established state holding companies, but three experiments have been particularly important. The Italian example was probably the most extensively referred to in Britain, but Sweden's adoption of the idea gave it added respectability. The Austrian case was referred to less often in the British debate, but is interesting, both because of the importance of state holding companies in the economy, and because it illustrates the flexibility which is the essential hallmark of the state holding company model.

The Italian example became influential in the British debate largely through the work of Stuart Holland who played a key role in Labour Party policy-making on industrial questions between 1970 and 1974 (Hatfield, 1978). In 1972, Holland published a book on the Italian state holding company system (Holland, 1972), which had originated as a Fascist response to the economic crisis of the 1930s. It was reorganized and expanded after the war, particularly through the creation of a state hydrocarbons corporation (ENI). Holland had few doubts that what he had observed in Italy held important lessons for Britain and other western industrialized countries. He spoke of the 'inspired extension in the postwar period' of the state holding company system in Italy as providing 'governments with a concrete example of what otherwise appeared difficult or impossible to achieve—state enterprise as efficient and dynamic as leading private enterprise groups, yet still directly serving the ends of government economic policy and the interests of society as a whole'[1].

Holland's later treatment of the Italian case strikes a more sceptical note (Holland, 1975) and it is certainly the case that the record of the Italian state holding companies looked less impressive at the end of the 1970s than it did at the beginning of the decade. The main state holding company, IRI, made losses of nearly L2500 billion in the three years to 1980 and was by then burdened with debts of L21000 billion. The hydrocarbons company, ENI, had enjoyed a high reputation abroad, but was rocked in 1979 by a scandal surrounding a supply contract from the Saudi petroleum company. The head of ENI, Snr. Mazzanti, was subsequently cleared of misconduct, but forced to resign. One of the smaller state holding companies, EGAM, collapsed with debts amounting to L1500 billion. Although IRI in particular has had some success in creating jobs in the south, all the companies have had to operate in a highly political environment in which key appointments are the subject of intense man-oeuvring between parties and factions within parties. Although the blame for this situation may be placed on the nature of the Italian political system, rather than the state holding companies themselves, it does show that the formula does not provide adequate insulation against outside political pressures.

Sweden has always been a source of inspiration for the mainstream of the British Labour Party and the establishment by the Swedish Government in 1970 of a state holding company (AB Statsföretag) undoubtedly gave an additional impetus to the political acceptability of the formula in Britain. Companies formerly under the jurisdiction of different ministries were brought together, primarily with the intention of promoting business efficiency. By one simple test of business efficiency, Statsföretag has been a failure. In its first ten years, it only paid dividends in 1973 and 1974 and accumulated a pre-tax loss of SKr 22 million over the decade. The Statsföretag management has tried to insist that state holding companies should be run to make profits, not to solve social and economic problems, but they have been unable to avoid taking on 'lame ducks' whose losses have outweighed the profits made by their other companies.

Austria has the largest public sector of any OECD country, one of the most successful western economies, and an approach to public ownership which is based largely on market principles. One-third of Austria's industry, eighty per cent of its transport, and fifty per cent of its banking are within the public sector[2]. Most heavy industry, including the largest iron and steel concern, the electrical, electrical power and oil industries, almost all coal mining, shipbuilding and heavy engineering, and a section of the chemicals industry, are under state control. Austria has an enviable record of economic success, having managed the simultaneous achievement of a low rate of inflation and continued growth of employment. Undoubtedly, much of this record of success has little to do with the scope and organization of the public sector. The Austrian economy is closely tied to that of the BRD, which takes around a quarter of its exports, and has benefitted from the continued growth of the West German economy. The effective pursuit of wage moderation through incomes policies has been eased by a tradition of corporatist co-operation between the parties which outlasted the end of the grand coalition which governed the country until 1966.

The principal state industrial enterprises are controlled by Oesterreichische Industrie Verwaltung AG (OeAIG), a holding company established in 1970. Garner has observed that 'the most striking characteristic of Austrian government policy as it affects public enterprise is that there is so little policy: or, alternatively, where there is a policy as in the case of regional development, that in respect of public enterprise . . . is left to operate through inducements and restrictions common to both public and private enterprises, with no special pressure on public concerns if they reject the inducements'[3]. The basic philosophy is that 'Enterprises in the public sector must meet the test of the market in the same way as private enterprises.'[4] The Austrian case shows that a large state holding company is not incompatible with a successful economic policy; it also further illustrates the different ways in which the state holding company model can be deployed.

Some general lessons can be drawn from this brief survey of foreign experience with state holding companies, even if they are of a negative character. First, one can only understand the state holding companies in terms of the economic and political context in which they operate: this point is graphically illustrated by the contrast between the neighbouring countries of Italy and Austria. Second, the state holding companies respond to, rather than influence, trends in the national economy: in so far as they influence the course of events, it is in relation to particular policy programmes, such as the success of IRI in creating jobs in the south of Italy. Third, state holding companies are extremely flexible instruments which can readily be adapted to pursue new goals. In the context of the British political system, which is more adversarial than any of the other three countries discussed, this means that a new government can abandon the policies of its predecessors without changing the institutional format. It is doubtful whether this consideration was foremost in the minds of those who advocated the introduction of the state holding company into Britain.

5.2 Labour's NEB

The 1975 Industry Act provided the initial legislative framework for the NEB and was shaped by Harold Wilson's insistence that the new Board should 'have no marauding role'[5]. The NEB was established as a public corporation in 'an attempt to combine the advantages of public sector financial resources and the private sector's entrepreneurial approach to decision-making'[6] which sounds like a rather limp restatement of the traditional justification for using the public corporation format for nationalized industries, a formula that has worn rather thin over the years. Board members are appointed by the Secretary of State for Industry and Labour's NEB had a loose tripartite framework. Although the full-time Chairman (Lord Ryder to July 1977; then Sir Leslie Murphy) and the Deputy Chairman (at first Sir Leslie; then Richard Morris from Courtaulds) were drawn from the private sector, the eight (later nine) part-time members of the Board included four trade unionists, among them David Basnett, Harry Urwin (to 1979) and Hugh Scanlon (from 1977).

The NEB was given an initial statutory borrowing limit of £1000 million and by the end of March 1979 its commitments totalled about £850 million. Government acceptance of the NEB report on British Leyland in April 1979 led to additional commitments of £150 million, bringing the NEB up against its statutory limit. The 1979 Industry Act established a new borrowing limit of £3000 million, with provision for an extra £1500 million subject to Parliamentary approval. However, the NEB's borrowings were calculated in a new way, to include the external borrowings of all its subsidiaries—not just the wholly-owned ones—giving the NEB total commitments of £1800 million in 1979.

Although the 1975 Act set the framework for the NEB's activities, its development was influenced to an even greater extent by the statutory guidelines issued by Industry Secretary, Eric Varley, in December 1976. These guidelines had been the subject of a long process of consultation with the CBI in particular and, as Harold Wilson puts it, 'Contrary to the revolutionary hopes which surrounded the NEB when it was conceived in Opposition days, Eric Varley's department . . . ensured that it would not operate like an industrial rogue elephant. It had to operate within the existing rules governing the provision of industrial finance.'[7] For example, the NEB was generally required to charge commercial rates of interest and, in taking investment decisions, always to have regard to the profitability of the investments. All these general limitations on the NEB's powers, and specific ones such as the requirement that the NEB should dispose of any interest in a newspaper or magazine that it acquired (or at least not influence editorial functions), were intended to reassure businessmen that the NEB would work within, rather than seek to fundamentally alter, the existing economic system.

By way of contrast, the requirements in the guidelines concerned with industrial democracy seem to have had little practical effect. The 1975 Act stated that one of the functions of the NEB was the promotion of industrial democracy in undertakings which the Board controlled. The guidelines required the NEB to 'make appropriate arrangements with their subsidiaries, to the satisfaction of the Government, to ensure that management in these undertakings is playing its part in furthering government policies in this field'[8]. This requirement is difficult to reconcile with the NEB's belief in not involving itself in the day-to-day management of its companies, but as the Government itself never managed to develop a coherent or agreed policy on industrial democracy, inaction was not an unreasonable way of complying with the guideline. Although the presence of trade unionists on the Board could be represented as an example of the two-tier board form of industrial democracy, this represents the limits of the NEB's use of its freedom to conduct experiments in industrial democracy.

The philosophy of the NEB

Thus, the NEB as it developed was very different from the original conception of Labour left-wingers of an organization which would spearhead the transformation of Britain's industrial economy from capitalism to socialism (Forester, 1979; Coates, 1980). In fact, the NEB has operated within a philosophy that has sought to make the Board as acceptable as possible to the private sector. The first chairman, Lord Ryder, stressed that 'Although funded from public sources, the NEB has to exercise a commercial judgment in the same way as any other business.'[9] His successor, Sir Leslie Murphy, stressed that 'the strong commercial flavour which Lord Ryder imparted to the NEB will continue'[10]. The Board's former Planning Director has stated: 'The NEB is not playing and could not play an overwhelming role in determining the development of British industry. The claims that have never been made *for* it have never been made *by* it. The idea that the NEB could or even should regenerate British industry is absurd and it has never accepted the extension of public ownership as an end in itself.'[11] A similar philosophy was espoused by government. As Sir Peter Carey put it, 'we want in the National Enterprise Board to have a body which is operating as nearly as possible like a private sector body. That is to say, that is operating commercially in the open market, that is subject to market pressures and that is acting entrepreneurially.'[12]

One way in which the Board changed from the original concept was in the relative downgrading of the objective of creating employment. The 1974 White Paper, *The Regeneration of British Industry,* stated that the NEB was to be an instrument through which the Government would operate directly to create employment in areas of high unemployment. However, Lord Ryder made it clear that 'it is not part of NEB's policy to prop up non-viable companies simply to maintain jobs'[13]. Sir Leslie Murphy told the Public Accounts Committee that the Board was prepared to see a company through a sticky stage, 'But eventually the only way in which employment is created or safeguarded, is under successful companies.'[14] In practice, the NEB was prepared to face the Government 'with a number of harsh commercial decisions'[15]. For example, when it took over Fairey Engineering, it quickly closed a subsidiary near Newcastle -on-Tyne, Tress Engineering, which employed 330 people in an area of high unemployment.

The Board's priorities are revealed in its standard format for the submission of investment proposals[16]. Twelve aspects of the potential investment were considered, grouped under three headings: 'commercial assessment', 'economic assessment' and 'financial assessment'. The commercial assessment covered the market situation of the company; its production and technical capability; management; and industrial relations. The 'economic assessment' covered three areas which were concerned with the restructuring of British industry: importance of the company within its UK industry sector; potential for increasing exports or saving imports; and promotion of advanced technology. Only one of the matters considered had a 'social' character, the provision of productive employment, particularly in areas of high unemployment. The 'financial assessment' covered the kinds of questions that a merchant bank might be particularly concerned with: recent financial results; forecast of financial results; financial structure (gearing etc.); and adequacy of financial controls. Thus, of the twelve criteria, eight could well have been used by a private investor. Of the four criteria concerned with the NEB's 'wider national responsibilities', three were concerned with industrial restructuring and only one with employment.

However, it should not be supposed that the NEB under Labour was just like any private sector industrial holding company. As the NEB's first Annual Report stated, 'The NEB must base its investment policy on sound commercial criteria. At the same time it is expected to take a wider view of the national benefits and opportunities that flow from any investment.'[17] Members of its staff believed that the market did not work as well 'in the creation of the next generation of industries as it does in encouraging efficient production of current goods and services'[18]. In practice, this meant a willingness to take a longer than average view of the yield from an investment.

It should be borne in mind that during its first years of existence under Labour, the Board faced an unstable political environment in so far as the Government could be brought down at any time in the House of Commons, leading to a general election which might return to office a Conservative Party at that time pledged to the Board's abolition. It is therefore not surprising that the NEB's strategy was influenced in these years by the need to secure the organization's survival, not because the staff were worried about their jobs (many have since returned to good positions in the private sector), but because they genuinely believed that, given time, the NEB was capable of making a worthwhile contribution to the longterm revival of Britain's industrial economy. In these circumstances, it is understandable that 'The Board . . . avoided public controversies, believing that in the long run it was more important to act sensibly and produce worthwhile results than indulge in a political free-for-all.'[19]

Moreover, the Board was not afraid to risk upsetting the private sector when it considered that the matter at stake was of central importance to its longterm strategy. In 1977 it raised a storm of opposition in the City by taking over the ailing Fairey aviation and engineering group at a cost of some £20 million, defeating a bid from Victor (later Lord) Matthews of the Trafalgar Group. City interests were offended by the NEB competing with the private sector for what they saw as not much more than an assortment of small engineering companies linked by common ownership. However, the NEB saw a potential role for Fairey's hydraulics and nuclear subsidiaries in its strategic work of restructuring key industrial sectors.

The fact is that a great deal of ambivalence surrounded the work of the NEB, arising from its attempt to reconcile commercial criteria with its own conception of what was demanded by national industrial policy. It was not easy to reconcile a set of objectives which involved, as Marks has put it, bringing 'to the market place both a willingness to take the long-term view and a desire to make money while furthering the interests of Britain'[20]. This difficulty was reflected in the fixing of the Board's financial objectives. The NEB was required to achieve a return on capital employed (at historic cost, before tax and interest) of 15–20% on its investments, excluding the two biggest 'lame ducks' under its care, British Leyland and Rolls-Royce.

How was this figure arrived at? Sir Peter Carey has stated: 'Twenty per cent is our best estimate, in the Department at least, of the average return of large firms in the United Kingdom manufacturing industry in 1981. The range below this reflects, first of all, the NEB's statutory duties, which of course go wider than commercial considerations, and, secondly, the uncertainty of our own forecast and the difficulty for the National Enterprise Board of hitting any particular target in a particular year.'[21] In other words, the Industry Department chose a (rather high) figure based on its estimate of the likely return in the private sector, and took a bit off for the NEB's wider obligations, a bit off for the possibility that its own forecast might be wrong, and a bit off for the likelihood of the NEB not actually meeting its target. More generally, this procedure reveals the extent to which the NEB fits in with the notion of the mixed economy described in the first chapter as a modified market economy, an economy in which decisions are taken in accordance with market criteria, but in which some allowance is made for broader considerations which may not be adequately reflected in the operations of the market.

The NEB's performance under Labour

Not surprisingly, the NEB failed to meet its financial targets, partly because of the expense of setting up its 'green field' high technology companies. The return on capital employed in the manufacturing industry as a whole rose from 14.6% in 1975 to 14.9% in 1978, but the best that the NEB could manage in this period was 11.8%, well below its target, although not substantially below what private industry was achieving. However, in 1979, a year which still reflected NEB performance on the commitments acquired under Labour, the return on capital employed slumped to 4.8 per cent, a figure which the NEB itself admitted was 'poor'[22].

TABLE 5.1 NEB Performance

Year	Assets	Number of companies	Return on capital employed*
1976	£959M	13	11.8%
1977	£1132M	33	11.4%
1978	£1576M	46	11.3%
1979	£1502M	68	4.8%

*Excluding BL and Rolls-Royce
Source: *NEB Annual Reports*

The work of the NEB was dominated during the lifetime of the Labour Government by the problems of the four 'lame ducks' acquired from the government, particularly British Leyland and Rolls-Royce and, to a lesser extent, Alfred Herbert and Cambridge Instruments. Harold Wilson now admits that it was a mistake to hang these albatrosses around the NEB's neck. He states: '(The NEB's) preoccupation with Leyland, for example, has crippled its finances and to some extent depreciated its other achievements'[23]. Part of the reasoning at the time appears to have been an argument that it would be harder for an incoming Conservative Government to dismantle the NEB if it had substantial assets and responsibilities. The financial dominance of the transferred companies is illustrated by the fact that of the £777 million which the Board had received from public funds by March 1979, £699 million had been spent on transferred companies, largely British Leyland (£569 million) and Rolls-Royce (£95 million). Total expenditure on the Board's other three roles amounted to only some £17 million in 1976, £12 million in 1977 and £49 million in 1978.

However, excessive staff resources were not devoted to the 'lame ducks'. The NEB had two senior staff members dealing with BL and another two dealing with Rolls-Royce. In practice, the Industry Department was deeply involved in the affairs of British Leyland and Rolls-Royce, as is reflected by the fact that there was an arrangement whereby the NEB consulted the Industry Secretary about the appointment of the chairman, deputy chairman, chief executive and finance director of BL and Rolls-Royce, but not of any other companies. Although the Industry Department complained about receiving information about BL at second hand, they had contacts with the company through their sponsoring responsibility for the industry and direct personal links with Sir Michael Edwardes[24].

The relationship between the work of the NEB and the rest of the Labour Government's industrial policy was not always clear. Sir Peter Carey drew a distinction between the 'cheap money' provided by the

Industry Department in the form of selective assistance and NEB money which was provided 'on commercial terms and must be'[25]. In practice, the relationship between the two types of funding was rather more complicated, as NEB companies could themselves be the recipients of Industry Department assistance. Indeed, the NEB stressed that by working together with the Department, it was possible 'to offer an attractive financial package whereby equity finance from the NEB can be topped up by concessionary loans and grants from the Department'[26].

Reference was made in Chapter Three to disappointment expressed by some of the industrial strategy committees and working parties at what they saw as the lack of attention paid by the NEB to their findings. The NEB argued that it was one thing to identify difficulties and opportunities and another thing to act and 'Neither NEDO nor the Sector Working Parties are really in a position to organise this.'[27] The NEB used tests of market and profit prospects to select sectors on which to concentrate its efforts in its own version of the industrial strategy. The main sectors in which the NEB was interested were automotive products and aero engines (because of BL and Rolls-Royce) and, more significantly: computers and electronics; machine tools; scientific and medical instruments; office equipment; process control; telecommunications; power plant manufacture; construction and mechanical handling equipment; industrial engines; hydraulics; electronic test an measuring instruments; and offshore engineering. An ambitious plan to restructure the telecommunications industry foundered, but the NEB did make progress in computers and electronics. It had substantial shareholdings in two key companies, ICL and Ferranti, and created three new companies of its own: INMOS (to manufacture semiconductors); NEXOS (office equipment) and INSAC (computer software). The 'high technology' role of the NEB continued under the Conservatives and the NEB's progress in this area will be reviewed later in this chapter, as will its less successful handling of its small business and regional roles.

5.3 The NEB under the Conservatives

The 1979 Conservative Government, although weaned away from their original intention to abolish the NEB, were determined to define a substantially reduced role for the Board. They gave effect to their intentions in the 1980 Industry Act and in subsequent guidelines. The first clause of the 1980 Act deleted the 1975 Act's requirement for the Board to be responsible for 'extending public ownership into profitable areas of manufacturing industry' and instead stated that the NEB should be 'prompting the private ownership of interests in industrial undertakings by the disposal of securities and other property held by the board or any of their subsidiaries'. The NEB's top borrowing limit was cut back from £4.5 billion to £3 billion and the upper limit of new investments it could make without the Industry Secretary's approval was cut back from £10 million to £5 million. However, in 1981 the Government was obliged to secure the passage of a new Industry Act to increase the Industry Secretary's borrowing limit to £4400 million, with a power to increase that further to

£5250 million, to cover the needs of British Leyland after its transfer to the Secretary of State. The 1981 Act reduced the NEB's financial limits to £750 million for its other interests after the transfer of BL to the Industry Secretary.

Although pressure from the CBI, and the reality of a Board with substantial responsibilities, led the Conservatives to shed their original determination to abolish the NEB, there were fears that its role might be reduced to little more than an industrial 'casualty clearing station'. However, Sir Keith Joseph's statement to the House of Commons on the NEB in July 1979 was regarded by some Conservative MPs as not going far enough in limiting the Board's role. Sir Keith admitted that 'it will take some time to restore the full vitality of the private sector'[28] and in effect gave the NEB a renewed lease for five years.

The guidelines eventually issued to the Board showed a further softening of the Government's position. The draft guidelines required that the Board should develop projects only in partnership with the private sector, but the final version was modified by the insertion of the words 'wherever the board consider it practicable to do so'. The original draft referred to the NEB being 'restricted to' four specified areas of activity, but the final version used the phrase 'especially in connection with', thus allowing the NEB to undertake projects outside the four main areas. The four areas in which the NEB was to pursue what was termed a 'catalytic investment role' were companies in which the NEB already had an interest; companies engaged in the development or exploitation of advanced technologies; companies operating (or intending to operate) industrial undertakings in the English regions; and the provision of loans of up to £50000 to small firms.

Nevertheless, even leaving aside the fact that the membership of the Board has completely changed, the NEB is a very different organization under the Conservatives from what it was under Labour. The lame ducks such as BL and Rolls-Royce are no longer under its control; there is a much sharper emphasis on the high technology role; and there have been a number of important disposals. Between May 1979 and March 1981, the NEB sold holdings worth about £130 million, most importantly in the computer firm, ICL; the electronics group, Ferranti; and Fairey Engineering. Some smaller holdings were also sold, and a number of companies were closed, most importantly the British Tanners Products Group.

The Rolls-Royce affair

In November 1979, the entire Board resigned after a row over whether Rolls-Royce should continue to be controlled by NEB or transferred to the Industry Department. One consequence of the resignation of the trade union members was that the Board lost its loose tripartite character. Rolls-Royce was originally nationalized by the Heath Government when it ran into financial difficulties. The transfer of Rolls-Royce to the NEB when the Board was set up was not welcomed by the company and the difficulties that arose between the then NEB chairman, Lord Ryder, and Sir Kenneth (later Lord) Keith of Rolls-Royce were only resolved after the intervention of the Prime Minister and the conclusion of a formal 'concordat' which ushered in an uneasy truce.

In 1978 and 1979, Rolls-Royce made price offers on civil engine contracts which assumed that there would be a fall in sterling against the United States dollar. In a subsequent investigation, the Public Accounts Committee reported that 'The currency management policy previously followed by this publicly-owned company resulted in a prospective loss of over £58 million'[29].

In 1979, the NEB Chairman, Sir Leslie Murphy, took the unusual step of publicly criticizing the financial controls at Rolls-Royce, whilst Sir Kenneth Keith dismissed the NEB as a 'bureaucratic contraceptive'. The NEB was sceptical about Rolls-Royce's plans to seek up to £700 million of additional public money, largely to develop its aero engine range; they thought that the sum was too large and that some of the money could be raised in the City. Sir Leslie Murphy urged that Sir Kenneth Keith, who was planning to retire anyway, should be replaced; Sir Kenneth Keith wanted control of Rolls-Royce to be transferred to the Industry Department; Sir Keith Joseph had hopes of persuading GEC to take over Rolls-Royce. It became difficult to separate arguments about the merits of different arrangements for supervising Rolls-Royce from the personality clashes which tended to overshadow the whole affair.

Sir Leslie saw the solution as a change of management, but Sir Keith considered that he was not taking into account the problem of double supervision by the Department and the Board. Sir Keith commented: 'When I told (Sir Leslie), he reacted strongly and made a resigning matter of what I never really saw as a resigning matter.'[30] Sir Leslie commented: 'I have no confidence that Ministers advised by civil servants who have no business experience are competent to discharge the tasks previously carried out by the NEB.'[31] Sir Keith told the House of Commons that he had concluded that 'the friction is not a passing problem of personalities or a difference of opinion on the management of the company but is inherent in the relationship and would almost certainly survive a change of management. Rolls-Royce is a company of a scale and importance such that the supervision of its Board by another Board, however eminent and accomplished, is bound to give rise to strain.'[32]

Not only was Sir Keith Joseph able to reconstruct the NEB and transfer Rolls-Royce to the Industry Department's control, but the political row that followed the Board's resignation quickly subsided. The new chairman of the NEB, Sir Arthur Knight, was a former chairman of Courtaulds and the author of a book on government–industry relations in which he argued that the imperfections of the private enterprise system were such that there were many situations in which government action was needed (Knight, 1974). Sir Arthur had no interest in supervising lame ducks, and followed a strategy of removing the Board from the political limelight and concentrating on its high-technology role, a role acceptable to the Government.

The NEB and the National Research Development Corporation

In December 1980, Sir Arthur Knight surprised even his close colleagues by announcing his resignation as NEB chairman for personal reasons which were thought to include poor health and a dislike for such a public role. His successor, Sir Frederick Wood, the chairman of Croda International, was also chairman of the National Research Development Corporation (NRDC). Sir Frederick stated that he intended to explore the possibility of a merger between the NEB and the NRDC which are both concerned with providing financial support for technological ventures.

Such a merger would be a logical development from the NEB's increasing emphasis on its high-technology role and it might also serve to reinvigorate the NRDC. The NRDC was established by the 1948 Development of Inventions Act with the statutory function of securing the development or exploitation of inventions. Financial help is provided, largely to smaller companies, in two main ways: first, through joint venture projects in which the NRDC pays the client company an agreed proportion of the costs incurred in connection with the project and recovers this through a percentage levy charged on subsequent sales; and, secondly, through the provision of equity and loan finance. The NRDC has been criticized for supporting only a small proportion of the projects submitted to it and for being preoccupied with making profits rather than developing inventions. In fact, only a few of the NRDC's efforts to exploit inventions have been commercially successful, most importantly an important group of therapeutic and life-saving drugs (the Cephalosporins) (Makinson, 1976).

5.4 The roles of the NEB: an assessment

The lame ducks

With the transfer of BL and Rolls-Royce to the Industry Department, the collapse of Alfred Herbert, and the disposal of Cambridge Instruments, the NEB had lost all its original lame ducks by 1981. It is questionable whether it was ever sensible to give the NEB responsibility for these companies. In particular, the Board was placed in a position of either devoting a disproportionate share of its organizational resources to BL and Rolls-Royce; or of being accused of paying insufficient attention to their affairs. Although the Board would no doubt argue that it resolved this dilemma by concentrating on strategic issues, it was difficult for the Board to enjoy the same measure of autonomy in handling BL and Rolls-Royce as it did with other companies. Because of the economic and political importance of the two largest lame ducks, the Department of Industry had to be involved in their affairs to an extent that was not true of other NEB companies. This is not to say that the NEB was not a significant actor in decisions about the future of the two companies. For example, it could be argued that the NEB was largely responsible for stopping a commercially uncertain £150 million foundry programme planned by BL; for halting BL plans for a centralized engineering centre, when the real problem was a lack of engineers; and that the closure of the Speke No. 2 plant was only made possible by NEB support to BL management.

British Leyland and Rolls-Royce raised, in their different ways, important questions of national policy. The fate of Alfred Herbert, the biggest company to fail under NEB ownership, illustrates the difficulties that are encountered in any attempt to rescue a lame duck. Alfred Herbert was once Britain's biggest machine tool company but, of the companies inherited by the NEB, Herbert was 'in many respects in the worst position to face the future. Little work had been done to design new products and it faced a declining market position in its traditional machine tools.'[33] Nevertheless, in the early days of the NEB, Lord Ryder was confident that Herbert would be one of NEB's biggest successes[34]. Although experience showed that Herbert's deep-seated problems would take a long time to correct, Sir Leslie Murphy still felt able to talk in April 1979 of the transformation of the company from 'a low technology to a high technology machine tool manufacturer'[35]. However, of the £44.5 million put into the company since it was taken into public ownership in December 1975, £18 million had to be used to pay off pre-nationalization debts and much of the rest had to be used for stockbuilding rather than modernization. When the company collapsed in June 1980, it was found possible to sell off the major plants and thus preserve most of the workforce's jobs, the name being taken over by Tooling Investments. However, it could be argued that this would have happened without the expenditure of an estimated £56.5 million of public money[36] if the company had been placed into receivership as the Industrial Development Advisory Board had originally recommended.

The NEB also managed to divest itself of its fourth lame duck, Cambridge Instruments, a manufacturer of precision scientific and medical measuring instruments. The Board negotiated a complex package deal whereby it put another £6.5 million into the company, at the same time surrendering its control to an entrepreneur backed by a bank and the Industrial and Commercial Finance Corporation. Although Cambridge Instruments held some twenty per cent of the world market for electron microscopes, it had been unable to make profits on its prestige product, a scanning electron microscope which accounted for a third of its turnover.

Rescue operations are the most controversial aspect of industrial policy. Should shareholdings acquired through rescue operations be managed by state holding agencies like the NEB? On the one hand, it could be argued that bodies like the NEB have the relevant commercial expertise, although this did not enable the NEB to make a success of its lame ducks with the important exception of Ferranti. In practice, it will be difficult to insulate state holding agencies from the political pressures that led to the rescue operation in the first place and, if that is the case, it may be the better course of action to hold those who took the decision fully responsible for seeing it through. This may mean that a different minister from the one who took the original decision may have to handle the problem, but at least when the minister is directly responsible, the chances of public scrutiny are maximized.

High technology

The NEB's role has increasingly become that of undertaking, and participating in, high-technology ventures. Its efforts have been particularly concentrated on micro-electronics, although in 1980 it took a forty-four per cent share in a new biotechnology venture launched jointly with four City institutions. Celltech ('British Genes') will be concerned with the harnessing of living organisms to industrial processes, a technology with perhaps even more important implications for the future development of industry than micro-electronics. One of its tasks will be to place research contracts with leading teams of British genetic engineers to help to steer them towards products which can be profitably exported.

Of the three high-technology companies set up by the NEB in 1978, by far the most important in terms of the funding it has required, the political controversies that have surrounded it, and the long-run importance of its activities, has been the microchip venture, INMOS. The INMOS strategy has been to concentrate on the production of so-called 'standard' chips, manufactured in volume, and capable of a wide range of applications in computers, telecommunications and industrial control systems. Production was expected to be under way by the autumn of 1981 with two Random Access Memories (RAMs): a 16-K RAM and, even more important to the success of the venture, a 64-K RAM, smaller than a fingernail but able to manipulate more than 64000 bits of information.

Most of the £25 million provided by the Labour Government for INMOS was spent on setting up a research centre and production unit at Colorado Springs in the United States. The incoming Conservative Government was faced with the dilemma of deciding whether it should pull out of the project, and lose most of the money invested up to then, or approve the next tranche of £25 million to enable the project to continue. In fact, the Cabinet dithered for six months before Mrs Thatcher announced in July 1980 that a further £25 million would be provided. Apart from the philosophical problems that intervention of this kind poses for a 'social market' government, there were two more practical difficulties. First, it was hoped for a time that GEC might be persuaded to take a stake in INMOS, but this hope of 'privatization' came to nothing. Second, the project became embroiled in the politics of regional policy. INMOS wanted its first factory to be located near to its headquarters in Bristol, which was thought to be a more desirable location for its skilled staff, but the Government wanted the project to go to a development area. In the event, it was decided that the first factory should be built in South Wales. Subsequently, the Government provided an additional £35 million in regional aid and Government cover for various borrowing and leasing arrangements.

It should not be imagined that silicon chips would not be made in Britain if INMOS didn't exist. Although a joint venture between GEC and Fairchild was abandoned, a number of major US semiconductor companies, such as Texas Instruments, have decided to start production in Britain. Given that Japanese production is increasing rapidly, there is little risk of the shortage of certain key types of chip that developed on the world market in 1979. Indeed, if INMOS is going to be a financial success, it will have to break into a highly competitive world market. Whether INMOS will make a profit by 1984, as the NEB has claimed, remains to be seen. A high degree of risk must always attach to decisions relating to high-technology products and, at the end of the day, such decisions are based not only on commercial criteria, but at least as much on other, much broader questions such as whether it is desirable to be highly dependent on important technology.

The second NEB high-technology company, NEXOS, is concerned with what the NEB likes to call 'the office of the future' and undertakes the development of small business machines and communications equipment based on the latest micro-electronics technology. The venture is intended to stimulate the development of new products in an area hitherto dominated by foreign multinationals. The objective is to bring together the skills of existing UK companies, supplemented where necessary by technological joint ventures with foreign companies, and NEXOS itself concentrates on marketing and supporting the products. NEXOS was considerably strengthened by its acquisition of the Dowty subsidiary, Ultronic Data Systems, which licenses Ricoh word processors. In February 1981, the Conservative Government gave permission for the NEB's investment in NEXOS to be increased, in stages, from £15 million to £40 million.

The least successful of the three high-technology companies, INSAC, was formed to market software overseas. One complaint was that the company placed too much emphasis on exporting the Post Office viewdata system. In November 1979, INSAC was split in two, one company being concerned with viewdata (Insac Viewdata, later Aregon), and the other company being concerned with the rest of INSAC's business. This second company, Insac Products (IPL) was reorganized in March 1980, the previous requirement that the chief executives of the member companies had to sit on the central board being abolished.

The NEB's regional role

The establishment of NEB Regional Boards in the North and North West under the Labour Government was in large part a political response to demands to give the most deprived English regions some equivalent of the Scottish and Welsh Development Agencies. The NEB was not entirely happy with these developments, commenting that the devolution debate 'has tended to feed the appetite of the hard-pressed regions' and 'there is a danger that . . . greater expectations will be placed on our ability than are justified by the essential nature of the NEB'[37]. In fact, although the regional boards were given delegated powers to approve investments of up to £0.5 million in individual cases, their impact on the problems of their regions was, not surprisingly, limited. Sir Peter Carey admitted in 1979, 'It is one of the areas of NEB activity which has not taken off as much as either the previous Government or the present Government would have wished.'[38]

Outside critics saw what they regarded as 'very passive and tight-fisted regional boards' providing 'a useful pretence of special government action and concern'[39]. From the NEB's point of view, it has felt obliged to take on higher risk investments in the regions which then 'give more difficulties'[40] than its other companies. It is difficult not to sympathize with Sir Arthur Knight's comment when he was chairman: 'The problem has been around for fifty years or more and has taken up a lot of public money. I'm thinking about what difference the NEB can make.'[41] The NEB as an organization is particularly suited to pursuing those industrial policy objectives concerned with efficiency and international competitiveness, rather than the employment objectives which necessarily loom large in regional policy. The insistence that the NEB must have a regional role seems to be a reflection of the priority given by British politicians of all parties to regional aid.

Small firms

The NEB's small firms role is also one which it has found 'quite difficult'[42] to discharge. Sir Peter Carey has admitted that 'It is a matter of record that a number of these small investments has not been successful. That is so also in respect of the Scottish Development Agency (and) the Welsh Development Agency.'[43] In 1981, the NEB took a number of steps to improve its handling of smaller companies. A new NEB subsidiary, Oakwood Investments, with an initial budget of £1 million, was set up to make loans of up to £50 000 to small companies on special terms. The scheme was intended to help businesses having difficulty in raising money from other sources, but with potential for rapid growth, usually in high-technology areas. A subsidiary called Grosvenor Development Capital, was set up to take over a number of the NEB's smaller investments with the objective of eventually 'floating it off' to the private sector. The NEB also launched a venture capital project with a Californian businessman called Anglo-American Venture Capital.

All these initiatives should improve the NEB's ability to assist smaller firms. However, it is arguable whether the NEB should have such a role at all. The NEB is just one of several agencies trying to help smaller businessmen; among the others are the Department of Industry itself, the Scottish and Welsh Development Agencies, and the various rural development agencies. There might be a case for bringing the functions of all these bodies together in one 'Small Business Agency' which would have both a representational and a promotional function. As it is, the NEB's small business responsibilities must tend to divert its attention from other, and arguably more important, tasks.

5.5 The problem of accountability

The extent to which the NEB should be accountable to Parliament through the Public Accounts Committee has been the subject of a number of disagreements between the Board and the Committee. As the Committee has acknowledged, 'Such problems are in our view inherent in the extension of the mixed economy by way of such instruments of public policy as the NEB.'[44] In 1981, the Committee reaffirmed the position it has taken over a number of years by recommending that the NEB should be subject to the scrutiny of the Comptroller and Auditor-General[45].

Members of Parliament have been able to ask questions on the annual report and accounts of the Board and the Industry Secretary has also answered questions on matters of a general or strategic nature and on day-to-day matters which raised issues of urgent public importance. Witnesses from the Board have also appeared before the Public Accounts Committee on a number of occasions to answer questions. What is at issue is untramelled access for the Comptroller and Auditor-General to the

NEB's books. The Public Accounts Committee has taken the view that it was 'axiomatic that a body of the size and importance of the NEB and disposing of very large sums of public money should be accountable to Parliament to the fullest extent that did not undermine or seriously inhibit its functions'[46]. The Committee has argued that it cannot do its job properly if it is not adequately briefed by the Comptroller and Auditor-General, and such briefing is not possible without free access by the Comptroller and Auditor-General to the Board's records.

Apart from the extra burden of work that access for the Comptroller and Auditor-General could impose, and the risk that it might lead to the Board adopting more bureaucratic procedures, the NEB objected to such scrutiny because it conflicted with its self conception as a commercially oriented holding company. This view was supported by Sir Peter Carey for the Department of Industry who told the Public Accounts Committee: 'I imagine that it would alter the relationship of the firms within the NEB—the subsidiaries—if they believed that information that they had was going to be passed to Parliament . . . I think that they would regard this as a weakening of their competitive position by revealing commercial information . . .(it) would detract from the objective, which is to establish the NEB on as fully a commercial and competitive basis, working in the private sector, as is possible.'[47] The Committee's view was that if, contrary to their expectations, the Board's relationship with some of the private firms with whom it deals was prejudiced in any way, 'it would be part of the price to be paid for adequate accountability'[48].

The Board has argued that if Parliament wishes to increase the accountability of the NEB it should seek to strengthen the monitoring of the Board's overall performance through the Industry Secretary. The Board should be held accountable for its overall performance and not for individual decisions, viewed with the advantage of hindsight. The Department's monitoring arrangements have been the subject of some difficulty between it and the Board in the past. The Department were concerned about delays by the NEB in rendering relevant documents and also felt that they were not getting enough information about medium-sized companies in which the Board had an interest.

Two particular issues provoked disagreement between the NEB and the Department. In 1978 the NEB asked its auditors to carry out a management audit of all its procedures, but refused to provide the Industry Department with a copy on the grounds that the report was confidential to the Board and its auditors. By April 1979, the Board had been persuaded to let the Department have a copy of the report, which showed that the Board's procedures were generally satisfactory. With this dispute settled, the Department told the Board that they did not consider that its 1978-82 plan provided a clear statement of the prospects of NEB subsidiaries in which substantial sums of public money were at risk. The Board argued that the Department was seeking to extend the special arrangements for British Leyland and Rolls-Royce to other companies[49]. This argument led to what a senior civil servant called 'a period of discussion and controversy, but eventually it was resolved on the basis that they would give us the information'[50]. In other words, there was a row which the Government won.

These difficulties all occurred with the Murphy Board, and the Conservative Government agreed a new set of monitoring arrangements with the Board which took account of its diminished role. The annual submission of a comprehensive Corporate Plan was replaced by the annual submission of an investment programme emphasizing the NEB's financial duties. Quarterly meetings at an official level to discuss reports on the performance of NEB companies have continued. In the Industry Department's view, these and other arrangements amount to a 'fairly elaborate system of surveillance of the NEB's performance'[51].

The Public Accounts Committee would prefer to monitor the NEB's use of public funds on the basis of investigations by the Comptroller and Auditor-General, rather than through the secondary route of attempting to scrutinize the Industry Department's discharge of its monitoring functions. In the light of current demands for more open government, it might seem difficult to resist the Committee's request for access for the Comptroller and Auditor-General to the NEB's books and, indeed, at one stage, it did look as if the Labour Government might give way. In its 1980 Green Paper on the role of the Comptroller and Auditor-General, the Conservative Government reserved its position, stating that it would consider the question further when it had received comments on the Green Paper.

It should be noted that the Comptroller and Auditor-General is already the statutory auditor for the Scottish and Welsh Development Agencies and the Scottish Development Agency has told the Public Accounts Committee that this scrutiny has not hampered their commercial freedom. The NEB has disputed the relevance of this evidence, arguing that '90 per cent of the agencies' work ... is concerned with activities which bear no relation to ours'[52]. Nevertheless, the Comptroller and Auditor-General does audit those aspects of the agencies' functions which parallel the NEB's equity investment function.

The Public Accounts Committee has stressed its experience in handling issues involving commercial confidentiality, which in practice means 'asterisking out' sensitive passages in the public record. Thus, the Chairman of the Committee told the Scottish Development Agency when it gave evidence that, 'If when you have the written evidence, you find that there are matters that are embarrassing commercially, you will not find the Committee in any way difficult or ungenerous in acceding to requests that you may make for deletions.'[53] The difficulty with this approach is that it confines what is often the most interesting and important information to members of the Committee. Although ensuring that Members of Parliament are better informed is itself of value, the open government case for access is weakened if some of the information thus obtained is not available to the public. A jocular remark by the Chairman during one series of NEB hearings points to a more serious problem: 'I think, if I may say so, that we shall probably have our legs pulled by our colleagues when we eventually go back to the House and say that we spent a whole afternoon taking evidence from Sir Peter Carey and Sir Leslie Murphy and all we have got to show for it is just a few asterisks.'[54]

Moreover, there is some truth in Sir Leslie Murphy's comment that the problem 'is not so much the relationship between the NEB itself and Parliament but the relationship between Government and Parliament'[55].

Although the question of the relationship between Parliament and the NEB can be dealt with as a distinct issue, it raises a number of wider questions about the role of Parliament in an economy in which the dividing line between the public and private sectors has become blurred.

5.6 The development agencies

The Scottish and Welsh Development Agencies (SDA and WDA) established in 1975 are similar to the NEB in so far as they parallel its industrial investment function in Scotland and Wales where the NEB does not operate. However, they are also responsible for a much wider range of functions, including the building and managing of industrial estates, land renewal and (in Scotland), industrial promotion and urban renewal. Indeed, these other functions have tended to dwarf their industrial investment activities. Of £79 million spent on investments and projects by the SDA in the year ending March 1980, forty-nine per cent (£38.8 million) was spent on factories and industrial estates; thirty-three per cent (£26.3 million) was spent on land renewal; and only eight per cent (£6.5 million) on industrial investment[56]. Similarly, sixty-three per cent of the WDA's expenditure in 1979-80 was spent on industrial estates and factories; thirteen per cent was spent on land reclamation and environmental improvement; and only six per cent on industrial investment (including subsidized rural loans)[57].

The agencies have been a disappointment from a number of viewpoints. In business terms, they have not been a great success. The SDA was supposed to achieve a minimum average return on capital of fifteen per cent in 1980–81, but the average rate of return during the year ending March 1980 was a negative 0.8 per cent, admittedly an improvement on the negative 14.3 per cent for the previous year. Both agencies have suffered from the collapse of a number of companies in which they have invested. The SDA's biggest investment project, Stonefield Vehicles, which developed 'rough terrain' vehicles, had to be put into the hands of the receiver in August 1980 after the SDA had committed £4.7 million. The Scottish Office indemnified the receiver for the cost of keeping the plant going, and in March 1981 made a considerable contribution in the form of Industry Act assistance, to enable a Jersey-based company, Gomba Holdings, to purchase the company and keep production in Scotland. Scofisco, a fish and shellfish processing plant in Glasgow, in which the SDA had invested £825 000, also had to be put into the hands of the receiver. Similarly, a number of WDA's companies have gone into liquidation.

From a trade union and socialist viewpoint, there have also been disappointments. Danson has complained that the SDA has neglected Scotland's traditional industries, that its industrial policy has relied on attracting branch factories and that it is 'fundamentally trapped into accepting Scotland's increasingly peripheral economic position'[58]. David Jenkins of the Welsh TUC has argued that 'the performance of the WDA measured against its stated objectives has been disappointing ... the WDA has been both cautious and constrained in its approach to industrial investment and has opted for the softer options of industrial landlord and property developer ... the creation of new factory space has not made any meaningful impression on the wholesale displacement of jobs or the deterioration in the manufacturing base which has afflicted Wales throughout the last decade'[59].

The SDA has also managed to upset regional opinion within Scotland by appearing to concentrate on the Strathclyde region. There has been friction with the Scottish Office, and the SDA also caused offence within the government machine by the way in which it expanded its overseas promotion activities. The Committee on Scottish Affairs came to the conclusion that these overseas offices should be phased out and commented that they did 'not find the Agency's inward investment record impressive'[60].

Nevertheless, a number of defences can be advanced for the agencies. First, it could be argued that the agencies have insufficient funds to cope with problems of the magnitude which they face and that they have been saddled (particularly by the 1979 Government) with unrealistically high target rates of return. In particular, the SDA has complained that a staff of around 700 is too small to cope with its tasks[61] and that Civil Service Department rules have prevented it from having a much needed Director of Inward Investment[62]. Second, although it could be argued that the range of functions performed by the agencies leads to insufficient emphasis on the industrial investment function, land renewal and factory building do contribute to the attraction of industrial investment. Third, the criticism that the SDA is really a Strathclyde Development Agency is misplaced in the sense that Strathclyde is where the worst problems of industrial and environmental decay in Scotland are to be found. One should also not forget the innovations introduced by the SDA such as the task force concept which brings the agency into partnership with local authorities to tackle the problems of deprived areas. For example, the Glengarnock Task Force was set up under the leadership of the SDA with BSC (Industry) Ltd. and Cunninghame District Council to tackle the local employment problem resulting from the partial closure of British Steel's Glengarnock Works in 1978.

The scale of the problems facing the Scottish and Welsh economies ensures survival of the agencies, apart from the dangers of offending regional political opinion in the event of their abolition, and perhaps encouraging a revival of Nationalist sentiment. They have considerable importance as a symbol of a government commitment to do something to try and tackle the chronic problems of the Scottish and Welsh industrial economies. Indeed, the 1981 Industry Act increased the SDA's financial limit from £500 million to £700 million and the WDA's limit from £250 million to £450 million. However, the agencies do not have sufficient resources to make more than a marginal impact on the problems they seek to tackle, although it is unlikely that their activities could be substantially expanded within the present framework of relationships between England, Wales and Scotland.

Northern Ireland has its own Development Agency, set up in 1976, which replaced the former Northern Ireland Finance Corporation. There is also a Local Enterprise Development Unit set up in 1971 which is intended to help smaller businesses. Selective financial assistance is also available from the Department of Commerce which can amount to up to fifty per cent of the cost of new machinery, plant and building works. Indeed, 'generally speaking in Northern Ireland higher levels of grant are paid than in the Republic'[63], as is reflected in the aid package of over £70 million put together to attract the de Lorean car plant to Belfast. The 1979 Conservative Government reviewed the industrial development institutions and incentives in Northern Ireland, but decided to make no consequent changes, apart from the usual plea for improved co-ordination between the responsible bodies.

5.7 The future of the state holding company model in Britain

The future of the NEB will depend on the policy strategy being pursued by the government in power. Under a social market strategy, it is likely that it would complete its metamorphosis into a body largely concerned with mediating between the state and the private sector in the more arcane areas of high technology. Such a specialist body would be very different from the original conception of the NEB as a mechanism for state expansion into the profitable areas of manufacturing industry.

There is much to be said for a specialist body providing state support for private ventures concerned with the development and application of new technologies. There has been a longstanding concern that Britain has concentrated too much on pure research and development and not enough on the whole process of industrial innovation leading to the successful launch of a commercial product. There has also been concern about the disproportionate portion of Britain's research and development budget devoted to defence purposes with no industrial application. A specialist high-technology agency might be able to ensure that more money was spent on technical developments with commercial potential in industry. However, as has been pointed out at a number of places in the book, a single-minded concentration on high technology can encourage a kind of technological jingoism, of which the most expensive manifestation was the Concorde project.

Any attempt to use the NEB as part of a selective intervention strategy would have to solve two outstanding problems revealed by earlier experience. First, there is the problem of the relationship of the NEB to the rest of the Government's industrial policy. This is not simply a problem of developing, say, better institutional crosswalks with the NEDC. The concept of the NEB as an organization that works with the private sector (as distinct from a socialist NEB that simply acquires parts of the private sector) and therefore requires autonomy and confidentiality if it is to operate successfully is not entirely compatible with the idea that the Board should be answerable to, and guided by, some other body that is evolving an industrial strategy.

It is possible to envisage at least three alternative models for the development of the NEB's relationship with the rest of the industrial policy community under a selective intervention strategy. The first model would maximize the supposed advantages of autonomy and allow the NEB considerable freedom of operation within broad strategic guidelines. Such a model assumes that the work of the NEDC would be largely separate from (and, implicitly, of subordinate importance to) the work of the NEB which would use its resources to develop its own industrial strategy. An extreme version of this model would abolish the EDCs and sector working parties as an irrelevance. In contrast to this 'autonomy model', a second, 'tripartite model', would in effect (in its most extreme form) turn the NEB into an executive arm of the NEDC. The NEB would implement an industrial strategy developed by the NEDC and its EDCs. A third, 'departmental model', would involve the NEB being strictly controlled by the Industry Department. A separate body to hold state shareholdings would be kept in existence to free the minister and the department from day-to-day responsibility for running the companies and to facilitate relationships with the private sector which might be injured by direct government ownership. Which of these models is chosen depends on the different values attached to NEB autonomy, the importance of tripartite involvement in industrial policy-making, and the need for close departmental supervision of agency decisions.

A second outstanding problem is the NEB's relationship with the companies in which it has an interest. Although the NEB has usually put a NEB staff member or an external nominee (although not a NEB board member) on the boards of companies in which it has had an interest, this has not been an inflexible rule, and the NEB has generally maintained an 'arm's length' relationship with its companies, confining its interventions to strategic matters. Chairmen of the larger subsidiaries have not served on the Board, and it cannot be said that there has been much encouragement to subsidiaries to think of themselves as NEB companies. Under the 'tripartite' and 'departmental' models outlined above, the NEB would presumably involve itself more closely in the affairs of its member companies. Even under an 'autonomy' model, there might be a case for a closer relationship, if only in terms of inviting directors of some of the larger subsidiaries to join the Board so that there would be a two-way formal relationship between the NEB and the companies.

For socialists, 'Labour's original policy of direct state initiative is every bit as relevant today as it was in 1973.'[64] However, any effort to restore the NEB to its original interventionalist role would bring into play the political forces which neutralized the NEB after 1974. Of course, the balance of power between left and right would probably be different in a future Labour Government and it could be argued that the experience of the 1979 Conservative Government demonstrates the possibility of carrying out a policy based on ideological conviction rather than winning broad-based support. However, a left-wing government might face obstacles not encountered by a right-wing government. Perhaps all one can say with confidence is that the experience of the NEB demonstrates the flexibility of the state holding company as an organizational form and that the NEB has a good chance of surviving as an institution (in some form) whether future governments follow social market, selective intervention or socialist policies.

Notes to Chapter Five

1. S. Holland, 'Introduction' in S. Holland (Ed.), *The State as Entrepreneur* (London: Weidenfeld and Nicolson, 1972), pp.1–4, p.1

2. United States Department of Commerce, *Overseas Business Reports*, May 1979, OB79-17, Austria, p.9
3. M. R. Garner, *Relationships of government and public enterprises in France, West Germany and Sweden* (London: National Economic Development Office, 1976), p.48
4. Franz Nemschak, quoted in US Department of Commerce[2], p.7
5. H. Wilson, *Final Term* (London: Weidenfeld and Nicholson and Michael Joseph, 1979), p.33
6. *8th Report from the Committee of Public Accounts, 1977–78*, evidence by National Enterprise Board, Appendix VI, p.150
7. Wilson[5], pp.141–42
8. The National Enterprise Board (Guidelines) Direction 1976, paragraph 29
9. National Enterprise Board, *Annual Report 1976*, p.3
10. National Enterprise Board, *Annual Report 1977*, p.4
11. M. Marks, 'State and Private Enterprise', *Business Economist*, Vol. 11 (2), 1980, pp.5–15, p.12
12. *The Committee of Public Accounts[6]*, Q.2585
13. National Enterprise Board[9], p.3
14. *The Committee of Public Accounts[6]* Q.2523
15. Marks[11], p.12
16. Evidence by National Enterprise Board to the Committee of Public Accounts[6], p.152
17. National Enterprise Board[9], p.5
18. Marks[11], p.7
19. ibid., p.6
20. ibid., p.12
21. *The Committee of Public Accounts[6]*, Q.2414
22. National Enterprise Board, *Annual Report 1979*, p.6
23. Wilson[5], p.35
24. *6th Report from the Committee of Public Accounts, 1979–80*, Q.1543
25. The Committee of Public Accounts[6], Q.2425
26. National Enterprise Board[10], p.5
27. National Enterprise Board, *Annual Report 1978*, p.5
28. H.C. Debs. Vol.970, columns 2005–2007, column 2005
29. *30th Report from the Committee of Public Accounts, 1979–80*, p.xiv
30. *Sunday Times*, November 25th, 1979
31. *Financial Times*, November 22nd, 1979
32. H. C. Debs., Vol. 973, columns 754–5
33. National Enterprise Board[27], p.7
34. Interview with Lord Ryder, *The Observer*, 6th February 1977
35. National Enterprise Board[27], p.7
36. *Financial Times*, October 30th, 1980
37. National Enterprise Board[27], p.9
38. *The Committee of Public Accounts[24]*, Q.1573
39. Coventry, Liverpool, Newcastle and N. Tyneside Trades Councils, *State Intervention in Industry: a Workers Inquiry*, (Newcastle-upon-Tyne: Newcastle Trades Council, 1980), p.89
40. *The Committee of Public Accounts[29]*, Q.5497
41. *Financial Times*, September 25th, 1980
42. *The Committee of Public Accounts[29]*, Q.5399
43. ibid., Q.5444
44. *The Committee of Public Accounts[6]*, p.xxxii
45. *1st Special Report from the Committee of Public Accounts 1980–81*, p.xxxi
46. *The Committee of Public Accounts[6]*, p.xx
47. ibid, Q.2420
48. ibid., p.xxxii
49. *The Committee of Public Accounts[24]*, memorandum by Comptroller and Auditor-General, p.39
50. ibid., Q.1558
51. *The Committee of Public Accounts[29]*, Appendix V, letter from the Accounting Officer, Department of Industry to the Clerk of the Committee, 16th June 1980, p.61
52. *The Committee of Public Accounts[45]*, Q.970
53. 10th Report from the Committee of Public Accounts, 1977–78, Q.3575

54. *The Committee of Public Accounts*[6], Q.2799
55. National Enterprise Board[27], p.10
56. Scottish Development Agency, *Annual Report 1980,* p.8
57. Welsh Development Agency, *Annual Report 1979–80,* p.8
58. M. W. Danson, 'The Scottish Development Agency', *Public Enterprise,* Number 19, Autumn 1980, pp.12–14, p.13
59. D. Jenkins, 'The Welsh Development Agency: a Critical Analysis', *Public Enterprise,* Number 19, Autumn 1980, pp.11–12, p.12
60. *Second Report from the Committee on Scottish Affairs, 1979–80, Inward Investment,* p.25
61. ibid., Q.961
62. ibid., Q.948–951
63. ibid., Q.59
64. T. Forester, 'Neutralizing the Industrial Strategy', in K. Coates (Ed.), *What Went Wrong* (London: Spokesman Books, 1979), p.73

Chapter Six

Conclusions

6.1 The broader issues

Any attempt to suggest a more effective strategy for the conduct of
government industrial policy inevitably leads the analyst away from the
core of industrial policy itself, in the sense of efforts to influence the level
and pattern of industrial investment. Even the most well designed and
executed industrial policy cannot offset the impact of an economic policy
which handicaps industry. The development of a better framework for the
conduct of relations between government and industry is of little value if
hostile relationships exist between the management and the workforce.
There is little point in tackling employment problems through industrial
policy if what are really needed are changes in social policy and, indeed, in
social attitudes towards the nature of work. Hence, this chapter considers
some issues which are broader than those discussed in the rest of the book,
such as the debate about an economic strategy based on protection of
British industry; the impact of European Community membership on the
shape and conduct of British industrial policy; and the suitability of the
conventional firm as the usual basis for organizing units of industrial
production.

However, although all these issues are of crucial importance and must
not be neglected in any discussion of policies for industry, one must not
assume that industrial policies of the kind discussed in earlier chapters are
simply of residual importance. Before considering the wider issues outlined
above, the strategic questions emerging from the discussion of specific
industrial policies in earlier chapters will be reviewed. The general
argument presented in this book has been that industrial policy necessarily
involves a political choice between alternative strategies. In that sense, the
long-run consistency in policy advocated by many commentators on British
industrial policy is not attainable within the country's present political
framework, although it is possible to seek greater consistency within
particular policy strategies. Each strategy has its own inherent limits, but is
also capable of being developed more effectively through an enhanced
understanding of the nature of the strategy being pursued and the
consequential removal of self-imposed obstacles arising from imperfect
understanding on the part of policy makers.

6.2 Improving a social market strategy

In its first two years of office, the 1979 Conservative Government attempted to pursue a 'more market than social' version of the social market strategy, although the pursuit of the strategy was punctuated by a series of decisions inconsistent with the rhetoric of ministers. Apart from the electoral risks arising from the catastrophic decline in industrial output associated with the strategy, it was apparent by the spring of 1981 that it was beginning to lose the continuing and active consent of the centres of economic power necessary to its success. The unions had, of course, never endorsed the strategy, but the conditions brought about by recession made it difficult for a demoralized and often divided trade union movement to offer effective opposition to the Government's industrial policies, except in particular and essentially limited instances, such as the miners' defeat of the attempt to accelerate the pit closure programme. After outspoken criticisms of the Government's policies at its 1980 conference, the CBI published a major policy discussion document which called for a more positive industrial strategy. Even in the monetarist heartland of the City, there were signs of increasing nervousness about the possible economic and political consequences of the Government's policies. Only the political determination of the Prime Minister and her Industry Secretary seemed to stand in the way of a return to a 'as much social as market' industrial strategy.

If a social market policy is to have any chance of long-run success in a country like Britain, it must be as much social as market, and it must come to terms with the need to save capitalism from itself. This is particularly important when the attempt to create a favourable economic climate for industrial activity is not succeeding. As Sir Ian Gilmour has put it, 'the baby has to be preserved while the bath water is run away'[1]. The writings and speeches of Sir Ian Gilmour, who blends practical experience in government with the reputation as one of the leading British Conservative thinkers of his generation, offer a general intellectual framework for the kind of 'as much social as market' strategy which could find favour in a damper political climate. Of course, Gilmour does not set out to offer blueprints for action, stressing the overriding importance of 'circumstance' as a distinguishing mark of Toryism (Gilmour, 1978). For Gilmour, 'There is no ideal extent of governmental intervention. "The position of government in industry", as Mr Macmillan once put it, is "not a principle, it is an expedient."'[2] Nevertheless, even if it means going further in the direction of abstraction than Gilmour would tolerate, it is possible to extract from his work one strategic principle and three operational criteria for the conduct of industrial policy.

The strategic principle is to be found in Gilmour's belief that 'For a Tory, politics are more important than economics: political and social consequences are more important than purely economic considerations'[3]. The choice of policy measures then becomes not so much a question of what is demanded by the lessons extracted from currently fashionable economic theory, but rather a matter of what is politically tolerable: what is compatible with the continued existence of a free society with institutions which command respect and allegiance, which is free from excessive and avoidable social tensions, and in which individuals—even if they are not treated with perfect equity—are not the victims of undue harshness which results from an excessive zeal in the pursuit of economic efficiency and an indifference to social injustice. One can believe, as Gilmour does, that 'we would do better if we had more of a market economy'[4] and yet be conscious of the need to be aware of 'the social and political consequences of what we do'[5].

The first operational principle which can be extracted from Gilmour's work is the need to take heed of what other countries do. At the very least, Britain needs to 'match' the (often less transparent) industrial policies of other countries if the nation's industry is not to suffer a competitive disadvantage. More generally, other countries offer examples of what can be achieved by a positive industrial policy guided by long-run price and profit considerations. As Gilmour puts it, 'Some of the free market school have not always seemed to realise that even in countries with economies much freer than ours, there is a good deal of governmental interference and that even if our economy was working much more efficiently than it is there would still be plenty of scope for governmental activity'[6].

Second, there has to be action to correct market imperfections. As Gilmour points out, in some parts of the economy 'there is either a very imperfect market or none at all'[7]. Such intervention could remain consistent with a social market philosophy while going beyond the provision of a framework of rules to allow the market to operate to cover such matters as the dissemination of information to industry and government assistance to research and development.

Third, Gilmour's approach is influenced by a genuine concern about the problem of unemployment. He stresses, 'As unemployment rises rapidly . . . we will have to demonstrate concern not only for the social implications but also imagination about the reforms of the labour market and of pay bargaining which would help to create jobs rather than destroy them.'[8] Once again, Gilmour's approach is influenced by his strategic political concerns. As he points out, 'Lectures on the ultimate beneficence of competition and the dangers of interfering with market forces will not satisfy people who are in trouble. If the state is not interested in them, why should they be interested in the state?'[9]

Perhaps the main defect of the Gilmour approach to economic and industrial policy is that it is too reactive, too dependent on the intimations of 'circumstance', to provide the kind of forward-looking and anticipatory approach that modern industrial policy requires. As Macmillan pointed out in 1933, 'It would be an entirely false conception of the nature of the problem confronting British industry as a whole to imagine that it can be divided up into separate problems for separate industries, which can be solved bit by bit and industry by industry . . . (Such policies) cannot be regarded as a sufficient substitute for a comprehensive policy which would benefit industry as a whole and raise the level of production and of demand.'[10] These remarks are relevant today and serve as much as a criticism of selective interventionism as they do of social market policies. However, at least Gilmour's work provides a basis for a social market strategy which would be more coherent and more relevant to the problems facing British industry than the approach favoured by the Thatcher–Joseph tendency dominant in the Conservative Party.

6.3 Improving a selective intervention strategy

The record of achievement of selection intervention policies in Britain has, to say the least, been disappointing. Nevertheless, given the political attractiveness of such a strategy to both Conservative Governments (despite their determination to follow social market policies) and Labour Governments (despite their professed commitment to socialist policies), it is more than likely that selective intervention policies will sooner or later be tried again. Is there anything that could be done to pursue such policies more effectively next time?

As has been stressed throughout the book, inherent limits are set to such a strategy by its central insistence on preserving the autonomy of the firm. Some detailed suggestions have been made in the course of the analysis about how such policies could be improved, for example by giving greater emphasis to the development of mechanisms for the implementation of agreed tripartite strategies at the level of the firm or plant. More generally, the policy should be made more discretionary and more selective. For example, the 'automatic' Regional Development Grant should be replaced by a discretionary grant (or at least one with a substantial discretionary element) awarded in accordance with a set of priorities related to the objectives of policy. Above all, the balance between aid given to industry in the form of tax relief and aid given in the form of grants tied to particular forms of investment could be made more even. At present, for example, 'the relationship between the Inland Revenue and industry . . . is in volume terms ten times as important as the contribution of regional policy'[11]. The present dispersal of responsibility for industrial policy between a number of government departments can inhibit the vigorous pursuit of a selective intervention policy and some kind of strategic co-ordinating focus on the lines suggested in Chapter Two would be helpful. A selective intervention policy would also have a greater chance of success if the work of the state holding agencies such as the NEB was more closely integrated into industrial policy work as a whole. Their need for autonomy should not be allowed to lead to a disregard for industrial policy objectives.

Changes such as these would all have beneficial consequences which, taken cumulatively, might be substantial, but it would be foolish to pretend that they would fundamentally alter Britain's industrial performance. The crucial question that faces selective interventionists is whether it is possible to pursue such a policy successfully without the imposition of selective import controls. It could be argued that there is little point in using government funds to restructure an industry if, shortly afterwards, it is wiped out by foreign competition. Can one combine a selective intervention policy with an essentially non-discriminatory trade policy? Questions such as this one cannot be answered without reference to the debate about protection which is now at the centre of the discussion of alternative industrial policies in the UK.

6.4 The protection debate

The post-war period has seen the progressive liberalization of international trade through the General Agreement on Tariffs and Trade (GATT) negotiations. However, although tariff barriers have been substantially reduced, a variety of non-tariff barriers ranging from government procurement policies to customs documentation requirements remain important, with about half of world trade being managed trade in the sense that it is subject to some non-tariff control by importer, exporter or both (CBI, 1980). The 1973–79 Tokyo Round of GATT negotiations did lead to the evolution of a number of codes designed to bring non-tariff barriers under control, but whether they will be effective remains to be seen.

Trade liberalization and UK industry

Increasing concern has been expressed in recent years about the growth of import penetration in a number of manufactured goods sectors of the UK economy. Few sectors have escaped this trend, although it has been particularly marked in vehicles, instrument engineering, leather and leather goods and clothing and footwear. The problem is graphically illustrated by the case of the UK motor inudstry, with car import penetration of the British home market increasing from five per cent in 1965 to fifty-six per cent in 1979.

However, one must guard against the assumption that the association between trade liberalization and import penetration is a straightforward cause and effect relationship, and against taking the easy leap from that simplified conclusion to the apparent solution of import controls. Tariff reductions have been a major, but, not the only, or even the most important, influence on import trends (Morgan, 1978). There is, for example, evidence that the efficiency of the distribution network in the UK makes it easier for overseas suppliers to penetrate the home market (Industry and Trade Committee, 1981). Above all, it is important to remember that levels of import penetration vary considerably from one industry to another and that particular industries have been affected by particular policies. For example, the British paper and board industry has never really recovered from Scandinavian imports resulting from British membership of the European Free Trade Association (EFTA), but EFTA membership did not have a similar impact on other industries.

The new industrializing countries

An important feature of the debate about import penetration has been the expression of concern about the past and potential impact on the UK industrial economy of the so-called 'new industrializing countries', a loosely defined group of developing countries with export oriented industrial strategies[12]. These countries form a heterogeneous group, although attention has been particularly centred on a small group of Far Eastern 'super-competitives' including Hong Kong, Taiwan, South Korea and Singapore. The UK has, in fact, maintained a roughly constant and substantial surplus with the new industrializing countries (NICs) in finished manufactures and in 1977 they accounted for only some ten per cent of UK imports of manufactures, representing under three per cent of the sales of manufactures on the UK home market (Foreign and Commonwealth Office, 1979).

They have attracted attention because of their ability to surge forward and take a substantial share of a a particular market in a very short period with damaging consequences for a particular sector of UK industry. Thus, Singapore's share of UK imports of hygienic and pharmaceutical rubber goods increased from half a per cent in 1970 to thirty-six per cent in 1976, and imports of South Korean forks and spoons have increased rapidly from nothing to a position where they represent about half the quantity of imported stainless steel cutlery (Foreign and Commonwealth Office, 1979). These sudden surges are no accident, but are the product of a deliberate strategy which involves the selection of specific products and markets (OECD, 1979). Nevertheless, although industries such as clothing and footwear have been seriously affected by NIC competition, one study suggests that between 1970 and 1977 the increase of imports of manufactures from NICs is unlikely to have displaced more than two per cent of the labour force of the industries concerned and was largely offset by the employment effects resulting from increased UK exports of manufactures to the NICs (Foreign and Commonwealth Office, 1979). In fact, some of the sharpest increases in import penetration have come from other EEC countries and not from developing countries trying to find a niche for themselves in world trade.

Nevertheless, the real effects of NIC competition may not yet have been felt. More developing countries, particularly in Latin America, are likely to acquire NIC status and the greatest impact may not be on the UK home market, but in competition for exports to third country markets. As Jones points out, 'Because of its position at the lower end of the product sophistication spectrum, i.e. increasingly producing more mature products where price rather than non-price factors are important, Britain is likely to be one of the countries most severely affected by competition from the newly industrializing countries.'[13] The Foreign and Commonwealth Office study assumes as a working hypothesis that UK imports of manufactures by NICs will increase by fourteen per cent per year over the next ten years. Moreover, it is pointed out that 'the industries affected by increasing imports from NICs may well be more labour-intensive on average than the totality of UK manufacturing . . . many firms will react to cheap imports from NICs by adopting more capital-intensive and less labour-production methods'[14]. Some net displacement of labour seems inevitable and it is likely that it will be concentrated on less skilled labour, often in areas where there are few alternative jobs.

One solution that has been canvassed is the restriction of 'developing status' to the poorer less developed countries, thus depriving many of the NICs of their favourable special status in international trade agreements. However, the question of whether developing countries should be penalized the moment they start to achieve a measure of economic success raises broader issues of social justice which should not simply be treated as technical problems of trade management.

The case for import controls: a review

Import controls are advocated in two main and significantly different forms. First, there is the use of general, non-discriminatory import controls advocated by Wynne Godley and other members of the Cambridge Economic Policy Group. Second, there is the use of selective import controls to protect particular industries in difficulty, as advocated by the TUC and, more recently, the Labour Party. Godley dismisses the value of 'a policy of protection which is selectively directed towards those industries which are relative failures . . . the failures would be hospitalized and given some form of help, but the average industry, even the relatively successful industries and indeed the economy as a whole, would be committed to ever deepening depression'[15].

Godley advocates either a high tariff applied uniformly to all imports or an auction quota scheme whereby foreign exchange for importing would be sold in close correspondence to the foreign exchange earned by exports (Godley, 1979). It should be stressed that the aim of the Cambridge approach is not to reduce imports or improve the balance of payments but to reduce the import propensity of the economy so that fiscal expansion can occur without total imports being any higher. It is envisaged that a government adopting such a policy 'would simultaneously cut general taxation by enough to stimulate the economy so much that the total volume of imports is as high as it would otherwise have been'[16]. However, total output, employment and public expenditure would be higher than otherwise and, it is claimed, the current balance of payments would be the same.

Three principal objections to the use of import controls, whether of the general or selective variety, will be considered. First, it could be argued that such an approach deals with a symptom rather than the causes of Britain's industrial malaise. A recent review of British industrial performance by the National Economic Development Office (NEDO) states that 'In every respect the relative achievements of the UK have been, and remain, poor.'[17] The NEDO report shows that Britain suffered from much higher inflation than the rest of the EEC over the last decade; a fall in the relative quality or sophistication of UK exports, i.e. their non-price competitiveness; a poor record of productivity growth; and a faster fall in the rate of profit in the UK than elsewhere. Moreover, 'Current developments suggest that the structural weakening and consequent relative impoverishment of this country are both still continuing.'[18]

The facts reported in the NEDO booklet are well known, but there is little agreement about the causes of Britain's industrial decline. The Brookings study comes to the conclusion that 'Britain's economic malaise stems largely from its productivity problem, whose origins lie deep in the social system.'[19] However, it is difficult to reconcile this explanation with evidence presented in the same volume 'that the productivity performance in Britain, compared with those of other countries, varies significantly and persistently from industry to industry'[20]. If the social structure is so inimical to industrial activity, who do some industries prosper and why do some firms succeed in otherwise depressed industries?

One group of opponents of an import controls solution argue that the Cambridge Economic Policy Group approach, while correctly emphasizing the importance of the public sector deficit, distracts 'attention from the other central problem of the British economy, namely the incompatibility of full employment and stable prices . . . with the determination of wages by a process of free collective bargaining when some of the bargaining units are so powerful that they cannot be resisted either by employers or by the elected representatives of the people'[21]. However, one attempt to deal with this problem, the imposition of incomes policies, contributed to the downfall of three successive British Governments in 1970, 1974 and 1979.

Given the absence of agreement on what the problem is, it is difficult to reach a conclusion about the efficacy of particular solutions. However, the selective import controls approach which, in effect, represents an adaptation of the traditional infant industries case to plead the case for senile industries, could only make things worse. It would tend to slow down or prevent the disappearance of outmoded industries and would remove an important source of pressure for efficiency, and for international competition, on all industries. Godley's approach is more defensible. He admits that free trade may be an enemy of the inefficient, but maintains that a non-selective approach would still ensure the destruction of the relatively inefficient firm or industry. He accepts that, under his approach, 'the British economy *as a whole* is being featherbedded' but argues that 'a long period of uninterrupted expansion is a necessary condition for *increasing* investment and productivity. Individual industries may go bust under my assumptions, British industry as a whole cannot do so.'[22]

A second objection to the adoption of import controls by Britain is that of the likelihood of retaliation. The Conference of Socialist Economists admits that 'any challenge to the capitalist international order would be recognized for what it was, and would be met with appropriate disruptive response'[23]. Moss Evans has maintained that the answer to the retaliation argument is to be found in the Transport and General Workers' Union's ten-point charter for import controls and planned trade, but the statement in point ten that the retaliation argument 'should be utterly rejected both in the national interest *and* because the case for import controls makes sound common sense'[24] is not very helpful. The union's case rests in part on the argument that the removal of the 'import penetration constraint' would lead to an expansion of the British economy, and hence a net gain for world trade which would discourage retaliation. It also appears to depend on an assumption that other countries would develop trade policies based on direct or indirect barriers. The Cambridge case is more subtle, resting on the argument that the total level of imports would be as high as it would otherwise have been, and that, even if the composition of imports were changed, 'countries which lose trade to us can make it up elsewhere'[25].

However, even under the Cambridge approach, retaliation might well wipe out any benefits gained through the imposition of import controls. The character and extent of retaliation is unpredictable, but that is not the same as saying that it will not occur. Indeed, experience suggests that other countries tend to overreact to the use of import controls by Britain, even when they are imposed in accordance with international agreements. In 1980, the Indonesians reacted strongly against the imposition of quotas against their exports of clothing to the UK. As the Trade Secretary at the time commented, 'The result has been that by refusing to accept about £10 million of shirts and trousers Britain has lost major aerospace, process plant, scientific instrument and other orders to the tune of about £150 million. As much as another £500 million of business which was under discussion—and some of which would have come our way—has also been denied us.'[26] Similarly, the imposition of rather weak quotas to limit US synthetic fibre imports led to threats of retaliation against UK wool textile exports.

Once a trade war starts, there tend to be two (or more) losers, rather than one winner. There is the risk that unilateral British action might trigger off a chain-reaction which could lead to the disappearance, or at least substantial modification, of the existing liberal international trading system. 'No other major industrialized country exports such a high proportion of its gross domestic product'[27] and a collapse of exports following a decline in world trade could be highly damaging to Britain, quite apart from the effects of any individual retaliatory actions.

A third argument advanced against import controls is that they restrict consumer choice and/or push up prices. The Consumers' Association has argued that the Multi Fibre Arrangement, which regulates trade in textiles, has had the effect of pushing up the prices of basic imported clothing by fifteen to forty per cent and that the costs to the consumer of protection (in the clothing and textiles area, at any rate) outweigh the benefits achieved in terms of jobs saving. However, any losses sustained by citizens as consumers as a result of the imposition of import controls have to be balanced against losses that might otherwise be suffered by workers, bearing in mind that in the former case the benefits are relatively diffuse, and that in the latter case the losses are likely to be concentrated on particular groups of workers. As Godley points out, any restriction of consumer choice has to be balanced against anticipated gains in terms of higher real income and output and lower unemployment and 'the place not going down the drain'[28].

The difficulties involved in imposing wide-ranging import controls do not mean that Britain cannot take protectionist action of any kind, although since the UK joined the European Community, the conduct of international trade relations has ceased to be a matter of national competence. However, Britain has voluntary restraint arrangements with Japan covering about one-third of UK imports from that country, most importantly in relation to motor cars. Over ninety-five per cent of the UK's imports of clothing and textiles from low cost sources are subject to various forms of restraint (Industry and Trade Committee, 1981). Above all, it is possible to use national purchasing policy to assist domestic industries in a way that is often less transparent than the imposition of tariffs and quotas.

Import penetration does represent a problem facing the British industrial economy, even if it is a product of other deficiencies in industrial performance. Import controls on the lines advocated by the Cambridge Economic Policy Group could provide an economic framework within which industrial reconstruction could take place, although the strategy is a high-risk one because of the uncertainties surrounding the question of retaliation. Selective controls would prolong problems rather than solve them and might even lead to increased inefficiency in the industrial economy.

The domestic politics of protection

Protectionist policies have become increasingly associated in Britain with a left wing economic strategy, although in fact they are politically agnostic.

Although import controls now form part of the Labour Party's economic strategy, they are certainly compatible with Conservative tradition and might offer the 1979 Conservative Government a politically acceptable deviation from its initial policies. There is no doubt that protectionist sentiment gathered strength in Britain towards the end of the 1970s. For example, an attempt by a Conservative MP to introduce a Bill to give Parliament the right to introduce import controls unilaterally despite European Community regulations was defeated by only seventeen votes (153–136) in July 1980. Despite the fact that Mrs Thatcher had rejected import controls in a debate on the previous day, over twenty Conservative MPs supported the Bill in the division lobby.

Most interesting of all, there has been a shift in business opinion, as reflected in the changing attitudes of the CBI which has had to re-think its attachment to liberal international trade policies. At the CBI's 1979 conference, a motion calling for a degree of protection for UK industries was carried by 340 votes to 230 against the advice of the leadership. Subsequently, the CBI staff circulated a discussion document to members in which the idea of protection for core industries was discussed. It was not entirely clear which these industries were—the CBI maintained that the definition of the vital core would change over time—but given the fact that the CBI referred to the survival of industries needed 'to ensure a balanced economy, the production of essentials in time of war and the social wellbeing of the community'[29] it is clear that the concept was a wide-ranging one. If the CBI had adopted this idea as policy, its position on import controls would have been compatible with that of the TUC.

However, the majority of members consulted thought that a strategy of protection based on the core industries' concept would protect the inefficient. The CBI's 1980 strategy document on trade policy rejected across-the-board import controls, but called for vigorous and swift EEC action to protect industries against disruptive or unfair imports (CBI, 1980). Nevertheless, the persistence of protectionist sentiment among businessmen is shown by a London Chamber of Commerce survey published in 1980 which showed that nearly sixty per cent of manufacturing companies contacted in London and the South-East believed that selective import controls were vital[30].

Whatever the economic merits of protectionist policies, the political chances of Britain adopting protectionist policies on an increasing scale in the 1980s are high. The plight of the industrial economy is likely to worsen, at least in the medium term, and political pressure will increase for a solution that is not tainted by recent failure. Import penetration tends to have highly visible effects, leading to the closure of particular factories or even the collapse of whole industries. It is the kind of issue readily taken up by Members of Parliament in a geographically based Parliamentary system where the defence of constituency interests is given a high priority. Moreover, unlike some economic issues, it can easily be popularized in simple terms by the media.

It is likely that selective rather than general controls would be adopted. Selective controls confer specific benefits on favoured interests in a way that general controls do not; indeed, one of their drawbacks is that they foster vested interests which means that, once they have been adopted, it is politically difficult to dispense with them (Corden *et al.* 1980). As Corden points out, 'it is possible to think of many examples where protection was originally imposed because of a short-term decline and where the protection stayed on even when the urgent need has disappeared'[31]. Moreover, the adoption of selective controls, particularly if they were limited to a few industries, would be a less radical departure from existing policy than general controls and experience suggests that British politicians prefer the more cautious, incremental route where it is available.

6.5 The European Community and industrial policy

Supporters of protectionist policies in Britain often also advocate British withdrawal from the European Community. Certainly it is difficult to see how Britain could unilaterally impose import controls and remain a full member of the Community. Progress towards a European Community industrial policy has been disappointing, although one cannot assess the value of British membership of the Community solely in terms of the effectiveness of Community industrial policy. An important economic benefit is access to a wider market, although, as Wallace points out, 'The benefits to Britain's economy from access to a wider "home market" are shared by all other members of the Community; only Britain suffers the offsetting burden of budgetary and trade costs arising from the Common Agricultural Policy.'[32] There are wider, non-economic benefits, such as the ability of the Community to provide the major West European nations with a platform from which they can make a distinctive contribution to world affairs. Clearly, the assessment of all the benefits and costs of Community membership for Britain is beyond the scope of this book, and the analysis will concentrate on Community industrial policy.

The limitations of Community industrial policy

The development of an effective European Community industrial policy is inhibited by the Community's ideology, its organization, the national interests of its member states, and the conflicting interests of different industries within and between member states. The Community was formed at a time when it was assumed that a continually expanding West European economy would absorb any labour displaced from declining industries; hence, an interventionist industrial policy, even one designed to promote adjustment, was not seen as necessary. As Warnecke points out, 'The Treaty of Rome . . . neither mentioned the area of industrial policy nor granted the Commission those instruments through which national governments can exercise an influence over their own industries.'[33]

However, it became apparent that the creation of a customs union, the removal of technical barriers to trade and the pursuit of competition policy would not lead, in particular, to the creation of European firms operating on a scale that enabled them to compete effectively with American firms. This concern led to the Colonna Report on Industrial Policy of 1970; a commitment to the establishment of a single industrial base for the Community at the Paris Summit in 1972; and an action programme by December 1973. However, despite all this activity in 1972–73, 'little was really achieved beyond the acceptance of the idea that the EEC should have an industrial policy'[34]. Even supporters of the Community, like the CBI, have complained of the 'delay and uncertainty'[35] surrounding Community industrial policy.

Part of the problem is an organizational one. Particularly if one deducts translators from staff totals, the Commission has a small staff to cope with the immense problems it has to deal with. Responsibility for industrial policy is spread across a number of directorates, with DG III having a co-ordinating responsibility for industrial affairs. It often finds itself in conflict with the competition directorate whose commitment to liberal economic solutions is enshrined in the treaty in a way that the sponsorship tasks that DG III attempts to undertake are not. Calls for the strengthening of DG III, and for other changes in the Commission designed to enhance the organizational salience of industrial policy, are a familiar feature of prescriptive reports on Community industrial policy (CBI, 1976a; European Democratic Group, 1981).

However, the problem goes far deeper than a lack of adequate or properly located organizational resources within the Commission. The central problem is that each member state defines Community industrial policy largely in terms of its own self-interest, and pressure for a Community policy only arises when things have got so bad that an industry is beyond salvation on a national basis (Hodges, 1977). The Commission finds itself faced with a situation in which 'On the one hand the Governments of our Member States take differing positions on most issues; on the other hand a substantial part of the private sector in Europe in practice values its autonomy higher than the possible contribution the Community could make to its future.'[36] Given the absence of any positive political support for a Community industrial policy, it is the worst industrial problems that are most readily sent to Brussels. It is not entirely the fault of the Community if it cannot find soultions to problems which have defeated the national governments.

Sectoral policies

The steel sector is the one area where Community policies have had a significant impact. In relation to the steel industry, the Community has been able to achieve more than in other sectors because of the wider powers given to it by the Treaty of Paris which set up the Coal and Steel Community, the longer tradition of European co-operation in steel policy, the parlous state of the industry in recent years, and the energetic leadership of the responsible Commissioner, Viscount Davignon. A series of measures combining minimum prices and import controls, backed up by fines imposed on offending Community producers and a series of Voluntary Restraint Agreements negotiated with major steel-supplying third countries, culminated in the declaration in October 1980 of a state of manifest crisis in the Community's steel industry. After some concessions to the Germans, production quotas were agreed at the end of October.

However, one should not exaggerate the impact of Community steel policy on the policy of the British Government towards the steel industry.

The funds provided by the Community to help with the social consequences of restructuring the industry have been useful, and the Community has had some impact on imports from third countries and achieved
some degree of management of the internal market. Nevertheless, the 1979
Conservative Government's substantial cutbacks in BSC capacity,
although in conformity with the Commission's view that capacity should be
reduced, were a reflection of the Government's own policy priorities and
of the need to reduce the substantial public subsidies provided for the state
steel industry, rather than a response to any pressure from Brussels.

The difficulties that the Community faces in developing an adequate
policy even for industries that are in crisis are illustrated by the case of
shipbuilding. The Community would prefer assistance to the shipbuilding
industries of member states to be lower, but recognizes that, given the
price gap between European and Asian yards, most Community yards
would go out of business without such aid. However, the Commission is
also worried that 'such aids will drive back market forces and that the
economic selection of the most competitive yard will become a matter of
only secondary importance'[37].

The 1978 Fourth Directive on Aid to Shipbuilding did go some way to
providing a framework for a Community shipbuilding policy. The directive
required that aid and intervention should be progressively reduced, and
must be linked to the reduction of capacity. The draft Fifth Directive
attempted to tackle the more contentious question of aid to state owned
nationalized industries, the question of the controversial Polish Order
negotiated for British Shipbuilders by the Callaghan Government being at
the back of the Commission's mind. However, ambitious plans by Viscount
Davignon to parallel the Community's steel policy with a similar shipbuilding policy led to very little in the way of policy innovation.

The Community's impact in other industrial sectors has been even more
limited, although it has influenced sectors such as textiles through its
responsibility for commercial policy and the handling of negotiations for
the Multi Fibre Arrangement which provides for the restraint of the rate of
growth of imports of textiles into the EEC from low-cost countries. The
Commission is taking an interest in the Community's troubled motor
industry, and there has even been speculation about the possibility of
assistance for compensatory payments to redundant automobile workers.
As far as regional policy is concerned, ninety-five per cent of the Regional
Development Fund is carved up on a quota basis between member states,
and has been seen by successive British Governments as a means of getting
back part of the financial contribution made by Britain to the Community.

All too often Community industrial policy looks like a belated response
to changes in the industrial structure that have already taken place, rather
than an attempt to anticipate the problems of the future. The important
area of information technology offers a good illustration of this tendency.
The Community admits that 'The Nine have become concerned about this
only recently'[38], and it was not until June 1979 that the heads of state and
government meeting in Strasbourg asked the Commission to look into the
matter, a request which led to the submission of proposals by the
Commission to the Council of Ministers in September 1980. The proposals
centred on a traditional reliance on competition policy, combined with an

attempt to concert public procurement policies and the promotion of cross-frontier projects by undertakings. Member states are inclined jealously to defend their procurement policies because they offer a means of promoting 'national champions', and cross-frontier projects have hardly been a sparkling success in the past.

The general absence of effective sectoral policies is in large part a reflection of the social market orientation of the Community's approach to industrial policy. Those who would not want to see the integration process taken too far might argue that the ambiguities and ineffectualness of Community industrial policy is really a good thing, because it leaves member governments a freer rein to pursue their own national policies. However, although Community policy has not proved a significant constraint on the autonomous development of British industrial policy in the past, there are areas where conflict may occur in the future, even with a British Government pursuing a moderately interventionist policy. In particular, there are likely to be difficulties over state aids to the private sector and over the nationalized industries.

The Community and national industrial policies

Article 92(1) of the Treaty of Rome provides that 'Save as otherwise provided in this Treaty, any aid granted by a Member State or through State resources in any form whatsoever which distorts or threatens to distort competition by favouring certain undertakings or the production of certain goods shall, in so far as it affects trade between Member States, be incompatible with the common market.' However, Articles 92 (2) and (3) list a series of exemptions, one of which is so worded as to provide a means of allowing regional aid, and another which contains a clause which permits aid 'to remedy a serious disturbance in the economy of a Member State'. Much, then, depends on the way in which the treaty is interpreted.

In 1979, the Commission prohibited the Dutch Government from giving aid to Philip Morris International to enlarge a cigarette factory. The firm subsequently appealed to the European Court of Justice, the first time that a recipient of proposed aid has lodged such an appeal, and the decision of the Court in favour of the Commission is an interesting clarification of the Commission's power to prohibit state aids.

In its judgement dismissing the appeal, the Court pointed out that Article 92(3) gives the Commission power of discretion by stating that the types of aid listed 'may' be considered as compatible with the common market. The Court ruled that the Commission had rightly considered the standard of living and serious under-employment in the area in question not by reference to the national average in the Netherlands but in relation to the level throughout the Community. The compatibility of the aid in question with the treaty must be considered within a Community context and not simply in relation to one Member State[39].

Aid to the tobacco industry is controversial even at a national level and the Commission is on relatively safe ground in mounting a challenge to it. The Commission has kept out of politically more sensitive areas like state aid to the motor industry and has only gone through the motions of vetting the state aid, although this may change. There were hints from Brussels in

1981 that clearance for the latest Government aid package for British Leyland would not automatically be granted.

Another potential area of conflict concerns the nationalized industries. Article 90 of the Treaty of Rome provides that the relevant provisions of the treaty extend to public undertakings and gives the Commission the power to address appropriate directives or decisions to Member States. In June 1980, the Commission adopted what proved to be a controversial directive based on Article 90 which required each member state to place at the Commission's disposal data relating to the financial relationship between the state and public undertakings in each country. The Commission's stated objective in collecting this information was to 'be able to assess whether the public resources thus placed at the disposal of a public undertaking constitute, for example, an aid and must therefore be treated as such, or whether, on the contrary, the resources are being made available simply in accordance with normal practice in a market economy'[40]. Despite reassurances by the Commission that it did not intend to discriminate against the public sector, this directive concerned a number of member states and Britain, France and Italy launched a challenge against the Commission on the way it had used its powers in the European Court. The United Kingdom sympathized with the Commission's broad objective, but challenged the Commission on the technical grounds that the Commission could issue a directive on its own initiative under Article 90(3) only when it has been established that a member state is breaching the competition regulations, whereas the Italians based their case on the procedure and the principle. The underlying issue, which is likely to emerge again, is the Commission's belief that nationalized industries should follow market principles as well as private industries.

The impact of Community industrial policy

Even where conditions for a Community industrial policy are most favourable, i.e., where member states have a common interest in the problems resulting from the collapse of an industry, this common interest in the problem is often outweighed by conflicts of interest over possible counter-measures. Other Community policies often have more impact on industry than the attempts to develop an industrial policy. Thus, it has been argued that 'the trade agreement with the People's Republic of China will have a much greater effect on the textile industry than the Community's attempts to restructure the industry'[41]. All too often, the Commission tends to retreat into the pursuit of technicalities where it knows it will not encounter much opposition from the member states, even if the results it achieves have a minor impact on the industrial structure of the Community. Thus, it has achieved the passage of a whole series of directives on tractors, with work underway on the harmonization of the location and attachment of statutory plates and inscriptions to tractors, A directive on spa waters has been another area of activity. In many ways, the OECD has made a more positive contribution to the international debate on industrial policy, with its attempts to evolve an agreed framework for industrial policy which will shift the emphasis away from the short-term defence of weak sectors to a longterm strategy of adjustment.

A negative benefit of the absence of an effective Community industrial policy is that the British Government's pursuit of its own industrial policies has not faced serious interference from Brussels. However, much depends on the type of policy that the UK Government is following. A social market policy is likely to be generally compatible with the Commission's insistence that subsidies should be 'degressive'; a selective intervention policy is likely to require some delicate negotiation over areas of difficulty; and a socialist policy would be difficult to reconcile with the Commission's preference for an industrial policy based, at its most interventionist, on a philosophy of positive adjustment.

The Community's failure to make substantial progress in the area of industrial policy is a relatively minor item to be weighed in the balance when deciding whether or not Britain should remain a member of the Community. In any case, defenders of the Community would argue that industrial policy has been constrained 'not mainly by Community obligations, but by domestic political and economic obstacles and doctrinal inhibitions'[42]. Some commentators still cling to the public school 'cold shower' analogy to demonstrate the industrial benefits resulting from continued membership of the Community (Jones, 1980). This approach argues that Community membership invigorates management by exposing it to stimulating competitive pressures and also shocks government into giving more weight to efficiency, and less to the short-term preservation of employment, in its industrial policies.

Despite its hesitant steps towards an industrial policy, the Community remains attached to the free market philosophy embedded in the Rome Treaty and it is unlikely in the forseeable future that the member states, individual firms or the rather weak European industrial pressure groups will provide sufficient political impetus to shift the Community from that position. It is difficult to argue with the European Democratic Group's recommendation that 'Industry needs to be given equally important status and attention as Agriculture in the Community.'[43] However, that is unlikely to happen, given the institutional momentum behind, and cluster of interests associated with, the CAP. A conference sponsored by three major British policy institutes did suggest four lines of development for Community industrial policy which might assist the British economy: completion of the operation of the common market; extending the Coal and Steel Community model of assistance for industrial adjustment to other sectors under pressure; expanding the operations of the European Investment Bank; pressing for very substantial transfers to disadvantaged regions. However, it was recognized that Britain might have to offer a quid pro quo in the field of energy policy (Wallace, 1980). The price demanded by other Community countries in that respect might be too high.

The failure to evolve a satisfactory Community industrial policy, although it reduces the importance of a potentially significant constraint on British industrial policy, should not be a cause for rejoicing. The alternative is a competition for investment and jobs between the West European economies with transnationals as the main beneficiaries. The ultimate outcome might be a West European industrial economy dominated by a series of medium-sized national champions which would be highly vulnerable to Japanese, and possibly American, competition.

6.6 Raising capital for industrial investment

The level of industrial investment per employee in Britain has been considerably below that of other major industrial countries and one of the central concerns of industrial policy has been to try and stimulate a higher and more effective rate of industrial investment. Some of the blame for the low level of industrial investment has been attached to the way in which British capital markets are organized. Among the problems which have been identified are a less close relationship between banks and their industrial customers than is the case in major competitor countries; concern about the siphoning off of funds which might otherwise be available for industrial investment into housing investment through the building societies; the greater difficulties that smaller firms have faced in raising finance; and concern about the way in which institutional investors such as pension funds use the considerable sums of money at their disposal (Bayliss and Butt Philip, 1980).

The Wilson Committee on Financial Institutions found that it was not generally the case 'that real investment in the UK has been unnecessarily constrained by shortages in the supply of external finance'[44], although there were difficulties in the provision of finance for small firms. However, the fact that the Wilson Committee report gave financial institutions a relatively clean bill of health did little to quell worries about the provision of funds for industrial investment. Indeed, such worries have been sharpened by a growing concern that North Sea Oil revenues are not being used for industrial or infrastructure investment, but are being used to sustain a level of personal consumption which cannot be maintained in the long run. One popular remedy is to suggest that the Government's North Sea revenues should be transferred into a special industrial investment fund.

Whatever is done with North Sea oil revenues, it should be remembered that 'Retained funds within a company are the prime sources of finance for investment in the UK'[45]. The principal problem in the UK in recent years as far as finance for industrial investment is concerned has been that many firms have been locked into a vicious cycle of falling profits and inability to invest which government funds have not been able to offset. However, the use to which government aid has been put is often clouded in myths and misconceptions. For example, Sainsbury supports his case for an English Industrial Development Bank with the argument that interest relief grants under the 1972 Industry Act have gone to 'exactly the wrong companies. Instead of being used to help new industries or companies growing rapidly, they are used to prop up companies in structural decline.'[46] Although this may have happened in particular cases, the criteria under which such assistance is given ensure that it is used either to assist companies in difficulties to rationalize their production (which is rather different from 'propping up'), or to assist the development of new industries and products based on advanced technologies.

Moreover, the problem is not simply one of the level of industrial investment, but of the use to which it is put. The NEDO report on British industrial performance points out that 'There is evidence that in addition to investing rather less than France and West Germany, the UK has also obtained a lower "return" in terms of extra output from the investment actually undertaken.' Indeed, the evidence suggests that 'the extra output obtained from given investment in the manufacturing sectors in France was greater than twice that in the UK, and in West Germany was almost twice the UK figure'[47].

6.7 The future of the firm

By its own standards, the capitalist firm in Britain has not been doing very well in recent years. Rates of profit have been falling and the ultimate penalty of bankruptcy has only been avoided in a number of cases by government assistance or a tolerant (often government-encouraged) attitude by the firm's bankers. This state of affairs has naturally encouraged renewed demands for the replacement or radical reform of the firm as the basic unit of industrial organization, although managements in conventional firms would no doubt claim that their troubles are not largely of their own making, but are the consequences of changes in British society and in the international economic environment and of government mismanagement of the economy.

It would be possible to write a whole book on the arguments for and against the introduction of some form of industrial democracy which many commentators see as the panacea for Britain's problem of poor industrial performance. All that will be possible here is to briefly review the main arguments underlying the case for industrial democracy. A principal argument is that industrial democracy simply represents the extension of the basic democratic rights won in the 19th and early 20th century to the most important sphere of the life of men and women, the workplace. Democracy is the ultimate 'hurrah' word and it is difficult to object to any apparent extension of it. However, Tivey has pointed out that 'if participation in industry follows common experience, then it will mean more power for some than for others', resulting in an end state that he terms 'Zealocracy, the rule of the activists'[48].

A second theme in the debate is that industrial democracy would improve what might be termed 'the moral condition of the worker' by eliminating or reducing the alienation of the worker from his work. In fact, many of the forms of industrial democracy which are popularly advocated, such as the placement of a minority of worker directors on the boards of companies, would not give workers sufficient control over the work process to eliminate alienation in the classic sense. These weaker forms of industrial democracy are often justified in terms of the opportunities they present workers for the enhancement of job satisfaction. However, industrial democracy may inhibit the abolition of the more repetitive and less satisfying jobs by giving workers or their representatives increased opportunities to obstruct the introduction of new technology.

A third argument is of a rather different kind, being concerned with industrial efficiency rather than workers as individuals or as a collectivity. It is often argued that, if workers were more involved in decisions about the production process, their energies and talents would be more effectively harnessed, leading to improvements in industrial production. It is an argument which governments and management find attractive and which leads trade unionists to fear that industrial democracy is really a co-optive arrangement which employers hope to use to neutralize the leadership of the workers, with the worker representatives being converted into persuasive spokesmen for the management point of view. Certainly, there is some evidence from the worker democracy experiments in the steel industry and the Post Office that this can happen.

Although co-optive industrial democracy has been associated with industrial success in the BRD, other management styles have also been successful—for example, paternalism in Japan and authoritarianism in South Korea. Much, of course, depends on the cultural traditions in different societies, although there is evidence that Japanese management practices can bring successful results in Britain (Takamiya, 1979). The risk that the introduction of worker participation in the UK carries is that it might only serve 'to give increased weight to the old disfunctional attitudes'[49].

On the other hand, it is unlikely that an increasingly better educated workforce will be satisfied with token consultation on minor issues, or by the supply of more information on company decisions as seen from a management point of view. Like the imposition of import controls, the introduction of industrial democracy is a high-risk strategy because of the uncertainties associated with it. It might, however, have a better chance of producing successful outcomes than the incremental solutions to industrial problems which have been tried in Britain up to now.

Worker co-operatives

Despite the difficulties encountered by the so-called 'Benn co-operatives', only one of which survives and that in an emasculated form, the idea of worker co-operatives has enjoyed a considerable revival in recent years. As Smith points out, 'One of the attractions of co-operativism is its theoretical and operational flexibility, so that it appeals to idealist and technocrat alike as well as to most shades of political opinion.'[50] Thus, one finds economic liberals advocating worker co-operatives as means of making workers face up to the consequences of their actions in a market economy; political Liberals favouring them as a manifestation of the ideal of 'small is beautiful'; social democrats viewing them as one of the more tolerable aspects of British socialist tradition; socialists welcoming them as an alternative to bureaucratic and highly centralized state industries; while among some members of the far left, they are seen as an essential component of a form of anarcho-syndicalism. A political scientist tends to be suspicious of an idea which attracts such widespread ideological support, as it either means that people are not clear about their intentions, or that they will be disappointed by the results.

However, given the political respectability of the idea, 'hobbit socialism'[51] is likely to gain ground, if only as a 'soft option' alternative to industrial democracy in existing firms. It is likely that steps will be taken to further improve the facilitative legal framework for co-operative action and an enlarged Co-operative Development Agency, lending funds at preferential rates of interest to new co-operatives, can be envisaged. The path of a series of state-sponsored small-scale experiments in worker co-operatives might appear to be an attractive one. However, such experiments would be likely to be both disappointing and misleading. They would be disappointing in so far as, except in the smallest enterprises, the likely outcome is degeneration into a system of management and decision-making which, although outwardly different, would resemble that of the conventional firm. Thus, the John Lewis Partnership has developed 'an orthodox management structure, with strong emphasis on competitive efficiency'[52]. Such experiments would be misleading because an economy made up of, or dominated by, worker co-operatives would be very different from an economy with a fringe of worker co-operatives. In such an economy, the virtues of independence and competitive potential which worker co-operatives appear to possess might well be lost if all that developed was a 'collaborative network of employment-oriented concerns'[53].

The principal drawback of solutions to the dilemmas of industrial policy based on schemes for industrial democracy and worker co-operatives is their assumption that work will continue to play a central part in a person's life. Indeed, by emphasizing the primacy of work, they tend to reinforce attitudes which slow down the adaptation of new, labour-saving technology. The rate of adaptation of new technology is a function of many factors, such as the availability of relevant new skills in the labour force, but it can also be affected by the understandable fear of job displacement among workers. Solutions to industrial problems which emphasize the centrality of work in society carry an intellectual opportunity cost in so far as they shift emphasis away from the greater freedom from work which can result from the use of new technology.

6.8 Where do we go from here?

Many of the problems which industrial policy seeks to solve require action in areas which go well beyond the boundaries of industrial policy, however defined. Industrial policy has been deflected from its pursuit of industrial efficiency objectives by being required to cope with problems which really require a social policy solution; at the same time, these problems are not given sufficient priority in other policy arenas and hence remain unresolved. On the one hand, industrial policy needs to be more clearly separated from other policy arenas; on the other hand, it needs to be more closely integrated with other policy arenas. This is not such a paradoxical recommendation as it first sounds. The core of industrial policy should be concerned with measures which are designed to enhance the efficiency and international competitiveness of the industrial economy. This is not to say that employment objectives should be excluded altogether, particularly in such areas as regional policy. However, the social consequences of industrial change must be dealt with elsewhere in government than in the industry ministry. This is not to say that they should be neglected or treated as being of secondary importance; rather, it is being argued that they should be given a higher priority than hitherto and that more effort should be made to develop an integrated and coherent long-run strategy to cope with such changes. In particular, it has been suggested that there needs to be a high-level Cabinet minister concerned both with the promotion of industrial change and with the social consequences of such change.

The alternative to the approach outlined here is an industrial policy that fails because it is both attempting to cope with the social consequences of industrial change, and promote a more efficient industrial economy, with the result that both objectives become muddled and difficult to pursue; and a social policy that fails to cope with, because it does not always recognize, or give sufficient priority to, the social consequences of industrial change. There will, of course, always be some 'grey areas' where it is impossible to separate the two sets of objectives— for example, some rescue operations where the outcome is uncertain may be justified because, even if it is not found possible to save the firm in question for the industrial economy, at least the rescue operation will ensure that the process of rundown is carried out over a longer time period, making it easier for the displaced workforce to obtain alternative employment. British Leyland is a case in point: the primary objective of the rescue operation has been to preserve an independent British volume cars producer and, hence, maintain the viability of the British motor components industry. However, even if this objective is not achieved, the policy will have at least resulted in the rundown of the workforce over a longer period than would otherwise have been the case.

The future of work

The discussion of industrial policy ultimately leads to questions about the place and status of work in contemporary society. A central, if often implicit, objective of British industrial policy has been the preservation of employment. However, Britain is now in a position where the 'basic issue . . . is whether reasonably full employment can now be achieved by any combination of feasible policies'[54]. In such circumstances, it is appropriate to turn the problem on its head and ask whether we do not have too large a labour force rather than insufficient employment. These issues have been taken up by employers and trade unionists, with the CBI warning in a discussion document 'that unemployment may become so widespread that at any one time we will need to take a sizeable proportion of the population temporarily or permanently out of the labour market'[55]. In a broader review of the problem, Clive Jenkins and Barrie Sherman have argued that 'The expectation of a life at work . . . should be changed to life, with leisure and work taking equal priorities.'[56]

The relative merits of various 'worksharing' measures which either directly reduce the size of the workforce or reduce the amount of time worked by the existing workforce will not be discussed here, nor will it be possible to discuss the changes of attitude that may become necessary in a society which places a high moral value on work and reserves the label 'scrounger' for fit adult males not in employment. It is regrettable that the problem is often discussed through the revival of old prejudices, e.g. that married women should not work, and that there is a failure to appreciate the interrelationship between industrial policy and social policy measures. There is also a tendency to think in terms of the extension of existing solutions, rather than the development of new approaches. These points may be illustrated by reference to discussions about the statutory retirement age.

Harmonization of the retirement age for men and women at sixty would substantially reduce the size of the labour force. The main objection is one of cost: 'giving men a full pension at sixty would cost over £1½ billion a year, even if the vacancies left by those retiring earlier were filled by unemployed people, and once full pensions were generally available under the new pension scheme, the cost would almost double'[57]. In 1981, the DHSS stated that it found a common pension age with flexible retirement between sixty and seventy attractive as a longterm aim, but stressed that current constraints on spending prevented early changes[58].

A more innovative approach to the problem would be to encourage individuals to transfer to part-time work before the age of sixty. More jobs would be released, and one must also take account of the more diffuse benefit resulting from the reduction of political pressure on industrial policy-makers to undertake job preservation measures. Such a scheme would require social policy legislation to protect the pension rights of such individuals and changes in employment policy legislation to extend to part-time workers those rights which are at present largely confined to full-time workers. In the industrial policy sphere, such an approach would demand a more positive attitude towards industries such as tourism which, although they suffer from the disadvantage of not 'making things', earn foreign currency, are labour-intensive and provide part-time, seasonal occupations which could be followed by those taking early retirement.

Clearly, there are a number of problems with the policy strategy outlined, not least the technical difficulties which always arise in any attempt to revise state pension schemes without making them unduly expensive, inequitable and difficult to administer. However, the point of the example is not to suggest a specific reform, but to stress the need to view the problems that industrial policy attempts to tackle in a broader framework and to highlight the need for 'crosswalks' between industrial policy and social policy.

The industrial policies of successive British Governments have tended to be crisis-response policies, despite the good intentions of policy-makers and the ingenuity of civil servants in devising new schemes to revitalize industry. One only has to compare the far greater resources (in terms of staff and funds) that the Government devotes to the steel industry compared with the aluminium smelting industry. This difference cannot simply be explained in terms of the fact that steel is largely in the public sector, and that aluminium smelting is not; nor can it be explained in terms of the fact that there are fewer workers in the capital-intensive aluminium smelting industry. Rather, it reflects the longterm crisis in the steel industry and the absence of a comparable crisis in aluminium smelting. Industrial policy will always have to be reactive to some extent, as it is impossible to anticipate every problem in advance. What is really worrying is that the crises, once they arise, become longterm problems which appear to defy solution, as in the case of the steel and motor vehicle industries, whilst the number of relatively problem-free sectors is continually declining.

If Britain fails to devise and implement a more satisfactory industrial policy, the consequences will extend beyond industry itself so that eventually the social and political fabric of the country will be endangered. The alternative to a successful industrial policy is to 'risk the creation of a "Clockwork Orange" society with all its attendant alienation and misery'[59]. Unfortunately, it is difficult to be optimistic about the chances of success. A British commentator on an earlier draft of this book remarked: 'If people reject both the compulsion of the state *and* the constraints of the market, then they will end up in a kind of collective workhouse which perhaps may be regarded as fitting punishment for their refusal to face up to the need to make choices and to accept change.' Similarly, a German commentator remarked: 'In Britain, at least as far as the Labour Party is concerned, one often gets the impression that people think there is an alternative to technical efficiency and economic profitability, and that somehow the state or "the community" should be able to get resources from somewhere to permit non-competitive industries to survive.' A central theme of this book is that the industrial policy problem is essentially a political problem. The failure to produce an adequate political solution for the problems of the British industrial economy may eventually prove to be a fatal weakness for the British polity.

Notes to Chapter Six

1. Speech by the Rt.Hon. Sir Ian Gilmour, Bt., MP to the Cambridge University Conservative Association, November 8th 1980, 'R.A.B. Butler and the continuity of post war Conservatism', typescript, p.16. The author is grateful to Sir Ian Gilmour for providing him with a copy of this speech
2. I. Gilmour, *Inside Right*, (London: Quartet Books, 1978), p.236
3. ibid., p.229
4. Lecture by the Rt.Hon. Sir Ian Gilmour, Bt., MP at the Cambridge Union on 7th February 1980, typescript, p.30
5. ibid., p.22
6. ibid., p.31
7. Gilmour[2], p.234
8. Gilmour[4], p.24
9. ibid., p.19
10. H. Macmillan, *Reconstruction* (London: Macmillan, 1933), pp.29, 31–32
11. House of Commons Industry and Trade Committee, Session 1979 80, Minutes of Evidence, *Department of Industry*, Q.113. Answer by Sir Keith Joseph
12. The Foreign and Commonwealth Office's 1980 report lists twenty-three countries as NICs including India, Iran, Israel, Spain, Malta, Yugoslavia and Hungary. The OECD report is based on a list of ten countries, including four in Southern Europe (Greece, Portugal, Spain and Yugoslavia), and four in South-East Asia (Hong Kong, South Korea, Singapore and Taiwan)
13. D. T. Jones, 'British Industrial Regeneration: the European Dimension' in W. Wallace (Ed.), *Britain in Europe* (London: Heinemann, 1980), pp.115–133, p.122
14. Government Economic Service Working Paper No. 18, *The Newly Industrializing Countries and the Adjustment Problem* (London: Foreign and Commonwealth Office, 1979), p.44
15. W. Godley, 'Britain's Chronic Recession: Can Anything Be Done?' in W. Beckerman (Ed.), *Slow Growth in Britain* (Oxford: Clarendon Press, 1979), pp.226–233, p.231
16. ibid., p.231
17. National Economic Development Office, *Britain's Industrial Performance* (London: NEDO, 1980), Introduction (not paginated)
18. ibid., Conclusion (not paginated)
19. R. E. Caves and L. B Krause (Eds.), *Britain's Economic Performance* (Washington: The Brookings Institution, 1980), Introduction by Caves and Krause, p.19
20. R. E. Caves 'Productivity Differences among Industries' in Caves and Krause[19], pp.135–198, p.179

21. M. FG. Scott, W. M. Corden and I. M. D. Little, *The Case against General Import Restrictions* (London: Trade Policy Research Centre, 1980), p.9
22. Godley[15], p.233
23. Conference of Socialist Economists: CSE London Working Group, *The Alternative Economic Strategy* (London: CSE Books, 1980), p.100
24. Moss Evans, 'Import Controls are the Key to Industrial Planning', *Public Enterprise*, Number 19, Autumn 1980, pp.3–4, p.4
25. Godley[15], p.23–32
26. John Nott, reported in *British Business*, 14th November 1980
27. House of Commons Industry and Trade Committee, First Report, *Imports and Exports*, 1980–81, p.xvii
28. Godley[15], p.232
29. Confederation of British Industry, *International Trade Policy for the 1980's* (London: CBI, 1980), p.25
30. *Financial Times*, 11th August 1980
31. W. M. Corden, 'Relationships between Macro-economic and Industrial Policies', *World Economy*, Vol. 3(2), 1980, pp. 167–184, p.177
32. W. Wallace, 'Introduction and Comment on the Discussion' in W. Wallace (Ed.), *Britain in Europe*, (London: Heinemann, 1980), pp.1–24, p.6
33. S. J. Warnecke, 'Industrial Policy and the European Community' in S. J. Warnecke and E. J. Suleiman (Eds.), *Industrial Policies in Western Europe* (New York: Praeger, 1975), pp.155–191, p.168
34. C. J. Aislabie, 'Industrial Policy in the European Economic Community', *Journal of Industrial Affairs*, Volume 8 (1), 1980, pp.1–5, p.2
35. *Industrial Policy in the European Community – reappraisal and priorities*, a report by the CBI Europe Committee, November 1976, p.i
36. Christopher Wilkinson, 'European Community Industrial Policy', address to the Stagiares Conference, Brussels, 18th September 1980, typescript, p.7. At the time of the speech, Mr Wilkinson was Head of Division, Industrial Economics and Co-ordination.
37. Bulletin of the European Communities, Supplement 7/79, *Shipbuilding*, p.16
38. Bulletin of the European Communities, 9/1980, p.9
39. Court of Justice of the European Communities, Judgement of the Court, 17th September 1980, 'Aid to a cigarette manufacturer', in case 730/79. Translation LTS 1124/80/French/ MC
40. Bulletin of the European Communities, 6/1980, p.44
41. M. R. Martins and J. Mawson, 'The Evolution of EEC Regional Policy – Cosmetics or Major Surgery?', *Local Government Studies*, Vol. 6 (4), 1980, pp.29–56, p.46
42. Wallace[32], p.19
43. European Democratic Group, *Report on Industry Policy*, undated typescript, p.44
44. Cmnd.7937, *Report of the Committee to Review the Functioning of Financial Institutions*, p.372
45. ibid., *Evidence on the Financing of Industry and Trade*, Volume 1, 'The Provision of Funds for Investment', note by the Department of Industry and HM Treasury, pp.3–18, p.5
46. D. Sainsbury, *Government and Industry: a New Partnership*, Fabian Research Series 347 (London: Fabian Society, 1981), p.26
47. NEDO, *British Industrial Performance*[17], (Not paginated)
48. L. Tivey, *The Politics of the Firm* (Oxford: Martin Robertson, 1978), p.129
49. Caves[20], p.185
50. T. Smith, *The Politics of the Corporate Economy* (Oxford: Martin Robertson, 1979), p.180
51. D. Roy, 'The Road to Regeneration', *Public Enterprise*, Number 19, Autumn 1980, pp.1–2, p.2
52. Tivey[48], p.95
53. ibid., p.109
54. Corden, Little and Scott[21], p.24
55. Confederation of British Industry, *Jobs—facing the future* (London: CBI, 1980), p.46
56. C. Jenkins and B. Sherman, *The Collapse of Work* (London: Eyre Methuen, 1979), p.163
57. Cmnd.8173, *Growing Older*, p.17
58. ibid., p.18
59. Gilmour[1], p.23

References

ANGLO-GERMAN FOUNDATION, 1980. Alan Peacock with Rob Grant, Martin Ricketts, G. K. Shaw, Elaine Wagner, report for the Anglo-German Foundation for the Study of Industrial Society, *Structural Economic Policies in West Germany and the United Kingdom* (London: Anglo-German Foundation)

BAYLISS and BUTT PHILIP, 1980. B. T. Bayliss and A. A. S. Butt Philip, *Capital Markets and Industrial Investment in Germany and France: Lessons for the UK* (Farnborough: Saxon House)

BHASKAR, 1979. K. Bhaskar, *The Future of the UK Motor Industry* (London; Kogan Page)

BRUCE–GARDYNE, 1974. J. Bruce-Gardyne, *Whatever Happened to the Quiet Revolution?* (London: Charles Knight)

CAIRNCROSS, 1979. A. Cairncross, 'What is De-industrialization?' in F. Blackaby (Ed.), *De-industrialization* (London: Heinemann), pp.5–17

CBI, 1976a. *Industrial Policy in the European Community – Reappraisal and Priorities*, a report by the CBI Europe Commitee (London: CBI), typescript.

CBI, 1976b. *The road to recovery* (London: CBI)

CBI, 1978a. *Britain Means Business 1978* (London: CBI)

CBI, 1978b. *Investment Lead Times in British Manufacturing Industry* (London: CBI)

CBI, 1980. *International trade policy for the 1980s* (London: CBI)

COATES, 1980. D. Coates, *Labour in Power?* (London: Longman)

CONFERENCE OF SOCIALIST ECONOMISTS, 1980. Conference of Socialist Economists London Working Group, *The Alternative Economic Strategy* (London: CSE Books)

COOMBES and WALKLAND, 1980. D. Coombes and S. A. Walkland (Eds.), *Parliament and Economic Affairs* (London: Heinemann)

CORDEN, 1980. W. M. Corden, 'Relationships between Macro economic and Industrial Policies', *World Economy*, Vol. 3, (2), 1980, pp.167–184

CORDEN et al., 1980. M. FG. Scott, W. M. Corden and I. M. D. Little, *The Case against General Import Restrictions* (London: Trade Policy Research Centre)

DEAGLIO, 1966. M. Deaglio, *Private Enterprise and Public Emulation* (London: The Institute of Economic Affairs)

DELL, 1973. E. Dell, *Political Responsibility and Industry* (London: Allen and Unwin)

DEPARTMENT OF INDUSTRY, 1978. *Wool Textile Industry Scheme* (London: Department of Industry)

EUROPEAN DEMOCRATIC GROUP, 1981. *Report on Industry Policy*. (London: European Democratic Group)

FOREIGN AND COMMONWEALTH OFFICE, 1979. *The Newly Industrializing Countries and the Adjustment Problem*, Government Economic Service Working Paper No. 18 (London: Foreign and Commonwealth Office), typescript

FORESTER, 1979. T. Forester, 'Neutralizing the Industrial Strategy' in K. Coates (Ed.), *What Went Wrong* (London: Spokesman Books, 1979), pp.74–94

GANZ, 1977. G. Ganz, *Government and Industry: The Provision of Financial Assistance to Industry and its Control* (Abingdon: Professional Books)

GILMOUR, 1978. Ian Gilmour, *Inside Right* (London: Quartet Books)

149

GODLEY, 1979. W. Godley, 'Britain's Chronic Recession: Can Anything be Done?' in W. Beckerman (Ed.), *Slow Growth in Britain* (Oxford: Clarendon Press)

GRANT, 1980. W. Grant, 'Business Interests and the British Conservative Party', *Government and Opposition,* Vol. 15 (2), 1980, pp.143–161

GRANT, 1981. W. Grant, 'Representing Capital: The First Fifteen Years of the CBI', paper prepared for the British Sociological Association/Political Studies Association Political Sociology Group Conference, Sheffield, 8th and 9th January 1981

GUTHRIE and McLEAN, 1978. R. Guthrie and I. McLean, 'Another Part of the Periphery: Reactions to Devolution in an English Development Area', *Parliamentary Affairs,* Vol. 31, (2), 1978, pp.190–200

HATFIELD, 1978. M. Hatfield, *The House The Left Built* (London: Victor Gollanz)

HIRSCH, 1977. F. Hirsch, *Social Limits to Growth* (London: Routledge and Kegan Paul)

HODGES, 1977. M. Hodges, 'Industrial Policy: a Directorate-General in Search of a Role' in H. Wallace, W. Wallace and C. Webb (Eds.), *Policy-Making in the European Communities* (London: John Wiley), pp.113–135

HOGWOOD, 1979a. B. Hogwood, 'Analysing Industrial Policy: a multi-perspective approach', *Public Administration Bulletin,* Number 29, April 1979, pp.18–42

HOGWOOD, 1979b. B. Hogwood, *Government and Shipbuilding* (Farnborough: Saxon House)

HOLLAND, 1972. S. Holland (Ed.), *The State as Entrepreneur* (London: Weidenfeld and Nicolson)

HOLLAND, 1975. S. Holland, *The Socialist Challenge* (London: Quartet Books)

HOOD, 1980. C. Hood, 'The Politics of Quangocide', *Policy and Politics,* Vol. 8, (3), 1980, pp.247–266

INDUSTRY AND TRADE COMMITTEE, 1981. House of Commons, First Report from the Industry and Trade Committee, 1980–81, *Imports and Exports*

JONES, 1980. D. T. Jones, 'British Industrial Regeneration: the European Dimension' in W. Wallace (Ed.), *Britain in Europe* (London: Heinemann), pp.115–133

KAUFMAN, 1980. G. Kaufman, *How To Be A Minister* (London: Sidgwick and Jackson)

KNIGHT, 1974. A Knight, *Private Enterprise and Public Intervention* (London: Allen and Unwin)

LERUEZ, 1975. M. Leruez, translated by M. Harrison, *Economic Planning and Politics in Britain* (London: Martin Robertson)

LEVITT, 1973. T. Levitt, *The Third Sector: New Tactics for a Responsive Society* (New York: American Management Association)

LUND, 1976. P. J. Lund, 'The Econometric Assessment of the Impact of Investment Incentives' in A. Whiting (Ed.), *The Economics of Industrial Subsidies* (London: HMSO)

MAKINSON, 1976. W. Makinson, 'The National Research Development Corporation' in D. G. Lethbridge (Ed.), *Government and Industry Relationships* (Oxford: Pergamon Press), pp.117–134

MEEKS and MEEKS, 1979. Gay and Geoff Meeks, *Public Money in Private Industry,* Open University D323 course, Political Economy and Taxation, Unit 6 (Milton Keynes: Open University Press)

MINNS and THORNLEY, 1978. R. Minns and J. Thornley, *State Shareholding: The Role of Regional and Local Authorities* (London: Macmillan)

MORGAN, 1978. A. D. Morgan, 'Commercial Policy' in F. T. Blackaby (Ed.), *British Economic Policy, 1960–74* (Cambridge: University Press), pp.515–563

MULLER and BRUCE, 1981. R. Muller and A. Bruce, 'Local Government in Pursuit of an Industrial Strategy', *Local Government Studies,* Vol. 7, (1), 1981, pp.3–18

OECD, 1978. *Policies for the Stimulation of Industrial Innovation, analytical report.* (Paris: OECD)

OECD, 1979. *The Impact of the Newly Industrializing Countries on Production and Trade in Manufactures, report by the Secretary-General* (Paris: OECD)

OPEN UNIVERSITY, 1976. Radio programme for course D 203 (Decision Making in Britain), Programme 19, 'The Events of 1972: Industrial Policy'. (Milton Keynes: Open University)

OULTON, 1976. N. Oulton, 'Effective Protection of British Industry' in W. M. Corden and G. Fels (Eds.), *Public Assistance to Industry* (London: Macmillan), pp.46–90

OVENDEN, 1978. K. Ovenden, *The Politics of Steel* (London: Macmillan)

OWEN-SMITH, 1979. E. Owen-Smith, 'Government Intervention in the Economy of the Federal Republic of Germany' in P. Maunder (Ed.), *Government Intervention in the Developed Economy* (London: Croom Helm), pp.160–189

POSNER and PRYKE, 1966. M. V. Posner and R. Pryke, *New Public Enterprise,* Fabian Research Series Number 254 (London: Fabian Society)

ROBINSON and STOREY, 1980. J. F. F. Robinson and D. J. Storey, *Employment Change in Manufacturing Industry in Cleveland 1965-76,* County of Cleveland Planning Department, Report No. 176, typescript

SEDGEMORE, 1980. B. Sedgemore, *The Secret Constitution: an Analysis of the Political Establishment* (London: Hodder)

STOREY and ROBINSON, 1981. D. J. Storey and J. F. F. Robinson, 'Local Authorities and the Attraction of Industry – The Case of Cleveland County Council', *Local Government Studies,* Vol. 7, (1), 1981, pp.21–37

STOUT, 1980. D. K. Stout, 'Comment' in W. Wallace (Ed.), *Britain in Europe* (London: Heinemann), pp.133–137

TAKAMIYA, 1979. M. Takamiya, *Japanese Multinationals in Europe: Internal Operations and their Public Policy Implications,* International Institute of Management discussion paper IIM/dp79 – 86 (Berlin: Wissenschaftszentrum), typescript

TIVEY, 1978. L. Tivey, *The Politics of the Firm* (Oxford: Martin Robertson)

TUC–LABOUR PARTY LIAISON COMMITTEE, 1980. *Trade and Industry: a Policy for Expansion* (London: Labour Party)

WALKER and KRIST, 1980. G. Walker and H. Krist, *Regional Incentives and the Investment Decision of the Firm: a Comparative Study of Britain and Germany,* Centre for the Study of Public Policy, University of Strathclyde, Studies in Public Policy Number 57, typescript

WALLACE, 1980. W. Wallace, 'Introduction and Comment on the Discussion' in W. Wallace (Ed.), *Britain in Europe* (London: Heinemann), pp.1–24

WEISBROD, 1977. B. A. Weisbrod, *The Voluntary Nonprofit Sector: an Economic Analysis* (Lexington: Lexington Books)

WILKS, 1980. S. R. M. Wilks, 'Government and the Motor Industry With Particular Reference to Chrysler U.K. Ltd', Ph.D., University of Manchester, 1980

WORKERS INQUIRY, 1980. Coventry, Liverpool, Newcastle and N. Tyneside Trades Councils, *State Intervention in Industry: a Workers' Inquiry* (Newcastle-upon-Tyne: Trades Councils)

YOUNG, 1978. S. Young, 'Industrial Policy in Britain, 1972–1977' in J. Hayward and O. A. Narkiewicz, *Planning in Europe* (London: Croom Helm), pp.79–100

YOUNG with LOWE, 1974. S. Young with A. V. Lowe, *Intervention in the Mixed Economy* (London: Croom Helm)

Index

153